Coastal Sierra Leone

Against the backdrop of a threadbare post-war state and a global marine ecology in treacherous decline, Jennifer Diggins offers a dynamic account of Sierra Leone, through the examination of a precarious frontier economy and those who depend on it.

The book traces how understandings of intimacy, interdependence, and exploitation have been shaped through a history of indentured labour, violence, and gendered migration, and how these relationships are being renegotiated once more in a context of deepening economic uncertainty.

At its core, this is about the material substance of human relationships. One can go a long way towards mapping the town's shifting networks of friendship, love, and obligation simply by watching the vast daily traffic in gifts of fish exchanging hands on the wharf. However, these mundane social and economic strategies are often refracted through a cultural dynamic of 'secrecy', and a shared sense of the unseen forces understood to inhabit the material world.

Jennifer Diggins is Senior Lecturer in Social and Cultural Anthropology at Oxford Brookes University. Her ethnographic research focuses on fishing communities in coastal Sierra Leone, exploring how intimate social relationships have been shaped through histories of migration and economic change, and asks how men and women struggle to navigate precarious livelihoods through contexts of extreme poverty, insecurity, and environmental decline.

T0371472

THE INTERNATIONAL AFRICAN LIBRARY

General Editors

LESLIE BANK, *Human Sciences Research Council, South Africa*
HARRI ENGLUND, *University of Cambridge*
ADELINE MASQUELIER, *Tulane University, Louisiana*
BENJAMIN SOARES, *University of Florida, Gainesville*

The International African Library is a major monograph series from the International African Institute. Theoretically informed ethnographies, and studies of social relations 'on the ground' which are sensitive to local cultural forms, have long been central to the Institute's publications programme. The IAL maintains this strength and extends it into new areas of contemporary concern, both practical and intellectual. It includes works focused on the linkages between local, national, and global levels of society; writings on political economy and power; studies at the interface of the socio-cultural and the environmental; analyses of the roles of religion, cosmology, and ritual in social organisation; and historical studies, especially those of a social, cultural, or interdisciplinary character.

For a list of titles published in the series, please see the end of the book.

Coastal Sierra Leone

Materiality and the Unseen in
Maritime West Africa

Jennifer Diggins

Oxford Brookes University

International African Institute, London

and

CAMBRIDGE
UNIVERSITY PRESS

University Printing House, Cambridge CB2 8BS, United Kingdom

One Liberty Plaza, 20th Floor, New York, NY 10006, USA

477 Williamstown Road, Port Melbourne, VIC 3207, Australia

314-321, 3rd Floor, Plot 3, Splendor Forum, Jasola District Centre, New Delhi - 110025, India

79 Anson Road, #06-04/06, Singapore 079906

Cambridge University Press is part of the University of Cambridge.

It furthers the University's mission by disseminating knowledge in the pursuit of education, learning and research at the highest international levels of excellence.

www.cambridge.org
Information on this title: www.cambridge.org/9781108454681
DOI: 10.1017/9781108555647

First published 2018
First paperback edition 2020

A catalogue record for this publication is available from the British Library

ISBN 978-1-108-47116-9 Hardback
ISBN 978-1-108-45468-1 Paperback

This book is dedicated to Pa Yanker, who is the wisest person I know, and to Salta, who is the strongest.

Contents

Figures

Maps

Acknowledgements

This research was funded by a grant from the Economic and Social Research Council.

Issues of confidentiality prevent me from acknowledging the many people in Sierra Leone without whom this research would have been impossible. I owe particular thanks to Madame Doris Lenga-Koroma for welcoming me so warmly into her chiefdom.

I am extremely grateful to Andrea Cornwall, Chris Coulter, James Fairhead, Danny Hoffman, Adeline Masquelier, Elizabeth Mills, David Pratten, and Dinah Rajak for their careful comments on previous versions of this manuscript.

A note on translation

Tissana is a highly multilingual community. Almost all the conversations quoted in this book were conducted in the lingua franca, Krio, and translated by me into English. Where no adequate English translation exists for a word, I have retained the Krio terminology. However, ambiguity does occasionally arise as a result of the closeness between English and Krio. Below is a list of Krio terms used in the text, including a few that appear familiar but have a subtly different meaning to the one that English speakers might assume.

Alehn	A wharf town, or the act of migrating between wharf towns.
Baff	Large rubber tub used for measuring fish.
Banda	Smokehouse for drying fish.
Banda woman	Fish processor.
Bonga	The bony, herring-like fish that swim in large shoals through the Yawri Bay.
Boss-man	The owner of a boat, who may or may not also go to sea as the captain of the boat.
Bundu	Women's initiation society.
Devil	Nature spirit, occasionally embodied in the form of a masked figure. The word has no particular implications of evil.
Dreg-man	Lowly labourer.
Fetish medicine	Powerful esoteric substances that may be used to harm, heal, or protect from danger.
Fetish people	Ritual specialists.
Gbeshe	The person born after twins (who, in common with twins themselves, is usually considered a 'witch').
Ghana-boat	12–20-man fishing vessel.
Kongosar	Gossip or 'snitch'.
Kustoment	Respective partners in a long-term trading relationship.
Phone-man	A 'witch-eyed' fisherman able to hear fish moving beneath the water.

Plassas	A leaf-based sauce, eaten with rice and fish.
Plassas fish	Fish for household consumption, often given as a gift.
Poro	Men's initiation society.
Sell-gi	A monetary transaction with some of the social characteristics of gift exchange (literally: sell–give).
sim-boat	Onshore dragnet fishing method.
So'eh	Elder in the Bundu or Poro society.
Stranger	Migrant.
Swear	To put a curse on someone (typically the unknown or suspected perpetrator of a crime).
Tofi	To steal by witchcraft.
Tross	To loan money, or to sell on credit.
Turn-turn	To manipulate or charm.
Wap	To give fish away, free, to the people who come and beg on the wharf.
Witch	A person, sometimes described as possessing 'four eyes', who can see, and so can move, beyond the superficially visible landscape. The word does not necessarily imply evil.
Yele boat	3–5-man fishing vessel.

1   Introduction

**'When a person blesses you, that's how they add
[to your wealth]'**

Throughout the day in Tissana, almost every person's attention is trained,
even if only from the corner of their eye, towards the ocean: waiting.

Although it has a population of around 5,000 people – enough to
be considered a fairly substantial town by Sierra Leonean standards –
Tissana's homes and thatched smokehouses (*bandas*) straggle along such
a narrow, sandy strip by the shore that people are rarely more than a couple of minutes' walk from the sea. Together, a bundle of familiar stock
images – coconut palms, mango trees, and bright wooden boats – lend
Tissana a veneer of easy, tropical tranquillity. But this first impression
belies the anxious, youthful energy of life in this impoverished fishing
town. Moving back and forth along the two-mile beach that doubles
as the town's wharf and its main pedestrian artery, Tissana's residents
keep a vigilant eye on the horizon, scanning it for the appearance of a
familiar patchwork sail, or the recognisable silhouette of a canoe, heading
back to land. Even as women and men go about their work in gardens,
kitchens, and smokehouses further inland, their conversations are consistently drawn back out to sea, across the watery skyline: expressing
sympathy for the fishermen exposed to the oppressive sun or to the tor-
rential downpours of the rainy season; speculating where the fish might
be shoaling; worrying aloud which boats, if any, will return to town with
a decent catch.

By dusk, around a hundred boats will have been dragged out of the
water, to rest in single file under the trees that line the long wharf. Some
are tiny dugout canoes of the kind Sherbro men have used to navigate this
coast for generations. Nowadays, however, these traditional vessels are far
outnumbered by heavier, plank-built boats, the most impressive of which
require a crew of 20 strong men just to drag their heavy kilometre-long
fishing net from the sea.

A slight and softly spoken young man, Tito bore no outward resemblance to the bombastic 'big man' of West African cliché (Bayart 1993
[1989]; Strother 2000). Yet, as the owner of the longest fishing net in

1

Tissana, he was a prominent figure in the local economy. On a day-to-day basis, the crew of Tito's boat were as likely as any other to return from the sea disappointed. Occasionally, though, they succeeded in filling the long net to its capacity and, when they did, the catch would be spectacular enough to generate considerable commotion in town. Here, Tito is describing one such day. Long before his crew reached land, women up and down the two-mile beach had spotted the silhouette of his boat moving unusually heavily in the water, weighed down with the day's remarkable catch. By the time the fishermen finally drew up to their landing site, there were several hundred people awaiting them expectantly on the shore.

The fish that we gave people passed ten *baffs*![1] More than 500,000 leones [£100], if I had sold them. That's what we gave away to people. Big fish – fine fish . . . to the mammies, the girlfriends, the brothers, to all those people who just came and begged, no more – we gave them all. (Tito, boat owner)

Half a million leones is a substantial amount of money in Tissana. At the time of my fieldwork in 2010–11, it would have been enough to buy a small canoe complete with fishing tackle. But Tito was not exaggerating. I was there on the wharf that morning, as crowds of hopeful women waded chest-deep into the sea to press around his boat, and witnessed when this 'scramble for fish' eventually dispersed: dozens of people drifting home, relieved, each wielding a fine fish or two for their household's cooking pot.

This scene allows us to glimpse some of the most distinctive material qualities of life in Tissana, the frontier town that forms the ethnographic focus of this book. It points to the powerful sense in which maritime space is gendered: whilst most of my male neighbours led highly mobile lives, for women, time and watery space take on altogether different properties. They may be equally dependent on the ocean and its resources, but for Tissana's women the sea is an inaccessible space: a horizon across which they watch their partners disappear each morning, and from where, they hope, they will see them return bearing fish. Further, what is revealed in the image of dozens of hopeful supplicants pressed around Tito's boat is the visceral material urgency driving people's everyday pursuit of fish on the wharf. Day-to-day life for many people in Tissana is permeated with a profound sense of material insecurity: that the fragile, unpredictable fishing economy may one day soon fail to meet their most basic livelihood needs. In a town where many are only just managing to survive at the edge of subsistence, land-based fisherfolk invest an enormous amount of their creative energies, working to build and sustain the webs of social relations (*subabu*) that might enable them to 'catch' fish on land.

---

[1] From the English word 'bath', these large rubber tubs – about 1 metre across and 50 centimetres deep – are the standard measure by which smaller fish are sold on the wharf.

On a less exceptional fishing day, Tito's crew would have been content to have caught even half of the amount of fish that they gave away on that day. Yet, when I asked if Tito ever grew tired of being so relentlessly begged by neighbours and strangers on the wharf, he seemed rather taken aback by the question:

No! I don't get annoyed! If you do good, you yourself will get. When a person blesses you, tells you, 'Thank you, may God bless,' that's how they add [to your wealth]. But if you just hold [your catch] and say, 'This is only for me,' you never know what you will meet up with. This money, we find it now but we don't know how [long] it will last with us.

In Tissana, as in all places, economic transactions depend upon two people judging that, at that moment, the things they are exchanging are somehow 'equivalent' in value (Guyer 2004). The closer one examines this seemingly simple concept, its complexity multiplies, for nothing ever becomes 'valued' in a historical vacuum (Roitman 2007: 158). When we come across a surprising situation, such as a town in which poor fishermen routinely exchange the very substance of their subsistence for the spoken blessing of a stranger, it serves as a vivid reminder that, in any economic context, even the most routine daily act of valuation must inevitably connect to a much broader set of philosophical convictions about the substance of the material world they inhabit.

In this frontier town, fish are the substance through which relationships are nurtured, and are the subject of countless daily negotiations, both dramatic and mundane. Fish form the basis of almost every meal and the foundation of almost every person's livelihood: almost all men of working age are seagoing fishermen, and most women earn at least part of their living buying fish on the wharf and drying them to sell on at a marginal profit to the traders who gather here from across Sierra Leone. For many people, fish are also the source of profound, and deepening, anxiety. Fishing never was a predictable business, but it has become radically less so in recent decades. By the time I began fieldwork in 2010, a combination of local overfishing and damaging exploitation by internationally owned trawlers had left Sierra Leone's once-bountiful waters worryingly degraded (EJF 2012).

This juxtaposition of high levels of mobility and the urgent material need for close social networks generates a complex web of social tensions. So, as fish catches have become smaller and more erratic in recent decades, many fisherfolk reflect on their growing impoverishment through discourses that emphasise their *moral* ambivalence at being drawn into binding webs of interpersonal dependency. A tension animating many aspects of everyday life is how, through the strategic deployment of material gifts, people are able to nurture the *subabu* they depend upon for their survival, while simultaneously attempting to eschew other, less appealing social entanglements.

In common with many of Sierra Leone's fishing towns, Tissana has experienced rapid population growth in recent decades as a steady stream of marginalised young people, facing limited opportunities at home, have relocated to the coast hoping to find a new kind of life on the sea. As such, this frontier economy provides a window into broader patterns of youth 'navigation' (Vigh 2009) in contemporary Africa. Right across the continent, anthropologists have been describing the struggles young people face, as they attempt to come of age in precarious worlds shaped by extended periods of economic decline, political neglect, and violence. In many parts of Africa, youth have found themselves trapped in situations in which the 'possibilities of living decent lives are negligible' (Christiansen, Utas, and Vigh 2006: 9). In the 1990s and early 2000s, Sierra Leone provided a tragically brutal case in point. As the country spiralled into 11 years of civil war, violence came to be understood as a viable form of migrant labour and a unique opportunity for social mobility by a generation of frustrated young people who saw no opportunities for themselves anywhere else (see e.g. Peters 2010; Utas 2008; Vigh 2006).

Unlike most ethnographic studies to emerge from Sierra Leone over the past two decades, this is not a book about violence; nor is it even, explicitly, a book about post-war 'reconciliation'. I arrived in Tissana eight years after peace had officially been declared, at a time when the scars of fear and violence were gradually becoming less raw. And yet, this immediate legacy of societal collapse continued to shape people's everyday lives in profound ways – people who were struggling to build viable livelihoods in a context in which the political, economic, and moral fabric remained brittle and threadbare. At a personal level, this violent history had implications for individuals' ability to establish the trusting relationships they depend upon for their survival. In a town of migrants, it is often impossible to know what stories might lurk in one's neighbour's past.

The Sierra Leonean state, which was already extremely fragile even before its infrastructure was shredded by civil war, has yet to recover from the violence of the 1990s. It is in places such as Kagboro, which lack the infrastructure and political connections to attract outside investment, that the grinding pace of post-war reconstruction is felt most acutely. One might imagine that the decade following the end of violence would have been characterised by a growing sense of reintegration into post-war national politics, coupled with a steady increase in material security and well-being. But the people I knew in Tissana inhabited a landscape in which basic institutions remained in tatters: the police were ineffective; the health clinic and schools were desperately under-resourced; the only access road was all but impassable. Here, as Lorenzo Bordanaro recently observed in Guinea-Bissau, most people experience the state as 'irrelevant' in shaping their everyday strategies of survival and resilience (Bordanaro 2009: 39).

And yet, despite its peripheral position in relation to the state, there are other respects in which Tissana is part of a highly interconnected, cosmopolitan world. For all its apparent remoteness, the town depends for its very existence on its position within wider flows of people, cash, and fish. Sierra Leone's population depends on fish for 64 per cent of its dietary protein (Laurenti 2008: 64). Extending for almost two miles along the southern shore of the Kagboro Peninsula, Tissana wharf is located at the heart of the country's most productive fishery. Each week, traders converge here from every major market town as far as Koidu near the eastern border. Fish dried in Kagboro's smokehouses eventually find their way to household cooking pots in every corner of the country, from Freetown's crowded slums to the remotest forest village. The town is one of a cluster of bustling multi-ethnic wharf towns (*alehns*) that surround the busy fisheries of the Yawri Bay and the Sherbro Estuary. Fishermen move easily back and forth between these neighbouring coastal settlements. Where captains take their boats, or land their catch, will vary from day to day depending on where they believe they are most likely to encounter shoaling fish, or fetch the best price for their catch on the wharf.

Set against this backdrop, this book traces the material strategies adopted by men and women as they struggle to survive at the intersection between a depleted ecology, a threadbare post-war state, and a social order in which the basic rules of authority, kinship, intimacy, and trust are all perceived to be in a state of flux.

Materiality and morality in Sierra Leone's fishing economy

All along Sierra Leone's coastline, wharf towns began to mushroom from the 1960s onwards as rural migrants were attracted by new economic opportunities on the coast. In some respects, the social history of these burgeoning fishing communities echoes that found in accounts of frontier boom towns all across Africa. When large numbers of young people converge in an unfamiliar landscape, a space opens up in which new patterns of moral economy emerge (Mitchell 1956; Boswell 1969; De Boeck 2001; Walsh 2003). In a region in which we have come to correlate 'memory' with the collective scars of slavery (Shaw 2002) and civil war, Tissana's older residents look back with nostalgia to the youthful energy, conspicuous consumption, and seemingly easy 'freedom' of their town's brief boom years.

Nowadays, however, this boom-time narrative is wearing thin. The stagnation and marginalisation, experienced in most parts of post-war Sierra Leone, have been exacerbated in coastal communities by an ecological crisis with roots in the global political economy of fuel and fish. Climate change (Lam et al. 2012) and destructive over-exploitation by trawlers serving European fish markets (Lucht 2011; EJF 2012) have led to a collapse in fish stocks across West Africa. As is too often the case, an environmental crisis caused by over-consumption in some the world's wealthiest places is being felt most strongly by its poorest and most vulnerable populations. Tissana's fisherfolk are well aware that their impoverishment is shaped by broader structures of global economic injustice. But, operating from a position of powerlessness, they are more likely to focus their resentment and frustrations much closer to home. As catches become ever smaller and less predictable, this unrelenting material insecurity creates tensions that are ricocheting through the fabric of households and communities, putting new pressures on families, friendships, and gender relations.

What interests me in particular are the ways in which social and economic relationships are shaped by the material – and immaterial – fabric of this maritime world. Within this broad category, I include the physical contours of the coastal topography, as well as the specific substance of fish and other valuable livelihood resources, but I also include the particular social construction of space, value, and materiality.

At its core, then, this is a work about the substance of human relationships: of social bonds formed and lived under conditions of such stark economic uncertainty that, very often, 'love' and 'livelihood' are difficult to disaggregate – and even more difficult to trust. Relationships in Tissana often have a peculiarly concrete, ethnographically observable aspect: one can trace much of the town's fluctuating network of love, friendship, debt, and obligation simply by watching the flows of fish and rice weaving their shifting patterns through Tissana's social fabric. However, this region of West Africa also raises a particular set of problems for any ethnographer interested in the materiality of economic life.

Throughout the Upper Guinea Coast, a rich ethnographic literature attests to the importance of strategies of 'secrecy' at every level of social and political life (Bellman 1979; 1984). In the maritime economy, this diffuse regional aesthetic of secrecy intersects with a coastal topography that provides ample opportunity for people to move in and out of view, across the watery horizon. Within the contours of this physical and economic landscape, Sierra Leone's famed 'hermeneutic of suspicion' (Ferme 2001) finds palpable expression, and the weight of material urgency, in everyday gendered transactions between fishermen and their patrons, customers, and relatives on land.

Running as a thread throughout my ethnography is an examination of the ways in which pragmatic livelihood strategies are interwoven with material strategies that might appear to belong to the sphere of 'ritual' or 'esoteric' practice. Anthropologists working across West Africa have often pointed to the ways in which spiritual agencies are seen to inhabit material substances (Tonkin 1979; Soares 2005), in a context in which hidden, sequestered realms of knowledge and action play a central role in political life (Shaw 1996; Murphy 1980; 1998). This interweaving of material substances with immaterial agencies has been discussed both for its intrinsic interest as one facet of a complex regional cosmology (see e.g. Jędrej 1974; 1976; MacGaffey 1988; Tonkin 2000) and also for the ways in which it supports a regional model of charismatic power (Strother 2000).

What I trace through my ethnographic discussion is how these particular constructions of (im)materiality are both revealed and produced through the mundane practices of artisanal fishing, gift exchange, and relatedness. My approach is to treat the material value of fetish medicines, curses, and blessings not so much as a matter of 'belief', but rather as an economic fact with direct consequences for the ways in which people seek to balance their meagre livelihoods. The blessings Tito accepted in exchange for his precious fish encapsulate this problematic. Despite their communication through such an apparently ephemeral medium as speech, the people I knew in Tissana insisted that blessings carry a value far beyond that of mere expressions of gratitude or goodwill. Indeed (as I discuss in Chapter 7), fisherfolk describe spoken blessings, and exchange them, as though they were a material element of the economy.

But why does it really matter if a blessing is treated as being materially valuable, just as fish are? In an economy as impoverished as Tissana's, this surprising valuation has powerful consequences for people's livelihoods. It enables somebody with nothing to survive. By adopting an economic perspective, grounded in a detailed description of people's everyday livelihood strategies, we can begin to see how seemingly esoteric realms of knowledge – about the relationship between 'agencies, and their material forms' (Ferme 2001: 4) – become relevant in people's lives through their economic practices: through the decisions they make about how to invest their meagre resources, in fishing, trading, and building relationships.

The remainder of this chapter seeks to position the book within the anthropological literature on economic morality, both in West Africa and more broadly. In the first section, I introduce some key themes that emerge in existing accounts of Sierra Leone's rural economy. I consider how the autopsy of Sierra Leone's civil war revealed a seam of resentment among vulnerable young farmers, the depth of which appears to have been underestimated in earlier ethnographic accounts, and I discuss how these patterns of marginalisation were entangled in broader structures of neglect and economic exploitation.

In the second section, I contemplate where 'morality' resides in the economic order. I argue that people's sense of what is permissible or possible in economic life is usually taken for granted and that the 'morality' of economic behaviour is most likely to become the subject of explicit public reflection, available to ethnographic observation, at moments of important social rupture. As I begin to sketch in this chapter, certain characteristics of agrarian culture either have been undermined or have taken on new forms within the Yawri Bay's marine topography. A core proposition running through the book is that the anxieties preoccupying people in Tissana often gain salience through the juxtaposition of fishing life with memories of the agricultural world many fisherfolk left behind when they migrated to the coast. The chapter ends by returning to reflect in a more general way on how people's pragmatic judgements of exchange value may offer a window into their taken-for-granted knowledge of the material order.

A moral economy of rural Sierra Leone

While little research has been published on Sierra Leone's vibrant commercial maritime world,[2] my focus on the mundane contestations of economic life places this monograph within a well-established genre of regional ethnography. Some of the richest work to emerge from Sierra Leone in the pre-war period explored the everyday material tensions that ran half-hidden through agrarian households and villages (Richards 1986; Ferme 2001; Leach 1994). Across the broader West African region, anthropologists have highlighted the legacy of slavery in shaping the complexity and ambivalence of contemporary family relationships (Argenti 2010). There is a long-standing intellectual precedent, too, to my own interest in the ways in which people conceptualise and 'use' wealth, with ethnographers of Sierra Leone often describing the wealth of 'big' people as being measured in terms of their mastery of valuable 'secret' knowledge, and their ability to protect, provide for, and patronise a large number of dependants (d'Azevedo 1962b; Murphy 1980).

Rice farming in the forested regions of the Upper Guinea Coast is labour-intensive. Land itself is rarely in short supply and, in principle at least, anyone who begs permission from the head of a landholding lineage can expect to be granted access to an area of land to cultivate. Far more challenging is mobilising the labour required to clear the dense foliage and coax a harvest from the land's unforgiving soils. Against this ecological context, a constant preoccupation for the head of any farming household is how to cultivate relationships of dependency, through marriage, fostering, moneylending, and other forms of patronage (Leach 1994), with people who will then be obliged to provide labour on their farm. The flip side of this relationship is that, for most people in farming communities, their identity, safety, and well-being – even their most basic food security – are all contingent upon being able to rely on the

---

[2] Carol MacCormack's (1982) household survey of Katta village, conducted in the late 1970s, is one exception.

protection of some more powerful patron (d'Azevedo 1962a; Richards 1986).

It is difficult to understand the resonance of these power relations without some awareness of a not-so-distant history in which domestic 'slavery' (*wono*) was one of the region's most important institutions. Estimates vary but by some reckonings as many as three-quarters of the population of the Upper Guinea Coast were 'slaves' in the early part of the nineteenth century (Holsoe 1977: 294). They 'provided the basis, in fact, of the social system, and upon their labours as domestics depended, very largely, whatever agricultural culture [Sierra Leone] possessed' (Little 1967 [1951]: 37).

In 1928, domestic slavery was outlawed by the colonial regime, although it was not immediately clear to the British administrators what exactly it meant to be a 'slave' in Sierra Leone. Certainly, the institution bore little resemblance to the shackle-and-chains models of slavery familiar from colonial plantation economies (Rodney 1966; MacCormack 1977b). Precolonial European visitors knew very well that it was common for people to be bought, captured, or tricked into dependency, but they often had difficulty distinguishing these individuals from their 'free' neighbours by any visible measure of material wealth or lifestyle (Kopytoff and Miers 1977: 5). In a region in which social personhood is typically described as depending upon 'belonging' to a group 'in the double sense of the word in English – that is, they are members of the group and also part of its wealth, to be disposed of in its best interests' (ibid.: 9) – to be owned as a 'slave' was to occupy one position, albeit a particularly powerless and stigmatised one, within a social structure in which *all* persons were 'owned'. So, for example, migrants would sometimes voluntarily place themselves in a position of absolute dependency very similar to that of a 'slave' after fleeing their home following war or a personal dispute (ibid.).

Over 90 years have passed since slavery officially became illegal in Sierra Leone, but the legacy of these historical power structures continues to be strongly felt in rural areas today. It remains the case, for example, that the most powerful individuals in any village are invariably those able to demonstrate the longest genealogical roots in the land. More vulnerable people – the ones most likely to end up working as labourers on another person's farm – typically trace their descent from people who arrived in the village more recently, as client strangers or captured slaves (d'Azevedo 1962a; Sarró 2010; Berliner 2010).

Behind this apparently simple model of inherited power, commentators have repeatedly emphasised the subtlety of the ways in which people attempt to manipulate the labour of their weaker neighbours. So, while a person's high status is typically legitimised in terms of their direct descent from the village's original founding figure, it is apparently fairly common for elders to reinvent the public version of descent accounts to more closely mirror the lived reality of village politics, extending the ancestral roots of successful people deeper into their village's genealogical history (d'Azevedo 1962b: 510). Meanwhile, Caroline Bledsoe (1980; 1990a; 1995), Mariane Ferme (2001), and Melissa Leach (1994) all emphasise the range of covert strategies that enabled women (in particular) to manoeuvre successfully through this economic environment, even from a position of apparent weakness. Taken together, this body of literature has produced a highly nuanced image of how men and women in hunter-farmer villages worked to navigate a complex web of overt and covert relationships in order to balance fragile livelihoods in an unpredictable ecology.

Until the 1990s, ethnographers tended to emphasise the fact that, for all the evident stratification of village-level economics, 'differentials [of wealth] are fluid, even reversible' (Leach 1994: 185). However, examined retrospectively through the dark lens of civil war, the patronage system has come to be viewed by many with heightened misgivings, as a key source of the frustrations that eventually erupted so destructively in rural communities (Richards 2004; 2005; Murphy 2010; Knörr and Filho 2010; Peters 2010).

Civil war and economic life

Over the past two decades, much of the discussion of Sierra Leone's economic life has been preoccupied with making sense of the violence that ravaged the country during the 1990s. The conflict initially perplexed outside observers: Sierra Leone was not divided by any obvious ethnic or religious tensions, nor did the combatants seem able to articulate any coherent political motives for fighting. In any case, the violence was far more often directed against civilians than enemy soldiers. Nothing about this war made sense within traditional models of war as nation state politics. Then, towards the end of the 1990s, a new theoretical framework came to the fore, which appeared to render the conflict legible to Western observers: the violence, we were told, was driven not by political grievance but by the simple logic of economic 'greed' (cf. Collier 2000).

Starting from the common observation that all factions relied heavily on cash from the sale of alluvial diamonds, many commentators reasoned that the war had been, at heart, *about* diamond wealth (Douglas 1999; Gberie, Hazleton, and Smillie 2000); that everyone, from warlords to impoverished young fighters, had been drawn into the conflict by the promise that fortunes were to be made on the violent fringes of an illicit global trade. This explanation resonated powerfully in the international media, where, alongside emotive images of amputees and Kalashnikov-toting children, 'blood diamonds' have come to be seen as one of the key icons of the Sierra Leone war.

If this 'blood diamond' discourse can be read as a bleak meditation on the corrupting potential of incorporation into the global capitalist order, anthropologists with a more specific ethnographic knowledge of the region responded by drawing renewed attention to the fissures inherent in 'traditional' economic life. When anthropologists began listening to the accounts of ex-combatants, the narratives consistently painted a much more brutal image of village life than we were used to hearing. Again and again, young men claimed that they had been driven from their villages – and into one or other of the rebel factions – because they were routinely exploited by their wealthier neighbours, who abused customary law in what essentially amounted to patterns of indentured labour (Richards 2004; 2005; Peters and Richards 1998; Peters 2010; Humphreys and Weinstein 2004; 2006). In place of an earlier interest in the contingency and mutability of patron–client relationships, post-war ethnographers are much more likely to emphasise the brutal inequities of village life. A prominent thread in post-war ethnographic descriptions of agrarian life in Sierra Leone is summarised neatly by Paul Richards: 'The more docile among the descendants of the former farm slaves continue to work the land for subsistence returns. Others, less willing to queue in line for increasingly uncertain patrimonial scraps, default on their fines, are hounded into vagrancy, and end up as protagonists of war' (Richards 2005: 585). This book is strongly informed by the work of scholars, including Paul Richards and Krijn Peters, who emphasise the importance of this deeper history in understanding the tensions that characterise contemporary Sierra Leonean society. However, we need to be careful of sliding towards teleological narratives of how Sierra Leone's history of slavery led, inevitably, to a violent modern war (Jackson 2005). The danger is that we arrive at an image of peacetime life as inherently – inevitably – pathological (see Reno 2003: 156).

A crisis of youth?

In the rural context, most rebel fighters described themselves as participating in a 'revolution' against the injustices of a gerontocratic society. The bridewealth system, combined with patterns of formal and informal polygyny, excluded the poorest rural men from marrying (Peters 2011). In a context where social maturity has long been defined by one's ability to marry and support a family, these long-term bachelors found themselves trapped in an indefinite state of 'waithood', unable to make the transition into adulthood (Honwana 2014).[3]

However, these local frustrations cannot be disentangled from wider patterns of political exclusion and economic inequality. For much of the

---

[3] As the Poro society has gradually declined in prestige, participation in the society's initiation rituals is no longer sufficient to achieve adulthood.

twentieth century, men who were excluded from 'coming of age' in the agrarian economy were able to escape the limited opportunities of village life by pursuing new kinds of livelihoods in Sierra Leone's emerging urban centres, or in the diamond-mining and gold-mining regions that were fuelling the nascent national economy (Dorjahn and Fyfe 1962). By participating in new, European forms of education and labour, rural migrants were able to transform themselves, accumulating sufficient resources to return home and establish themselves in the centre of society (Utas 2003: 140). By the middle of the twentieth century, Sierra Leoneans had fully incorporated the 'myth' (Ferguson 1999) that their country was destined to continue developing along an inevitable path towards ever greater prosperity and global integration. The personal aspirations of young people were linked to this broader narrative of national modernisation, through the expectation that high-quality Western-style educational and well-paid employment opportunities would increasingly become available (Utas 2003).

But history failed to live up to this promise. In the 1980s and 1990s, the International Monetary Fund (IMF), the World Bank, and other international donors imposed severe limitations on state spending, as part of a neoliberal programme of reform that was supposed to lead to economic growth. Instead, these structural adjustment policies left Sierra Leone – like much of sub-Saharan Africa – spiralling into an extended period of economic decline and stagnation. The radical reduction in funding of state services led to a decline in the quality of education, a reduction in the number of job opportunities, and dwindling salaries for the few still able to access paid work (Utas 2008: 116). As Sierra Leone's economy collapsed, young people in urban as well as rural areas found themselves politically, socially, and economically blocked from participating in the modernity they yearned for. Ferguson has written powerfully about the profound sense of 'abjection' (1999) experienced by many across Africa, as their promised future retreated into an imagined past:

Once modernity ceases to be understood as a telos...the stark status differentiations of the global social system sit raw and naked, no longer softened by the promises of the 'not yet'...Rather than poor countries being understood as behind 'the West'...they are increasingly understood as naturally, perhaps even racially, beneath it. (Ferguson 2006: 186, 190)

The perception, common among Sierra Leone's youth, that they had been stripped of their futures by forces beyond their influence was to become 'socially explosive' (Utas 2008: 112) during the war. As the economy collapsed, violence came to be perceived by some as a rare opportunity to escape the 'social death that otherwise [characterised] their situation' (Vigh 2006: 31). For these 'abject' youths, joining a rebel faction appeared to offer a new promise of upward mobility and respect in a system that no longer offered any other hope of social transformation.

Most literature about youth in Sierra Leone focuses on the perspectives of ex-combatants. However, as Krijn Peters highlights, about 98 per cent of young Sierra Leoneans never took up arms (Peters 2011: 130). These young civilians have remained relatively overlooked, particularly in rural areas. Peters' recent research has demonstrated that non-fighters in rural areas shared many of the ex-combatants' grievances. If asked, they would complain about selfish elders, the inequity of the customary marriage system, and the lack of education and employment opportunities that leaves them stranded in an open-ended state of 'youth-hood'.

Anne Menzel's (2016) post-war research in Sierra Leone's second city, Bo, points to a similar frustration about the lack of 'good' patronage (cf. Bolten 2008). Menzel describes how, seven years after the official declaration of peace, people in Bo were so frustrated by the continuing levels of poverty and youth unemployment that many feared an imminent spiral back into civil war. While these fears were not fulfilled, her ethnography demonstrates John Davis's argument: that war 'is continuous with ordinary social experience; and people place it in social memory and incorporate it with their accumulated culture' (Davis 1992: 152). In many parts of post-war Sierra Leone, peace was experienced as fragile and provisional. Indeed, from the perspective of Menzel's young informants, 'there would not be peace as long as able-bodied young men like [them] remained unable to even properly feed themselves, let alone provide for a family' (Menzel 2016: 85).

'Post-war' Sierra Leone

Social scientists are only just beginning to understand the ways in which Sierra Leone's social fabric has been transformed over the past three decades (Højbejerg, Knörr, and Murphy 2016). Some recent literature emphasises the new spaces for social creativity that were produced by the ruptures of war, 'in the formation of new identities and cultures' (Ibrahim and Shepler 2011: viii). And yet, 11 years of conflict did almost nothing to resolve the underlying 'crisis of youth' that had propelled so many to participate in the violence. The war left behind a crippled national economy, a devastated infrastructure, and a legacy of massive peri-urban overcrowding. While there have been attempts to rebuild the state, these have been fragmented and incomplete, 'leaving a situation of uncertainty for many people on the ground' (Leach 2015: 826). Indeed, for large sections of the population, life opportunities are even more precarious now than they were in the 1990s (Peters 2011; Hoffman 2011), creating a situation described by Bürge in which 'practically everyone' is anxious about the 'omnipresent pending danger to remain or become youth, that is to say, not a full member of society' (Bürge 2011: 62).

Danny Hoffman (2007) provides another striking image of youth in urban Sierra Leone in the early 'post-war' years. Despite the official declaration of peace, the young men in Hoffman's ethnography moved through a fluid regional economy in which violence remained one of the few available livelihood options. As they traversed national borders, scraping a living from whatever opportunities they could access, his informants also slid fluidly between identities: sometimes trying their luck as diamond miners, or posing as refugees to claim international aid; sometimes smuggling goods across national borders, or joining one of the army factions in Liberia or Côte d'Ivoire. The image he paints is of a terrain in which young men – whether or not they had ever been combatants – were leading radically unstable, fluid lives. Echoing Simone's (2003) account of the postcolonial metropolis as a site of constant, restless movement, Hoffman argues that the urban economy of post-war Freetown was indistinguishable from that of the broader war zone – a social world in which 'no social category . . . signifies or guarantees stable habitation, and everyone is potentially on the market' (Hoffman 2007: 418).

In 2013 and 2014, the Ebola crisis that ravaged Sierra Leone, Liberia, and Guinea stood as a stark illustration of the limits of post-war recovery in this region. In all three countries, attempts to control the outbreak were handicapped by such desperately neglected health systems (Abramowitz 2014; Ferme 2014), such threadbare national infrastructures, and such a profound absence of trust between populations and those in power (Leach 2015) that the outbreak spiralled into an epidemic of a previously unimagined scale, eventually infecting over 25,000 people (WHO 2015).

As Melissa Leach and Annie Wilkinson have argued, the scale of this crisis can only be understood in the context of a much deeper history of structural violence, operating at a global as well as a regional level (Wilkinson and Leach 2014; Leach 2015).

The 'weakness' in health systems in the region needs to be seen not just as technical but as the result of particular political economies of neglect – including those fostered by the aid system. (Leach 2015: 823)

These 'interlacing' histories of injustice and exploitation stretch back to the Atlantic slave trade, and extend to include the hollowing out of state services through programmes of structural adjustment, as well as more recent patterns of extractive economic development. In the post-war period, internationally financed schemes to annex land for the mining of iron ore, diamonds, and gold have proved extremely lucrative for a small elite, and led to an official gross domestic product (GDP) growth of 21 per cent in 2013 (ibid.: 821). Yet such projects have brought negligible benefit for the majority of the population, and, in many cases, have undermined local livelihoods and institutions. In this respect, contemporary patterns of resource extraction appear to reinforce one of the war narratives already discussed: that, in this region, global economic forces have been deeply destructive for local well-being and stability.

There is one final point I want to emphasise about the different explanations for Sierra Leone's civil war, and the scepticism shown by local communities to global actors in the post-war context. Whether violence is understood as a grass-roots 'slave revolt' against distinctively local forms of exploitation (Richards 2005: 580) or as the tragic by-product of a global greed for local resources (Gberie, Hazleton, and Smillie 2000), what is striking is that both narratives locate the root cause of the country's terrible implosion in the catastrophic moral failure of one or other economic system. So, while the discussion is rarely framed explicitly in these terms, these arguments represent two quite different standpoints on a broader debate that has preoccupied social anthropologists for decades, and that is also a major concern of this book: what is the relationship between 'economics' and 'morality'?

The intersection of economies and moralities

The past 50 years have been a period of dramatic social and economic upheaval along Sierra Leone's southern coast, as settlements such as Tissana have been transformed from subsistence hamlets to busy hubs of commercial fishing, fish processing, and trade. Elsewhere across the postcolonial world, a rich ethnographic literature attests to the fact that members of recently subsistence economies often respond with deep moral ambivalence to newly introduced market-based systems of reckoning value and mobilising labour (Bohannan 1959; Ong 1988; Burkhalter and Murphy 1989; Hutchinson 1992). Historically, this unease was often interpreted by anthropologists as a 'natural' response to the moral vacuity of market relations (Taussig 1980; Luetchford 2012), which were thought to erode the moral bedrock of society.

Over the past couple of decades, these polarised models of economic life have been challenged from a number of different directions. Firstly, following Bloch and Parry's (1989) important edited volume, it is nowadays well recognised that people around the world appropriate, represent, and use money in a whole range of different ways. Ethnographers elsewhere in West Africa have stressed that – far from going hand in hand with 'individualism', as Western models tend to assume – the circulation of cash is inseparable from the production of social relations. In rural Ghana, for example, Sjaak van der Geest found that 'money does not sever relations, it binds people together' (1997: 555). Important relationships that, at one time, would have been maintained by other forms of gift exchange are nowadays linked with the flux of money, making cash an indispensable means of realising reciprocity (cf. Cornwall 2002; Barber 1995; Hasty 2005). Van der Geest's observations could be taken as one illustration of Appadurai's (1986) more general argument that *all* 'things' are capable of acquiring quite different social meanings as they circulate from one context to another, often shifting from an anonymous commodity to a highly personal gift and back again.

More recent ethnography emphasises that market systems are in fact infused with, and shaped by, moral discourse – and not only in the sense that commercial supply chains (Tsing 2013) and industrial labour regimes (Sanchez 2012; Rajak 2011) often depend on personalised relationships of the kind anthropologists tend to associate with 'gift' economies. In certain circumstances, the very concept of 'free market' trade can become an *ideological* aspiration (Otto and Willerslev 2013: 15), typically entangled with ideals about individual freedom, personal expression, and the potential for social mobility (Browne 2009; Carrier 1997). Whatever we might think of the real-world consequences of economic liberalism, its ideological potential is visible in many contemporary development initiatives: for example, those that aim to 'empower' poor people through credit-lending projects in which 'adapting to the market has been presented as an ethical imperative' (Elyachar 2005: 9; cf. Dolan and Scott 2009).

One difficulty with studying the 'morality' of economic life is that, for most people most of the time, morality is essentially indistinguishable from custom or habit (d'Andrade 1995; Howell 1997). Zigon has argued that it is only when people come up against some kind of social rupture that they become tangibly aware of having to negotiate right from wrong, and that it is in these crises, as 'persons or groups of persons are forced to step away from their unreflective everydayness and think through, figure out, work on themselves and respond to certain ethical dilemmas, troubles or problems', that moral reasoning becomes an active social process, open to ethnographic study (Zigon 2007: 140).

As we have already seen, civil war – and the sense-making that follows it – is one context in which previously unquestioned aspects of economic life might become the focus of widespread moral commentary. Another, less brutal situation in which moral rupture is likely to become a common feature of daily life is when people find themselves navigating through a period of dramatic social change. It is no coincidence, for example, that the very term 'moral economy' was first coined by the social historian E. P. Thompson (1971) to describe one such moment of rupture: in this case in eighteenth-century England, at a time when rural economies had been shifting away from older paternalist models of food marketing towards a newly capitalist order in which landlords were absolved of their responsibility to protect their tenants in times of dearth. While

Thompson is most often cited for his analysis of the market as 'heartless' and 'disinfested of intrusive moral imperatives' (ibid.: 89–90), the more general point worth stressing is that the protections that peasants had once taken for granted became the subject of an active moral discourse (in this case, in the form of food riots) only at the moment when they were stripped away (Thompson 1991; Edelman 2012).

Over a century later, and facing the demise of the twentieth-century welfare system, Andrea Muehlebach made a similar observation: 'Many of Europe's most famous public intellectuals ... [are] engaged in their own acts of grieving; a grieving quite ambivalent in that it is directed toward an object *never quite loved*' (Muehlebach 2012: 6, emphasis added). In both cases, the experience of living through a moment of important economic *change* is what instilled in people a heightened sense of the moral complexity of their economic lives. As Joel Robbins described in relation to his fieldwork with the Urapmin, a Papua New Guinean society recently converted to Pentecostal Christianity: 'For those caught living between a traditional cultural system and one they have newly adopted, morality is likely to provide the window through which they can see the contradictions with which they have to live' (Robbins 2004: 14).

Bearing this in mind, and given that ethnographers have so often worked in societies freshly reeling from their exposure to the hegemonic forces of global capital, it is not terribly surprising that the anthropological literature on economic change should be particularly rich in examples of people responding with moral unease to the unfamiliar logic of wage labour and colonial currency. It is in these liminal spaces of social history, where people find themselves consciously working to reconcile their experience of participating in two quite different socio-economic systems, that the everyday economic order is most likely to become the site of active moral reflection. What we ought to be careful of, however, is sliding from this important *methodological* point towards a more generalising set of assumptions about what *kinds* of economic change are likely to disrupt people's sense of natural morality, and why.

My own ethnography points to a quite different history of economic change, and of the moral anxieties it stimulates. The strongest motive farmers cited for leaving home to seek a new life on the sea is that commercial fishing appeared to offer an escape from a long-resented 'traditional' rural economy of bondship and pawnship. By the time of my fieldwork in 2010–11, Tissana's commercial heyday was already a memory. With fish stocks in noticeable decline, my neighbours reflected upon their creeping material impoverishment through a discourse that emphasised the changing character of their personal relationships. According to popular perception, the 'free' economic transactions of Tissana's boom years are being encroached upon once more by sticky bonds of debt and social obligation.

The material form of the landscape and its resources

In recent years, a growing number of writers from across the social sciences have become interested in exploring the extent to which people's lives are shaped by the material *substance* and physical spaces of the worlds they inhabit (Ingold 2007; Harvey 2006; Miller 2005). Within Africanist ethnography, a good example of this broad resurgence of interest in the material 'stuff' of economic life can be found in the work of Maxim Bolt. His ethnography, set in a farm workers' settlement on the Zimbabwean-South African border, examines how the substance of cash becomes relevant within the particular landscape of a border work camp. In a world 'characterised by transience and a conspicuously absent police force, money's *form* matters. Cash is a burden' (2012: 2, original emphasis). Bolt demonstrates that his interlocutors were motivated to spend their wages fast, and subsist for the rest of the month on credit – not because of any cultural associations with cash as inherently 'hot' or 'polluting', as has sometimes been claimed in frontier towns elsewhere in Africa – but rather because, living in dorms and often surrounded by strangers, the most likely alternative is to be robbed. In any economic world, there will always be important social repercussions arising from the fact that the things we consider valuable and want to possess have particular material properties. However, the 'materiality' of social life is not limited merely to the things we exchange and consume. 'As human beings . . . we live our lives surrounded by, immersed in, matter' (Coole and Frost 2010: 1). Fully acknowledging this means exploring how economic relationships play out within the physical contours of a particular topography.

One cannot live long among fisherfolk without developing an acute awareness that, as Acheson puts it, 'marine adaptations are one of the most extreme achieved by man' (1981: 277). In a context such as coastal Sierra Leone, where rainy season storms are ferocious and navigation technology rudimentary, the force and danger of the ocean are rarely far from people's minds. Indeed, it is striking that many aspects of the Yawri Bay's commercial fishing economy have developed, in a relatively short space of time, to mirror those described in commercial fisheries elsewhere. From the fluid migration patterns (Jorion 1988; Marquette et al. 2002), deliberate valorisation of 'living in the moment' (Astuti 1999), and highly charged gendered relationships (Allison and Janet 2001; Béné 2007; Westaway, Seeley, and Alison 2007; Seeley 2009), to the widespread air of competition and mistrust (Andersen 1980; Beuving 2010; McGregor 2008), I repeatedly came across examples of how life in Tissana appeared to conform to the global stereotypes of fishing life. Each of these characteristics will be fleshed out in detail in the ethnographic chapters of this monograph, but I devote a few pages here to a brief contextualisation of these social changes within their regional ethnographic setting.

The material assumptions that underpin economic behaviour are most likely to be raised to the level of visibility and called into question at moments when people find themselves navigating between two markedly different systems of reckoning value. To begin with an obvious and powerful example: I have discussed Sierra Leone's history of domestic slavery and its continuing importance in shaping the more subtle forms of social 'ownership' that persist in rural areas today. These patterns of reckoning wealth in terms of 'people' are now recognised as a characteristic feature of life in farming villages across this region. However, as Walter Rodney (1966; 1970) famously argued, it was only through their dealings with European slavers that African elites first learned to view other human beings as a potential form of *property*.[4]

While Rodney was describing a period of radical rupture in West African history, the general theoretical point holds true in moments of less violent upheaval. Any newly emergent way of understanding property inevitably brings with it new patterns through which relationships can be mediated materially (Busse 2012: 120–1). In the post-industrial world, for example, we are living through a historical change in the material substance of the things we value and want to claim as property. An increasing number of things once assumed too fluid, too minute, or otherwise incapable of being 'owned' are being privatised for the first time. In a global economic order in which genetic sequences (Boyle 2003), company brands (Foster 2013), and atmospheric carbon (Dalsgaard 2013) can all have a monetary value, it no longer seems nonsensical to claim that 'intangible assets are worth more than brick-and-mortar assets' (Foster 2013: 59). Just as we see taking place in public debates across the post-industrial world, as people adjust to the trend towards privatising 'intangible assets', Sierra Leone's recently burgeoning fishing population has had to respond to the changing material basis of their economic lives by grappling to figure out afresh what exactly 'value' is and where it resides in the world.

---

[4] In fact, the economic value systems in both West Africa and Western Europe were challenged and transformed through their long economic encounter with the other. In a series of extraordinary articles, for example, William Pietz illustrated how even that apparently most archetypical African valuable – the 'fetish' – emerged as a distinct category in both continents' economic discourses only as a result of centuries of miscommunication around exactly this 'mystery of value' (1985: 9). When, in the fifteenth century, members of European feudal and West African lineage economies faced one another on the coast for the first time, each came up against the problem that their new trading partners judged the allure of things according to a logic entirely different from their own (Pietz 1987; 1985). Portuguese merchants derided as *fetiço* (witchcraft) any object that their new trading partners valued as powerful and precious, but that fell outside Portuguese assumptions about what kind of materials were capable of holding value or commanding respect.

History and space

Around the world, most coastal communities regard the ocean as too wild a space to be divided up in order for it to be claimed – or indeed inherited – as private property. As we will see in Chapter 6, this often leads to intense competition between rival fishermen, all of whom are able to make an equally legitimate claim on the same 'commons' resource (Andersen 1980; Schoembucher 1988). A further consequence of fluid 'commons' wealth is that it effectively undermines the relevance of ancestral history as a source of social privilege.

As mentioned above, most classic ethnographic literature on the Upper Guinea region is concerned with describing hunter-farmer forest villages. In agrarian communities of this kind, the most eagerly sought-after resources fall into two broad categories. Firstly, a person's relationships to living and dead members of the landholding lineages determine whether they will be able to claim a 'natural' right to farm the land. Secondly, certain resources enable farming households to coax a successful harvest from that unforgiving forest landscape: plenty of hard human labour, and the esoteric knowledge to enable the land's capricious productive forces. The value placed on these particular resources helps reproduce a pattern of social hierarchy and cosmological power that is literally grounded in the land and its history. In Sherbro farming communities in the 1970s and 1980s, for example, MacCormack (1986) described how ancestors and ancestresses of village-founding lineages were considered to inhabit the contemporary landscape, and were revered as the ultimate source of good and bad fortune. The implication was that there was an apparently direct correlation between the depth of a person's historical roots in the land, the extent of their legitimate knowledge of the forces of nature concealed within it, and their ability to claim moral and material authority over other members of their community. So, although it was recognised that even a poor stranger could potentially become a powerful patron, such a radical reversal in status was conceivable only through the 'strategic, *though illicit*, exploitation of secret knowledge of the landscape' (Ferme 2001: 2, emphasis added).

For those migrants who chose to leave their farming villages behind to pursue livelihoods as fisherfolk, uprooted from the land, there have been far-reaching repercussions. Even for the minority of people whose ancestors had inhabited this coastline for several generations, Tissana's transformation from a subsistence fisher-farming village to a commercial fishing town entailed a radical reorientation away from value rooted in the productive forces of the land and its history. Reliant instead upon a slippery and highly mobile underwater quarry, members of Sierra Leone's burgeoning commercial fishing economy have learned to develop new, quite different modes of negotiating social belonging and economic power – not only between 'landlords' and their tenants (Dorjahn and Fyfe 1962; McGovern 2012), but also more broadly across a shifting fabric of households (Chapter 5), business partnerships (Chapter 4), and boats (Chapter 3).

Gender, concealment, and space

Perhaps the single most striking way in which the physical topography of the Kagboro coast shapes how people are able to negotiate their social relationships is that men and women are empowered to move in quite different ways through the maritime space. Tissana's seagoing fishermen lead highly mobile lives, pursuing their quarry across the Yawri Bay. If they judge that it may increase their chances of landing a good catch, boat captains often choose to base their boat, and land their fish, on a rival wharf for a period of days or weeks. As wharf towns all along the shores of these fishing grounds have flourished, the bay itself has become an increasingly congested – though unequivocally *male* – space, in which rival crews actively compete with one another to hunt the same limited, elusive shoals of fish. For Tissana's women, reliant upon the success of their male business partners at sea, yet unable to venture out to sea themselves, the oceanscape is regarded through a lens of half-trust and uncertainty (see Chapters 4 and 6).

This emphasis on the hidden nature of gendered agency connects with one of the strongest recurrent themes in Sierra Leonean ethnography. Gendered initiation societies play a central role in customary politics and have been capturing the imagination of European visitors for at least the past 200 years (Winterbottom 1803; Aldridge 1894). Although often described in English as 'secret societies', the label does not refer to a society whose *membership* is secret. On the contrary, almost all men join the lower echelons of the Poro, while practically every woman is a member of the Bundu. Rather, the institutions' 'secrecy' resides in the powerful esoteric 'medicines' (*ifohn*) that form the core of each sodality's identity.

At one time, young people of both genders would have spent several months or years secluded in their respective societies' 'bush': a sacred space carefully segregated beyond the limits of the public landscape of the village. During this period of separation, children were transformed into fully gendered adults, passing through a series of physical ordeals and bodily transformations as well as receiving gender-specific instruction on life skills ranging from farming to military tactics, childbirth, and the confection of their society's most common *ifohn*. Much of the research focusing directly on initiation societies has been concerned with exploring the relationship between secrecy and power. Even though they imparted some basic knowledge to initiates, it was the elders' mastery of other, more powerful, esoteric knowledge that imbued them with the charisma to exercise almost indisputable authority over junior members (Little 1966; Murphy 1980; Bledsoe 1984). Already by the 1940s, Kenneth Little was describing the Poro as an institution in decline, its importance undermined by the introduction of colonial forms of education and political authority (1948: 8). And yet, six decades on, sodalities show no sign of disappearing from Sierra Leone's political landscape. The picture in Tissana, for example, was mixed. Nowadays, Poro initiation is a simple, day-long ceremony and most of the men I knew were keen to stress that the society held little coercive power in their lives anymore. The Bundu society had experienced no such decline and continues to play a central – and celebrated – role in women's everyday social lives.

In the 1970s and early 1980s, societies drew considerable attention from feminist anthropologists, in part because of the evident political power wielded by female society leaders (MacCormack 1982; 2000). What seemed even more resonant at the time was that the *process* of initiation appeared to encapsulate the central argument being made in anthropological theorisations of gender: that gendered difference is not biologically given, but rather socially produced (Lamp 1985). So, for example, in her fieldwork among Sherbro speakers in the 1970s, Carol MacCormack (1980) emphasised that Sherbro men and women were both active in what we might gloss as 'public' and 'private' spheres of social life. Both laboured on the farm, engaged in commercial trade, contributed to training children, and invested considerable creative energy nurturing networks of social relations. Sherbro speakers expressed a strong and explicit ideology of gendered difference, but central to this ideology was the knowledge that gendered difference had to be actively produced through rites of spatial separation, cultural training, and bodily transformation.[5] One thing that is striking about the commercial fishing economy is that 'men's space' has come to be segregated from 'women's space' in additional, quite different, ways with profound repercussions for the ways in which people of both genders are able to manage their social and economic lives.

Plenty of ethnographers before me have suggested that the aesthetic of secrecy, so clearly epitomised by the high fences and esoteric practices of the region's sodalities, also finds expression across a whole range of more 'banal' contexts (Bellman 1984; Gable 1997; Piot 1993). In the maritime context, this broader 'hermeneutic of concealment' (Ferme 2001: 6) intersects with a watery topography that provides both an unusual level of opportunity and particularly powerful material incentives to be strategic about how much of their lives they reveal to their neighbours, lovers,

[5] Far from viewing pregnancy and birth as inevitable functions of their female bodies, Bundu women, 'with their secret knowledge, public laws, legitimate sanctions, and hierarchical organisation, bring women's biology under the most careful cultural control' (MacCormack 1977a: 94).

business partners, and rivals (cf. Palmer 1990). My focus in this book is not on temporary gendered separation per se but rather on the frictions that emerge for men and women in the highly charged spaces where their two worlds re-converge on the shore (see especially Chapters 4 and 6).

Fish and the substance of relatedness

Back on land, the particular material qualities of fish work to foster certain distinctive patterns of relationships. Tissana's economy exists because of fish, and almost every individual in town depends for their subsistence on being able to catch, dry, or exchange them. Fish are the basis of almost every meal, the foundation of almost every household economy, and the subject of a thousand daily dramas, large and small. From my own perspective, it sometimes seemed as though they were the very substance out of which Tissana's shifting social fabric was woven. Sitting on the wharf as the fishing boats returned from sea, or in the busy shared kitchen of my own compound as residents distributed their rice in dishes of various carefully calibrated sizes, I observed who was giving what to whom, in exchange for what, and under what circumstances.

Such a materialist approach would resonate well with my neighbours' own accounts of their interpersonal lives. In many cases, the people I knew were negotiating tenuous livelihoods close to the edge of subsistence. As other ethnographers have found in similarly impoverished settings elsewhere in this region, people's daily priorities are very explicitly focused on meeting their basic material needs; almost all other aspects of their relational lives are ultimately refracted through that lens (Leach 1994; Whitehead 1990). In particular, this book could be read as building on Caroline Bledsoe's (1980; 1990b; 1995) excellent research among Mende and Kpelle speakers in the 1980s, in which she paints an uncompromisingly honest picture of the tough personal choices poor men and women are sometimes forced to make: nurturing certain relationships, and neglecting others, in the basic struggle to balance viable livelihoods.

However, fish are not just *any* commodity. They have a specific physical form, and that form has powerful consequences for the ways in which people in Tissana are able to use them to establish social and material relationships. Firstly, as property, fish rot quickly. In a town with no refrigeration technology, this simple fact injects economic life with a peculiarly heightened urgency. Boat captains must sell their catch or give it away as soon as they return to land, or otherwise watch helplessly as the source of their sustenance and wealth decays into a pungent health hazard. Secondly, as prey, fish are mobile, invisible, and highly unpredictable. This not only encourages fishermen to adopt similarly fluid migratory patterns themselves, but also requires people to invest an inflated amount of creative energy and material resources in nurturing the social networks that will enable them to survive when their catches fail.

And their catches *will* fail. It looks increasingly likely that the existing crisis in Sierra Leone's fisheries will deepen even further in the coming years. In addition to the current problems of fisheries management and defence against illegal trawling, ecologists identify West Africa as one of the regions most vulnerable to climate change (Lam et al. 2012).[6]

These factors combine to mean that Tissana lends itself unusually well to a study foregrounding the materiality of social life. One can go a long way in tracing the town's ever-shifting lattice of kinship, love, and obligation simply by watching gifts of fish and counter-gifts of rice weaving their complex patterns, in real time, through Tissana's social fabric. However, as I explore in the following section, relationships are not only forged through tangible exchanges of fish, rice, and cash. They are also cultivated and manipulated in other, less visible but equally material ways: through the movement of concealed fetish medicines and bodily substances, for example; or through the strategic mobilisation of spoken blessings or curses. A central observation of this book is that these things are integral to the everyday business of economic survival, in ways that challenge any intuitive ontological distinction between the material and immaterial, the 'supernatural' and the banal.

Immaterial forces and the substance of relatedness

My experience in Tissana forced me to relearn what exactly counts as material in the world of economic transactions. In Tissana, the work people invest in managing their stretched livelihoods often incorporates the use of curses, blessings, amulets, and 'fetish' medicines: substances and technologies that we might instinctively gloss as belonging to the world of 'religion' or 'ritual', but which are, in fact, integral to the mundane economic order. To some extent, this is not particularly surprising. There is a large literature within historical and contemporary ethnography highlighting the absence of any sharp, conceptual distinction between material and spiritual domains. In Giovanni da Col's recent account of Tibetan 'cosmoeconomics', for example, he tells us that 'transactions of forces such as fortune, luck, and vitality materially inhabit economic exchange and conceptions of value' (2012: S191). Steven Gudeman's (2012) description of a Colombian peasant economy offers a similarly compelling account in which he describes how the 'energy of life' circulating through crops and the bodies of livestock and human beings is

---

[6] Rising sea temperatures are expected to have an adverse effect on marine resources, exacerbating existing threats to the livelihoods and well-being of fishing communities. Some models predict that the number of people able to make a living in fisheries-related work will have shrunk by half by 2050 (Lam et al. 2012).

conceptualised as a form of currency. But, if this talk of materially valuable 'forces', 'energies', and 'blessings' all sounds rather exotic, we might
do well to remember that the value of money could quite reasonably be
construed as equally mysterious. On a day-to-day basis, we are not called
upon to wonder *why* those tatty pieces of paper can be exchanged for
a week's groceries, nor, more bizarrely still, how it is possible that the
weightless numbers in our bank accounts can be digitally swapped for a
piece of furniture.[7] I am struck by the parallels between this 'suspended
disbelief' about the value of banknotes and Olivier de Sardan's comments
about the power of sorcery, spirits, and magic charms for the people he
knew in Niger:

> The practical efficiency of fetishes goes without saying. All that is banal. Ances-
> tors, spirits, sorcerers or magic charms are all familiar concepts in regard to which
> 'disbelief is suspended', and which need no justification. There is no question of
> believing or not believing: it is not a case of belief, but of fact, not of the fantastic
> but of the routine. (Olivier de Sardan 1992: 11)

In Sierra Leone, the interweaving of unseen agencies within material culture can be seen, for example, in the fact that spoken words are often considered a powerful ingredient in the confection of amulets and medicines
(Bledsoe and Robey 1986; Shaw 1997a), or in the fact that seemingly
inert objects are credited with the power to catch and punish criminals
(Jędrej 1976; Tonkin 2000). However, scholars have tended to discuss
this construction of (im)material agency within a very particular framework: as one facet in the underlying workings of the 'politics of secrecy'.

Marianne Ferme's erudite description of 'the underneath' of a Mende
agrarian landscape achieved something that no earlier study had quite
managed: it captured the extent to which unseen forces weave through
the entire material fabric of Sierra Leonean life, reaching far beyond
explicitly ritual contexts.

> [S]ome of these agencies, and their material forms, appear to coincide with
> others that drew the attention of scholars of comparative religion...But this
> continuum also includes transformative powers of incompletely controlled forces
> and materials whose history in Sierra Leone is linked not so much to religious
> belief as to the material experience of modernity and the magic associated with
> it. (Ferme 2001: 4)

However, for Ferme too, the study of (im)materiality seems analytically inseparable from the study of 'secrecy'. Her argument is that Sierra

---

[7] There have been repeated moments in Western history when the materiality of money,
the stuff it is made of, has changed. During each of these transitions – whether with
the introduction of paper banknotes, the removal of the gold standard, or the currently
soaring value of the stateless internet currency 'Bitcoins' (Maurer 2011) – changes in the
materiality of wealth have sparked considerable existential uncertainty, as people have
been forced to question what really is holding together their economy and, by extension,
their society.

Leone's culture of secrecy developed out of its violent history of slaving, during which there had been very real dangers associated with speaking or acting openly. Other ethnographers had already highlighted the layers of ambiguity and conflicting meaning that run through spoken discourse in this region (Bellman 1984; Piot 1993); however, Ferme went further, seeking to reveal how ambiguous meanings are concealed beneath, and produced through, the material landscape, in the 'tension between surface phenomena and that which is concealed beneath them' (2001: 1). Ferme thus set herself a considerable challenge of deciphering for an English-speaking readership how the topography of Mende farms, villages, and forests might be read as a shifting text of hidden metaphors and metonyms, the 'semantics' of which evaded all but the most skilful of her Mende informants:

> The ability to recognise these clues, and to make one's own interpretation of them gain acceptance among many, forms the basis of the achievement of power in Mende society. However, this process is characterised by struggles, whose outcome is rendered all the more uncertain by the shifting grounds of a hermeneutic of ambiguity, which has been activated by a violent history. (Ferme 2001: 20)

The subject of Ferme's analysis, like mine, is the material fabric of 'everyday' economic and political life – including a whole range of ostensibly rather mundane activities, such as braiding hair, weaving nets, and making cloth. However, her analytic approach emphasises that the true 'meanings' carried within these material practices are legible to only a very small minority of Mende people.

Without seeking to contradict Ferme, I was motivated to explore the relationship between the tangible world and its unseen agencies for quite different reasons. My starting point was simply to describe the ways in which my informants were working to *survive* under conditions of extreme material uncertainty: the things they exchanged, and the ways in which they sought to build and nurture relationships. However, as I have suggested in this section, people's pragmatic, everyday assessments of material value can be a window into a diffuse field of practical knowledge about the substance of the material order, and the scope of human agency within it. This embodied knowledge of the world is akin to what Foucault (2005 [1966]) called an 'episteme'. Unlike previous scholars of the history of knowledge, his interest had not been to explore *what* people knew at other times in history, but rather to excavate the shape of the 'epistemological space' (ibid.: x) that set the most taken-for-granted limits within which it was possible to know the world or act within it. Similarly, my own interest in this book is not to decipher the layers of hidden 'meaning' that preoccupy Ferme in her study of the Mende landscape; rather, I explore how the lived anxieties of precarious livelihoods are both shaped by – and produce – a particular field of shared knowledge about the moral and material 'order of things' (ibid.). One point I want to emphasise is that, while the political use of secrecy and complex understandings of material agency are both important facets of social experience in Sierra Leone, it does not follow that they are always two aspects of the same phenomenon. In the ethnographic chapters that follow, I describe how men and women in Tissana navigate these bonds of debt and obligation, and I explore how they invest their limited resources: in the attempt to access fish and money, but also to accumulate the spoken blessings of strangers. I examine how people work to build and manage their vital webs of social and economic relations through material gifts of fish and rice, but also through the strategic use of fetish medicines. Through this detailed description of everyday material negotiations, we can begin to see how seemingly esoteric fields of knowledge – about the scope of the material world and the limits of human agency within it – are relevant to *all* people's livelihoods.

Map of this book

The five ethnographic chapters of this book were conceived of and written as a series of interrelated empirical studies, rather than elements of a single linear argument. Each reveals a different facet of a material, social, and economic order that is in flux. The structure unfolds in a pattern that broadly echoes the structure of this introduction. The early chapters discuss how the specific tensions I observed in Tissana speak to a broader anthropological discourse on 'morality' in times of economic change. The second analytical thread, which comes particularly to the fore in the final two substantive chapters, explores how people's knowledge of the material order both shapes and is simultaneously shaped by the practical challenges and micro-political struggles of economic survival in a rapidly changing economic order.

Chapter 2 sets out the context of my research, introducing Tissana as a town of apparent paradoxes: a lively, cosmopolitan space that is also a site of economic exclusion and decline. The chapter sketches a brief economic history of the town, tracking the successive innovations in fishing technology that enabled its rapid growth from a subsistence fisher-farmer hamlet 50 years ago to a commercial fishing town. It ends with a discussion of my research methods and limitations.

Chapter 3 speaks strongly to regional ethnographic debates. It tells the stories of some of the young men who chose to risk everything, to leave their farming villages and establish a new kind of life on the sea. The migrants' accounts often closely mirror the grievances expressed by young rebel fighters in the aftermath of Sierra Leone's civil war, circling around the themes of patriarchal exploitation. The chapter discusses the migrants' hopes that the fishing economy might offer a level of personal autonomy that would be unthinkable within the patron–client strictures of agrarian life, but ends by acknowledging that many vulnerable men in fact find themselves drawn rapidly back into extractive forms of patronage.

Chapter 4 continues to explore this tension between people's hopes for 'independence' and their experience of becoming rapidly re-entangled in more binding patterns of economic relations. Through the lens of gendered negotiations, between fishermen and the women who buy and dry their fish, I develop a picture of the constricted forms of material agency available to Tissana's most vulnerable residents. We see, for example, that for the very poorest crewmen, choosing to work with a strong female customer can provide them with a vital safety net while allowing them to avoid outright dependency on the owner of their boat. This chapter also explores the repercussions of the Yawri Bay's declining fish stocks for patterns of gendered power. As the balance of supply and demand slides ever further out of their favour on the wharf, *banda* women have learned to invest an ever greater proportion of their creative energies and material resources, working to build enduring *social* relationships with the fishermen whose catch they want to buy.

Set against a broader regional context in which a person's most basic well-being depends upon being embedded in networks of supportive kin, Chapter 5 describes some of the practical ways in which people work – by exchanging gifts of fish, rice, and other substances – to create the networks of kinship that offer the only security net in a highly precarious environment. In such a highly mobile population, the resultant tangle of relatedness bears little resemblance to the neatly hierarchical lineage structures described in classic ethnographic accounts of this region (d'Azevedo 1962a; Little 1967 [1951]). Yet, for all their apparent inclusivity, 'potato rope' families come with their own risks. Where ties of kinship can never simply be taken for granted, but must instead be continually recreated materially, then, without sufficient material resources, even the most seemingly 'natural' family bond is vulnerable to atrophy or collapse.

Running throughout the first three ethnographic chapters, we will see repeated examples of 'fetish' medicines (*ifohn*) circulating through the everyday economic order and forming an integral element of people's mundane livelihood strategies. However, Chapter 6 marks a gear shift away from the tangible patterns of exchange to dwell more explicitly on the ways in which people's economic lives are threaded through with material strategies of a less visible kind. There are multiple layers of hiddenness that run through Tissana's topography. This is a world in which men disappear across the horizon each day, into a watery topography only half-imagined by their neighbours and relatives inland. Similarly, a large proportion of Tissana's population is assumed to have access to an invisible space – sometimes referred to as 'the witch-world' – that maps onto the visible surfaces of the townscape. My goal is to explore the phenomenology of felt ignorance and mistrust that permeate economic life in a context in which much of that which affects a person's livelihood is necessarily hidden from their view. Finally, Chapter 7 returns to the problem introduced at the beginning of this introduction, asking why it matters – practically and theoretically – that people in Tissana value spoken words as a material element of the world of transactions.

2   Context, history, methods

Context

The road to Shenge-Tissana

In post-war Sierra Leone, travellers are hardened to the discomforts of a long-neglected transport network. Yet, even by such poor national standards (in 2010–11), the traders I knew felt a special horror when contemplating the journey to Shenge. If travelling by land, wherever their journey begins, they must eventually fork off the tarmac road at Moyamba and follow the short, 80-kilometre 'Highway' that runs like a spine down the length of the Shenge Peninsula.

Much as contemporary British cities have 'Haymarkets' and 'Canongates', the fact that this route should be known as a 'Highway' at all is a remnant of a former age: a time before the war, when, I was told, the road had been so smooth and fast you could travel its entire length in a single hour. In the early 1990s there had even been – and this part of the tale is recounted in a tone of wonderment – *government buses* plying its route. Later, in the 1990s, the Highway had become one of the busiest thoroughfares in Sierra Leone. During that decade of devastating violence, the Shenge Peninsula had been almost the only part of the country to escape rebel attack.[1] So, when all other routes in and out of Freetown had been blocked by armed fighters, this peripheral region found itself transformed, albeit temporarily, into one of the busiest trading hubs in the country, channelling food and other essential supplies to towns throughout the southern provinces.

Travelling the dilapidated road today, it is not easy to conjure these images in one's mind. Nibbled away on either side by hungry, tropical vegetation, the Highway's sandy earth has been carved by successive rainy season downpours into gullies and potholes so deep as to leave the road all but impassable. In some places one can make out valiant but largely unsuccessful efforts by work teams from local villages to salvage the road

---

[1] People in Shenge usually agreed that the reason rebel soldiers never ventured as far as their town was for fear of becoming entrapped on the peninsula, surrounded by water on three sides.

Figure 2.1 The Highway, the only land route to Shenge

from complete self-destruction, packing tree trunks and sacks of sand into the deepest trenches in its surface (see Figure 2.1).

> This is what has been promised, promised, promised with every government that comes: 'We'll mend the road, we'll mend the road, we'll mend the road.' If they could mend the road, even as far as Moyamba, things would be very easy for us. (Pa Albert, elder, Shenge)

For the fortunate few who can afford the considerable expense (as I could), it is possible to charter a motorcycle to carry you, weaving and bumping, on the three-hour journey from Moyamba to the coast. For everybody else, only a single, small, unreliable passenger vehicle attempts the journey each week. This road remains the only land artery serving a chiefdom with a population of well over 30,000 people (Sierra Leone Statistics 2004: 11). Yet, as evidence of just how sparse traffic had become, in the rainy season we would often pass villages in which people had spread their laundry across the entire width of the Highway, utilising a channel of rainwater to rinse their clothes.

The terrain we are passing through is one of the last remaining pockets of Sierra Leone in which Sherbro is the most commonly spoken language. Extending some 50 kilometres inland along either side of the Kagboro River inlet, the landscape of Kagboro Chiefdom is a patchwork of sandy soils and salty mangrove swamps, as difficult to cultivate as it is to navigate. The farmers who eke out their livelihoods from these unpromising soils are among the poorest, remotest communities in one of the poorest countries on earth (UNDP 2012). Having once dominated the entire length of Sierra Leone's coastline, Sherbro speakers nowadays have such a low national profile that when I travelled elsewhere in the country I often encountered people who told me, with confidence, that the language no longer exists. The fact that, even in a country as small as Sierra Leone, it is possible for their existence to be so completely overlooked highlights how marginalised Kagboro's 20,000 Sherbro-speaking farmers have become:

People wait and expect the government to do things for them, like build a path to their village, but I tell them, 'Listen. The government will not come here. [President] Bai Koroma will never ever come here ... No minister will ever come here. We have our Member of Parliament, [but] she can only go where motorcars go. If we want a path, it is only we – it is only we who have to do it.' (Pa Albert, elder, Shenge)

But if Sierra Leone's government sometimes appears to have abandoned Kagboro altogether, its fish traders cannot. Such is the nation's demand for dried fish that once a week lorryloads of urban traders take a deep breath, count their money, and clamber aboard a truck to brave the uncomfortable journey to Shenge (see Figure 2.2). These massive vehicles, which on their return journey are piled precariously high with a seemingly impossible load of fish and passengers, must creep and sway so tentatively across the Highway's hostile terrain that, in the wet season, it often takes two days to complete the short, 80-kilometre route. 'That vehicle is dangerous! You sit on top, like a two-storey building! And the road is *so bad*! Sway-swaying, all the way. I don't want to die!' (Lucy, fish trader).

After a long, painful day cramped aboard one of these lumbering fish trucks, traders finally grind to a standstill in Shenge's 'vehicle park': a peaceful, open, leafy space. Around the perimeter are dotted a few wooden stalls, selling an assortment of small luxuries from cigarettes and powdered milk to pens and mobile phone credit. At its far end, the passengers get their first glimpse of the sea, where a steep ramp leads down to a small wharf and a now-decaying jetty.

Although it may not be obvious at first glance, Shenge was consciously oriented to an international world from the very date of its foundation in 1854 (Caulker-Burnett 2010; Fyfe 1962). Today, the townscape is littered with so many abandoned buildings – once-fine compounds being swallowed back into the forest or teetering precariously on the brink of an eroding bluff – one sometimes gets the impression that, at any moment, nature might reclaim for itself the entire peninsula upon which the town

Figure 2.2 Fish traders preparing for a journey along the Highway

is built. By far the most striking of these ruins is a massive, derelict fish-processing facility on the edge of town. Built by the Food and Agriculture Organization of the United Nations (FAO) in the 1980s, the hulking buildings that once housed ice factories and state-of-the-art machine workshops now stand empty and decaying, a poignant monument to the crumbling interventionism of a previous era.

The view from the sea

It does not take long to realise that this first impression of retrenchment and decay is only a tiny part of Kagboro's story. In fact, this stretch of coastline is anything but stagnant. Nor is it isolated – no more than it has been at any point in its centuries of recorded history. Facing the sea, the view from Kagboro is entirely different. The Shenge Peninsula protrudes into some of the richest, most navigable – and busiest – fishing grounds in West Africa (see Map 2.1). To its north lie the expansive intertidal mudflats of the Yawri Bay; to its south and east, the wide estuary of the Sherbro River, protected from the ocean by Sherbro Island to the south. Whereas fishermen elsewhere on the Upper Guinea Coast have no choice but to brave the fierce, unforgiving depths of the open Atlantic, the shallow seas around Shenge provide comparatively sheltered conditions for

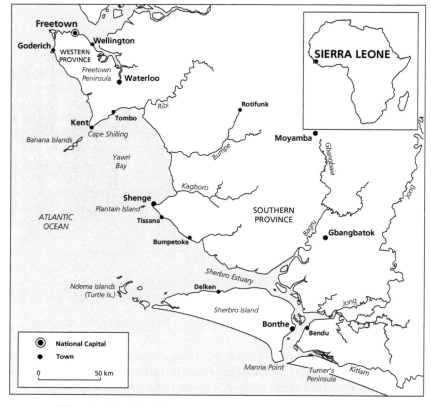

Map 2.1 The Yawri Bay and the Sherbro Estuary

breeding fish and for vulnerable fishing vessels. As experienced fishermen such as Pa Gberiwa will tell you: 'The reason there are so many fish here is that fish like rivers. There is no fishing ground like this fishing ground; like this Kagboro fishing ground. It is the best in the whole country. We in Shenge, up to today, we supply the whole country.'

In fact, when Sierra Leoneans elsewhere in the country talk about 'Shenge', what they are most likely to be referring to is the cluster of bustling, multi-ethnic satellite towns that surrounds it: Katta and Shenge-bul to the north; Plantain Island to the west; and, sprawling for almost two miles along the south-western shore of the peninsula, my field site, Tissana Wharf. These satellite towns have been attracting a steady stream of fresh migrants for most of the past century. Many of these settlers are experienced fisherfolk from elsewhere along the coast. Just as often, however, young people relocate here from towns and farming villages inland, attracted by the hope of new opportunities on the sea. Such has been the rate of migration to the coast in recent generations that, along the ocean-facing fringes of Kagboro Chiefdom, Sherbro speakers are now only one of many minorities in a complex polyglot society:

We Sherbros have always lived on the coast... All the other people who came and based themselves here, they all migrated here. Most of them are northerners – Temnes – from Makeni, from Port Loko... They came here. We taught them how to fish, and now some of them are professionals more than us! We have a lot of tribes. Loads and loads of tribes have come and based themselves here. Aside from we – the actual citizens, the actual landowners, we the Sherbros – we have Temnes here, we have Mendes, Limbas, we have Fulas. Even some Senegalese are here. (Pa Sese, elder, Shenge)

So, however remote Tissana may appear on first encounter, it is, in fact, a highly cosmopolitan world. The Shenge Peninsula sits almost exactly at the centre of Sierra Leone's most congested fishing zone, the coasts of which are peppered with at least a dozen busy wharf towns (*alehns*). Tissana's fishermen can reach any one of these towns fairly easily in the space of a day; and, if they judge that it will give them better access to the waters where the fish are currently shoaling, boat captains often choose to base themselves for a period or days or weeks in one of these other *alehns*.

This image of the waters of the Yawri Bay, filled with a busy traffic of migratory fishermen, fits very neatly with our currently fashionable view of seascapes as spaces of connectivity. It had once appeared fairly self-evident to historians and social scientists that, for 'terrestrial mammals' (Ingold 1994: x), coastlines marked the edges of human space. Oceans were socially relevant, largely insofar as they formed a natural barrier between one land-based community and another. Over the past few decades, however, in tandem with our own ever-quickening experience of globalisation, there has been a steady reorientation towards considering seascapes in exactly the opposite light: as the medium that connects peoples across distances.

Sidney Mintz (1985) and Paul Gilroy (1993) were among the first in this important trend in global history to 'invert scholarly convention' (Wigen 2006: 720) by exploring what happens when they shift their gaze from land-based societies to 'ocean-centred realities' (Wigen 2007: 17). In two quite different but equally influential studies of Atlantic history, both authors revealed an image of the ocean not as a vast dividing space but rather as a busy communicative network, criss-crossed with a constant traffic of ships, bearing people, commodities, and ideas that would radically transform the societies on all of its coastlines.[2] Making a related argument for the Pacific Ocean, Epeli Hau'ofa (1993) has argued that

---

[2] This argument builds on Fernand Braudel's (1995 [1966]) influential history of the Mediterranean.

European traders and colonisers consistently misrepresented Oceania when they described it as a scattering of tiny, isolated islands. Far from being cut off from the wider world by the tracts of water that surrounded them, Hau'ofa claims that Oceanic peoples had always experienced their universe as a 'sea of islands': not divided, but connected, by the water.[3]

Although ethnographic studies of actual seascapes remain surprisingly rare (Ballinger 2006), social anthropologists have become interested 'in rethinking the world in fluid terms' (Helmreich 2011: 137); enlisting images of watery 'flows' and 'circulations' whenever we want to allude to the increased mobility and interconnectivity of the globalising world (Appadurai 1990). If islands had once been the ethnographic field site of choice, precisely because they were assumed to be isolated and self-contained (Gupta and Ferguson 1997), seascapes have now found a place in the anthropological imagination as the metaphor of choice for interconnectedness.

My initial sense had been that I ought to find some way to compensate for the fact that, as a woman, I was unable to move through the seascape with these migratory fishermen. Throughout my early months of field-work, I travelled widely around the fringes of the Yawri–Sherbro fishing zone, on what I had originally conceived as a series of 'reconnaissance' trips, looking for the multiple field sites that would enable me to capture this fluid maritime economy from as many perspectives as possible. I took several trips to the frenetic Plantain Island, as well as to the Yawri Bay's most urban fishing centre, Tombo. I visited Gbangbatoke and Banana Island, and also spent several days in Ndema Chiefdom – the scattering of remote, low-lying islands on the far side of the Sherbro Estuary, where the Sherbro-speaking communities continue to subsist on the kind of low-intensity canoe fishing and cassava farming that characterised Kagboro's coastal economy a couple of generations ago.

While it was enlightening to catch glimpses of the broader topography through which the fishermen moved, I eventually rejected the idea of a truly multisited ethnography. The longer I lived in Tissana, and the more absorbed I became in the lives and dramas of my immediate neighbours, I realised that, although their social lives and material livelihoods were heavily shaped by the relentless comings and goings of fishermen and traders, most of the people whom I knew best led rather sedentary lives

---

[3] Similarly, recent ethnography by Judith Scheele (2012) has challenged the long-standing image of the Sahara as a social 'void'. While she is certainly not the first to note that people, ideas, and goods always moved across the Sahara, Scheele's ethnography reveals the Sahara as a dynamic social space in its own right. Through multisited ethnography, she traces relationships that unfold, often across considerable distances, between people whose livelihoods require them to move back and forth across the borders of Algeria, Mali, and Niger.

on a year-to-year basis.[4] For most of Tissana's women, children, and non-seafaring men, urban markets and foreign wharfs were present in their lives primarily as imagined spaces. Some made occasional hair-raising boat trips to Tombo, but, whether for lack of need or out of a well-founded fear of those notoriously dangerous passenger boats, most never strayed from dry land at all.

When faced with screens that obscure our vision, we tend to assume that 'what lies beyond the façade – the backstage rather than the front stage, the face rather than the mask – is where the core of culture lies' (Gable 1997: 215). Certainly, there were multiple levels on which I was excluded from important aspects of Tissana's social, economic, and onto-logical order. However, to one extent or another, the majority of people in Tissana found themselves in a similar position. Very few of my neigh-bours had been initiated into the deepest secrets of their respective ini-tiation society, for example; and only a fraction were familiar with the distant urban marketplaces upon which, ultimately, all their livelihoods depended. To the extent that the sea was an ever-present 'focus' in the lives of Tissana's women – and it certainly was – it was so only in the sense we might use to describe renaissance draughtsmanship: a focal point on the horizon where one's gaze is drawn but where, in fact, all lines are destined to converge and vanish. The ocean remained for us a potent but largely imagined space – a skyline under which men disappeared in their boats each morning and from whence, we hoped, they might return bear-ing fish. To this extent, my own pervasive sense of felt ignorance was not only a limitation but also, in itself, a form of ethnographic participation (Mair, High, and Kelly 2012).

The spiritual landscape

In the precolonial period, most people in the region we now call Sierra Leone had combined local ritual practices, such as those associated with the Poro and Bundu societies, with varying degrees of Islam. Over a period of several centuries, Mande traders and clerics became increas-ingly established in towns and villages across the region, forming a flourishing network of long-distance trade and missionary activity, inter-marrying with the indigenous elite, and founding mosques and Islamic schools wherever they settled (Cole 2008). The influence of Islam con-tinued to grow throughout the colonial era – particularly in north-ern parts of the country – as Islamic concepts, values, and rituals

---

[4] It was common for women, children, and non-seafaring men to have relocated several times over the course of their lifetimes – but they did not move at the same restless pace that characterised the lives of fishermen.

gradually became intertwined with pre-existing religious ideas and practices (Skinner 1978).

Having spread into coastal West Africa from the Sahara, the influence of Islamic beliefs and practices was less strongly felt in the south-western regions of Sierra Leone. By the mid-nineteenth century, when British colonial authorities began encouraging Christian missionaries to open schools in southern districts of the protectorate, the religious landscape of Kagboro Chiefdom remained largely unshaped by Islam. In 1857, American Methodists leased a piece of land in Shenge to establish a church and missionary school, one of the first in Sierra Leone's hinterland. After a difficult start, the mission established a network of schools throughout Sherbro country (Aldridge 1910: 261), giving Christian missionaries their first cultural foothold outside Freetown (Little 1967 [1951]: 262–3). Whatever their initial indifference to the Christian religion, Sherbro people were quick to identify the value of Western literacy, just as they had long valued Arabic literacy, as a source of exotic power and prestige (cf. d'Azevado 1962b: 30).

The form of Methodist Christianity that was to become established on this coastline was – and remains – striking for the extent to which it accommodated local rites and spiritual practices. Attempts to discredit local African gods and spirits by 'diabolising' them were a feature of missionary Christianity elsewhere in West Africa at this time (Meyer 2004: 455). However, in Shenge – and in many other parts of Sierra Leone's hinterland (O'Brien and Rashid 2013) – the relationship between Christianity, Islam, and spirit-based religious practices remained highly fluid and syncretic.

Nowadays, almost all Sherbro-speaking people in Tissana formally identify as Christian, although only a fraction attend church on a regular basis; they are discouraged, at least in part, by the fact that both local churches are 40 minutes' walk away, in neighbouring Shenge.[5] However, given the extent of migration into the fishing economy from predominantly Muslim regions of northern Sierra Leone, Tissana's population is now dominated by people who formally identify as Muslim.[6]

While everyday conversation is saturated with allusions to God or Allah, and almost every public meeting begins with Christian and Islamic prayers, there is very little sense of these two religions forming bounded faith groups. Intermarriage is extremely common and, given the frequency with which domestic groups reconfigure themselves through remarriage and fostering, a great many children grow up in mixed households in which at least some members belong to the 'other' faith. When

[5] Although there is a new Pentecostal church on the outskirts of Shenge, the older Methodist church remains, for now, the dominant Christian institution.
[6] About 70 per cent of Tissana's population identify as Muslim, and 30 per cent identify as Christian.

one adds to this the fact that attendance at formal religious services is decidedly patchy across the board, it is not simply that there is a high level of religious 'tolerance' between the two faiths. Most people I knew, if ever probed on the matter, were vague bordering on indifferent as to what, if any, were the significant theological differences between Christianity and Islam. Regardless of whether they attend mosque or church, almost everyone in Tissana believes in – and actively engages with – at least some of the figures in the Sherbro, Temne, and Mende spiritual pantheon. As a striking illustration of this religious flexibility, few people saw any contradiction in the fact that Kagboro's current Paramount Chief is a retired Methodist church minister, the former headmistress of a Christian girls' school, and ceremonial leader of the Poro society. Almost all women – including those who attended church each Sunday, or who piously fasted over Ramadan – remained enthusiastic members of the Bundu society.

An economic history of the Kagboro coast

This section outlines the economic history of the Kagboro coastline, beginning with its precolonial heritage as an important hub in the Atlantic slave trade. I trace the various waves of migration and the shifts in fishing technology and culture that have seen Tissana develop from a tiny subsistence village into the busy, cosmopolitan fishing town it is today.

Research in Sierra Leone, as elsewhere in Africa, is bifurcated. On the one hand are the 'classic' village ethnographies, with their emphasis on the customary politics of kinship and secrecy, of powerful elders, and of deeply entrenched lineage-based patterns of inequality. At the other extreme, studies that explore the self-consciously cosmopolitan, unstable youth culture of the city seem to represent an almost entirely separate subdiscipline within Africanist anthropology. As a town that is unquestionably remote and yet vividly in flux, Tissana's story offers the opportunity to unsettle these binaries, and, in doing so, to bridge an important gap in ethnographic discussions of this region (Fumanti and Rajak 2013).

The town's history offers one window into a much broader set of social and economic changes that have been taking place across maritime Sierra Leone since the mid-twentieth century, in which previously discrete fisher-farming communities have increasingly been assimilated within a highly integrated commercial fishing world. As I explore here, this trajectory has not always been experienced as one of unambiguous 'progress'. Set against a backdrop of national political violence, civil war, and, most recently, a precipitous decline in fish stocks, people in coastal Kagboro have sometimes responded to these transformations with profound ambivalence.

Precolonial era: slavers and chiefs

The precolonial history of Kagboro Chiefdom – like the history of the Upper Guinea Coast in general, in fact – is usually narrated as a violent story of slavers and warring chiefs (Fyfe 1962; Caulker-Burnett 2010; Manson and Knight 2012). The first Europeans to reach these shores were Portuguese traders in the mid-fifteenth century. From their arrival, the strangers established themselves under the patronage of local Sherbro landlords, exchanging imported metals and textiles for African ivory, animal hides, and, most lucratively of all, slaves. The profits to be made dealing with the white traders attracted an increasing number of Africans to the coast and to the creole settlements that were growing up there (Rodney 1970).[7] As the New World plantation economy expanded over the next three centuries, the market for Sierra Leonean slaves steadily accelerated, gradually usurping all other trade goods and fuelling a commerce that was to have profound and destructive repercussions throughout the region, as local wars were repeatedly orchestrated to meet the insatiable European demand for African bodies (Rodney 1966).

Although it is hardly the subject of day-to-day conversation, my neighbours in Shenge-Tissana knew very well that their coastline had once been among the busiest, most profitable ports in the export of human beings to the New World. As a foreigner, I was often asked if I had visited the crumbling remains of the slave fort that can still be seen on Plantain Island, a couple of miles off the coast. Nor is it any secret that their proud chiefly family traces its heritage to a mixed-race dynasty of slave traders.[8] In front of an audience of American anthropologists in 1977, the then Paramount Chief of Kagboro, Madame Honoria Bailor-Caulker, made this startlingly frank admission:

Yes, the Caulkers were slavers. They ruled the shores of the Yawri Bay... and their territory included Plantain and Banana Islands. Those islands were busy slave trading centres, regularly visited by ships from Europe; the Caulkers grew rich and powerful on the slave trade... but history cannot be eradicated... furthermore, powerful chiefs frankly prefer their ancestry to be rooted among the strong that ruled rather than among the weak that were enslaved. (quoted in Reader 1997: 379–80)

There was a centuries-long period during which the Caulkers had been one of the wealthiest and most powerful families on the Upper Guinea

---

[7] Even now, many centuries since the decline of Portuguese influence in this region, both the Sherbro and Temne languages are peppered with hundreds of Portuguese loanwords (Turay 1979).

[8] Thomas Corker arrived on the Sherbro Coast in 1684 as an agent of the British Royal African Company, and married the daughter of Kagboro's Chief. Their son, Skinner, inherited his grandmother's extensive coastal kingdom at the very peak of the Atlantic slave trade, at a time when 4,000 to 6,000 slaves were being dispatched from Sierra Leone each year.

Coast (Fyfe 1962; Jones 1983). In common with many of the slaving dynasties in this region, they worked hard to maintain the prestige of their transatlantic heritage, often sending their children to be educated in England. However, when the British abolitionist movement finally took hold in the early nineteenth century, their fortunes began to wane. When the crown colony of Sierra Leone was established at the other end of the Yawri Bay as the centre of British efforts to police the Atlantic trade, the slave fort on Plantain Island rapidly fell out of use.

The Caulkers relocated to mainland Shenge in a bid to control the emerging 'legitimate' trade in timber. However, with the British channelling their commerce ever more exclusively through their colony, Shenge's prominence in the Atlantic economy continued to decline. At the turn of the twentieth century, the British had coaxed provincial chiefs – including the Caulkers – into signing a contract that, in theory at least, was supposed to bring their territories under the 'protection' of Freetown (Little 1967 [1951]: 46). In reality, though, both the British and Freetown's emerging urban Krio elite kept their direct interference in hinterland regions to a minimum. Having been a prominent node in the long, brutal history of Atlantic slaving, Shenge all but disappeared from published histories of Sierra Leone. So, viewed from the perspective of their once-powerful ruling elite, Shenge's twentieth-century history might be told as one of stagnation and decline. However, there is another, quite different economic history to be narrated along this coast. As I discuss in the following section, the satellite fishing towns that surround Shenge have experienced almost a century of steady population growth and economic intensification.

Fishing from 1910 to the 1960s: immigration, innovation, and intensification

The Sherbro-speaking fishermen I knew were proud of their well-deserved reputation, famous across Sierra Leone, as uniquely skilled seamen and navigators. Cho was not the only one of my neighbours to have boasted to me, at length: 'Of course I can swim! Eh?! I am a Sherbro! We are fishermen. We have *always* been fishermen! If you saw me in the water, you'd think I was a fish!' However, while it is true that people on this coastline have been relying on the ocean to provide for their protein for as long as anyone can remember, the intensive focus on fishing, fish processing and trade, which now shapes so many aspects of social life on this coast, is a relatively recent development.

Paddling out to sea in tiny, streamlined canoes, fishermen such as Cho catch such small numbers of fish that they rarely make a substantial profit (see Figure 2.3). Unable to base their entire subsistence on fishing alone, most Sherbro-speaking households continue to invest considerable

Figure 2.3 Fishing canoe

time and energy in small-scale agriculture. In important respects, their livelihood patterns therefore retain a strong thread of continuity with that time – just on the cusp of living memory now – before commercial traders began to visit this coast; this was when Sierra Leone's fishing industry was, as Thomas Aldridge put it, a 'hand-to-mouth affair' (Aldridge 1910: 249). Here, Tissana's oldest living resident, Mi Yoki, is remembering Tissana as it had been, when she grew up there in the 1920s:

The place was small! Down there, there was a house. But all around here, it was just thick-thick-thick bush. We didn't know *anything*. We didn't know business. We didn't even have a *lappa* to tie [clothes to wear]. First time, there was no money in fishing.

In fact, although I ought to stress from the start that this differs from any version of oral history that was ever recounted to me by my own informants, Carol MacCormack has suggested that Tissana traces its origins to a community of domestic slaves, initially sent by their Sherbro masters to carry out the hard labour of clearing fresh farmland along the coast:

In the early nineteenth century, Tasso, at the mouth of the Sherbro River, was an important salt making site. Tasso salt was traded for Mende and Kono slaves, who then made farms for the 'owners of the land' [*ram de*]. Slaves were settled in villages around Tasso. One, Yondu, just up the coast from Tasso, means 'slave' in the Kono language; other slave villages were Marthin, Dibia, Pati and Tissana . . . In this area of villages clustered around Tasso, by the latter half of the nineteenth century, slaves and clients far outnumbered those who were *ram de*. (MacCormack 1977b: 192)

In other contexts, in agricultural areas further inland, anthropologists have tended to agree that the social memory of domestic slavery remains palpably imprinted across the landscape today, fossilised in the enduring power relations between a central town, inhabited by members of the landowning lineage, and the residents of its satellite hamlets, who, even now, are tacitly stigmatised as the descendants of former slaves (Little 1967 [1951]: 105). In his later work, Paul Richards (2005) has suggested that in some parts of Sierra Leone these inequalities continue to be so strongly felt – and so strongly resented – that they may be one of the reasons why smaller, more isolated farming settlements provided the most fertile grounds for recruiting rebel soldiers during the civil war.

Kagboro Chiefdom, however, bucks this trend. In terms of wealth and commercial vibrancy, older towns such as Tasso and Shenge have long been eclipsed by the now-thriving satellite settlements that, once upon a time, housed their slaves. In this sense, Tissana's name – which derives from the Sherbro *Tir Sana* or 'New Town' – has proven to be accommodatingly pliable. It may be that a settlement was once founded on this site as a new town for Kono and Mende slaves, but Tissana is now represented, in public at least, as a much newer town. In all my interviews, no elder I spoke to ever admitted to a knowledge of the town's history that stretched beyond a far more recent founding story, when Temne fish traders first began to arrive on the coast in significant numbers in the 1920s and 'begged' permission to settle there. In this story, only a single family is mentioned as having inhabited the land near Tissana Wharf prior to the Temnes' arrival. The head of this family, Pa Humpa Togbe – who was to become landlord and patron for the entire first wave of Temne settlers – is now remembered publicly as the 'first' of Tissana's original inhabitants.

When the Temne people started coming here, in the 1920s, 30s . . . it was first they who made these big smokehouses [*bandas*], like you see now. They started buying fresh fish from our canoes, and smoking them, and taking them away – far away, inland – to sell. They'd buy them cheap-cheap, and go and make a lot of money. So this fish trading flourished. (George Thomas, retired politician)

This was a time of rapid change across much of Sierra Leone, as the colonial regime made its first serious attempt to integrate hinterland regions into its broader modernising project for the state. Perhaps the most significant development over this period was the construction of a railway running south-east from Freetown, along which a string of new towns emerged as 'centres both for native and modern trade' (Little 1967 [1951]: 68). The demand generated by these emerging urban centres helped drive the intensification of the commercial fishing economy. By the middle of the twentieth century, Kenneth Little was describing 'quite a large local trade ... in dried fish, mainly *bonga*,[9] which has been brought from places like Bonthe and Shenge on the coast' (ibid.: 67).

In the early 1950s, the Shenge Highway was built, connecting the Kagboro coast with an overland route to the interior for the first time. With this increased connectivity came an accelerating trickle of migrants. Before long, the newcomers were not only processing and trading fish, but also going to sea themselves, building larger canoes than Sherbro fishermen had typically constructed, with the aim of catching fish for trade on the commercial market. In this respect (and others), we can see striking parallels with the patterns reported in Kono's alluvial diamond centres around the same time, when informal mining first began attracting large numbers of young people from farming villages throughout Sierra Leone and beyond (Dorjahn and Fyfe 1962).

However, the truly radical shift in Tissana's economy came quite abruptly in 1959 when the first of several waves of Ghanaian migrant fishermen arrived in the towns around Shenge, bringing with them vastly larger boats, longer nets, and more productive deep-water fishing methods than had ever been seen in this region before. Fante speakers have a reputation across West Africa as remarkably accomplished seamen. For many years they had been migrating up and down the coast of Ghana, following the seasonal movements of shoaling *bonga*. From the 1940s, Fante fishermen began travelling much greater distances in search of underexploited waters, eventually reaching as far as Nigeria and Senegal (Marquette et al. 2002).

As Tissana's last remaining Ghanaian elder, Pa Goaso, put it to me: 'We came because there were so many *bonga* here and the [local] people didn't know how to fish yet.' Jacob had been a young boy at the time, but this quote captures some of the wonder local people had felt on their initial encounter with the foreign fishermen:

They arrived, paddling, paddling in their boats. Big boats! So big ... [Their boats were] sharp at both ends, with a sail. Three or four boats would come in one day! And when they arrived, there were maybe 30 people in each boat – because they were coming with their wives, their children, their pots, everything ... They settled in Patti, Shenge, Plantain, Katta. They stayed by themselves; they built their own houses. Eeeeeee, that time there! If you saw the fish they caught! Those people, they know how to fish!

---

[9] Bony, herring-like fish that swim in large shoals in this region of West Africa.

While Kagboro's fishermen were reliant on dugout canoes, the vast Fante vessels went to sea with crews of up to 15 men. Where they saw evidence of *bonga* shoaling beneath the water's surface, they would paddle rapidly around them, casting their kilometre-long net in a wide loop so as to trap the entire shoal. Perhaps unsurprisingly, local fishermen were alarmed initially by the massive volumes of fish being caught each day in the nets of these foreign boats:

Ahhh, people became angry. With our canoes, we'd catch a few dozen fish, and these Ghanaians, with their big boats, would catch a hundred thousand fish or more! Our people said, 'This is *a lot* of fish! These Ghanaians have come to finish our fish! No no, we will not take it!' There was a big row, big palaver. (Harry, Tissana)

Local fisherfolk considered their livelihoods to be under such direct threat from overfishing that the men's Poro society mobilised to attempt to drive away the newcomers by force.

Pa Goaso: When people saw that every day we Ghanaians would catch a canoe-full of *bonga*, they became jealous! They used their society to go and trouble the fishermen in the sea.
Jacob: Yes! They used our society to organise the attack – the Poro society.
Pa Goaso: Because we Ghanaians are not Poro men. So, they went and started to fight our fishermen in the sea.

Eventually, following the intervention of the colonial governor,[10] an uneasy truce was reached, with Fante boat captains agreeing to take local men to sea with them and teach them their methods. At its peak, there were well over a thousand Ghanaian fishermen in the towns around Shenge, along with their wives and families. Then, as suddenly as they had arrived, they left again. In 1967, for reasons that were never made explicit in Shenge, Siaka Stevens' newly elected government deported all the Fante fishermen en masse back to Ghana. Nowadays, only Pa Goaso remains.

Yet in their short, eight-year residence, these migrant fishermen sowed the seeds that would transform the entire character of Kagboro's economy. Today, full-scale 'Ghana boats' remain a potent – and, for most fishermen, wholly unattainable – emblem of wealth. However, the four- to five-man '*yele* boats' (see Figure 2.4) – now by far the most common model of fishing vessel in the Yawri–Sherbro region – are essentially a scaled-down replica of those impressive Fante vessels, and use similar methods. Pa Moses' experience is typical of a man of his generation:

When I first came here, from Temne land [in the 1950s], I began to go to sea, fishing with those small nets. With that fishing, you couldn't catch a hundred dozen [fish]. You couldn't do it! So, when the Ghanaians came, I joined their

---

[10] This was during the dying years of the British colonial presence in Sierra Leone.

Figure 2.4 *Yele* boat

boat. We left our own boat and followed them to sea, to learn how to fish . . . Once we'd learned, then we left the Ghana men and built our own *yele* boat.

The 1970s and 1980s: Tissana's boom years

The compound where I lived was known across Tissana and all its neighbouring towns as 'Site'. The name is a throwback to the period some 30 years ago when an ambitious young Minister of Parliament, George Thomas, made this the largest construction site ever seen on this stretch of the Sierra Leonean coastline. The majority of homes in this region are built of mud and thatch. Those relatively few people wealthy enough to invest in modern building materials, such as concrete and corrugated iron, continue to build homes that closely resemble the traditional style in both design and layout. Although now seriously dilapidated, Site – with its open yard leading to a wide, pink façade, with its large windows, iron-railed veranda, and spacious parlour – continues to look completely different from a typical Tissana home.

George Thomas was the son of the young sub-chief who had welcomed that first trickle of Temne-speaking settlers, back in the 1920s, when Tissana was still a tiny fishing and farming hamlet. By the time Pa Thomas was an adult, the character of the entire Kagboro coastline had been radically transformed by the accelerating flow of Temne migrants. Carol MacCormack's (1982) survey of Katta Village, conducted in 1976, provides a valuable snapshot of the dizzying rapidity with which these transformations took place. Situated a few miles away, on the northern shore of the Shenge Peninsula, Katta is very similar in size and character to Tissana. At the time of MacCormack's survey, it was a very new town indeed. Only a decade after its population first began to mushroom in the 1960s, Katta had well over a thousand residents and had already surpassed Shenge as the largest town in Kagboro Chiefdom.[11] Even as early as the 1970s, only 9 per cent of the households MacCormack surveyed were headed by a Sherbro-speaking person. Even more striking is the fact that almost half the adults she recorded were unmarried, male 'strangers', unrelated to the person in whose compound they were living.

It was young strangers like these who formed George Thomas's support base when he first ran for parliament in 1973. The only previous Minister for Kagboro had been a prominent member of Shenge's old elite Caulker lineage. When the 'foreigners' in Shenge's erstwhile slave towns succeeded in electing their candidate for political office, this stood as a powerful symbol that profound social changes were under way. By the end of my 18 months of fieldwork, there were certain stories about Pa Thomas's time in office with which I had grown very familiar indeed. Throughout the 1970s and 1980s, Pa Thomas had bankrolled members of the Orjeh society to perform almost every evening with their masquerade devils. A predominantly Temne initiation society, the Orjeh is, to its followers, the most exuberantly 'fun-making' of all Sierra Leone's sodalities; and, as these two veteran supporters of Pa Thomas retell, the society's high-profile presence in Kagboro was explicitly conceived as a party-political campaign tool:

Mama Digba: Before, when this man was in power, there was so much gladdy-gladdy [joyfulness] here! We danced every day. We'd play-play, play-play with the Orjeh men.
Pa Brima: People would dance; the [masked] devils would dance! People would enjoy!...Ah, this place was famous...We didn't sit down! We'd go all over [the chiefdom]. For two weeks at a time, we'd be out; we would campaign. We would dance.

[11] Plantain is now the most populous settlement.

In common with many of Pa Thomas's most vociferous supporters, Mama Digba and Pa Brima were first-generation settlers on this coastline. However, from the start, this 'foreign' society was feared by many longer-term Kagboro residents as an aggressive move to usurp the once-incontrovertible authority of Shenge's own Poro society. Given that I was living as a guest in Pa Thomas's property, it was some time before the darker side of his reputation was revealed to me. But eventually an increasing number of my neighbours began to recount that the very same people who had delighted crowds with their exuberant, rum-fuelled performances would take anyone who dared to voice dissent from Pa Thomas's leadership to punish them in the sinisterly named 'naughty corner' (*fitei* corner) on the edge of town. For most of this period, Shenge's Paramount Chief of the time, Honoria Bailor-Caulker (herself a powerful and extremely controversial figure), sought refuge in Freetown for her safety. When the findings of the country's Truth and Reconciliation Commission were published in 2004, they singled out Kagboro as emblematic of all that had been most problematic in Sierra Leonean politics in the decades leading up to civil war (2004: 33).

Whatever their ethnicity or political allegiance, almost everyone I knew in Shenge-Tissana represented the long-running conflict between the Poro and Orjeh societies as the single most salient theme in their regional political history – more noteworthy, even, than the civil war that came so frighteningly close to their coastline in the 1990s.[12] This history of conflict between the Poro and the Orjeh reflects a more general characteristic of life on the Kagboro coast, where areas of social life we might intuitively want to gloss as 'esoteric' or 'ritual' are often integral to the concrete, everyday workings of power. Just as we saw a decade previously, at the moment of the Ghanaians' arrival in the Yawri Bay, these so-called 'secret' societies emerged to play a very public – and violently decisive – role in mediating economic conflicts.

Underlying the power struggle between the old chieftaincy capital and its erstwhile slave settlement, a fundamental reorientation was taking place in Kagboro's economy. As we have seen, the Sherbro-speaking residents of this coastline had historically been subsistence fisher-farmers. While perfectly capable of covering long distances in their streamlined canoes, their social identities and material livelihoods had remained strongly rooted in the land. However, alongside the important technological innovations of the 1960s and 1970s had come an even more dramatic shift in the character of fishing society. What Kagboro's fisherfolk learned

[12] See Pratten (2008), Bentor (2008), and Nunley (1988) for a discussion of the politics of initiation societies.

from the Fante example was that it is possible for commercially successful fishermen to sever their dependence on agriculture altogether.

Thus, freed from any economic need to have roots in the land or its history, a radically new kind of fishing economy began to evolve, with repercussions that penetrated deep into people's social and moral lives. The Yawri Bay's fast expanding wharf towns developed between them a distinctive form of maritime cosmopolitanism, as fishermen learned to migrate back and forth across the watery region in search of the richest fishing grounds. The new fluidity of the fishing society is perhaps illustrated most vividly by Plantain Island's dramatic efflorescence as a commercial fishing town from this period onwards. Despite being too small and too sandy to support even a single productive farm, Plantain is now home to the largest and most frenetically busy town on Sierra Leone's southern coast.

Here, it is worth recalling Honoria Bailor-Caulker's strident statement, cited earlier in this chapter, that 'history cannot be eradicated [and] ... furthermore powerful chiefs frankly prefer their ancestry to be rooted among the strong that ruled rather than among the weak that were enslaved' (quoted in Reader 1997: 379–80). We can now see that she was staking a defiant claim to conservatism at a moment when her chiefdom was experiencing profound political and economic transformation. The fact is, even as she was speaking in 1977, the importance of history *was* being rapidly eroded (if not 'eradicated') by the clamour of migrant hopes for newly forged futures. As the fishing economy continued to intensify over the following decades, the real basis of wealth across coastal Kagboro has become ever more thoroughly dislocated from the ancestral claims upon which Bailor-Caulker's framing of herself as a 'powerful chief' depended.

The latter decades of the twentieth century are remembered wistfully in Tissana as a period of seemingly inexorable boom. As more and more fishermen abandoned their dugout canoes in favour of new techniques that emulated the Ghanaian style, the quantity of fish being landed on Tissana's wharf always seemed to outstrip demand. The early 1980s saw another apparently great leap forward in fishing technology, this time in the form of large-scale dragnet fishing that local people refer to as '*sim*-boat'. This innovation was brought by a migrant from Sierra Leone's northern Bullom Coast, having originated in Côte d'Ivoire. The method involves using a boat to cast a net in a kilometre-wide arc through the shallow coastal waters. Two teams of people then wade out into the sea and gradually draw the net up onto the beach, corralling the fish into a large mesh sack at its centre (see Figure 2.5). At the time of its introduction, *sim*-boat fishing was far more efficient than any pre-existing method, and yielded vastly greater quantities of fish.

Figure 2.5 Men and women *sim*-boat fishing (dragnet fishing)

It would be difficult to overstate the general sense of nostalgia with which people remember the relative affluence of that period, when Tissana's waters seemed to contain unlimited riches. Mammy Hawa's effusive tone here is typical: 'Ah! This country was sweet! A sweet-sweet country, you see here. This country, which has become so hard now. Sweet!' By contrast, as Mammy Hawa suggests, the past two decades are often narrated as a tale of encroaching hardship. Despite the enormous influence of technological innovations imported from elsewhere in West Africa, international efforts to consciously 'develop' Sierra Leone's fishing economy have had a far more limited effect. The FAO funded a flagship fisheries project in Shenge in the 1980s, including a large fish-processing complex. The project's heyday was short-lived, however; after war broke out in 1991, it fell rapidly into disrepair.

The 1990s to the present day

An alternative war story The war years are remembered in Tissana with profound ambivalence. On the one hand, the local Kamajor 'civil defence force' governed Kagboro with considerable harshness. I heard countless stories, too, of families fleeing their homes in the middle of the night, to hide in the bush or to paddle out to sea.

As Jacob recalled, 'There was this fear. There was this fear around the area. We always thought that the rebels were on their way.' Those traders who continued to travel inland to sell fish had much more direct and traumatic exposure to the violence that was tearing their country apart.

However, the Shenge Peninsula was one of only a few tiny pockets of Sierra Leone that were neither attacked by rebels nor became the site of their own rebellions. Indeed, economically at least, Shenge thrived. Its now-sleepy 'vehicle park' was transformed into a heaving marketplace, as massive quantities of goods, shipped by boat from Freetown, were loaded onto trucks destined for towns across the southern provinces: towns that, were it not for this lifeline, would have found themselves entirely under siege. For several years, the Shenge Highway, built to sustain the light traffic of a provincial town, became the busiest thoroughfare in Sierra Leone.

This was the only way to the provinces: Moyamba, Bo, Kenema, Kailahun, Makeni. This was the *only* way you went there. Every day, every day, vehicles were coming, vehicles were going, vehicles were coming, vehicles were...just like that. (Pa Modu, elder, Shenge)

Although the war was rarely the subject of open discussion in Tissana, my neighbours would occasionally recall their wartime experiences in private conversations with me. Rosalind Shaw has argued that, in the immediate aftermath of war, many in Sierra Leone preferred a strategy of deliberate public 'forgetting'; they feared that, by giving discursive reality to past violence, they would only risk 'encouraging' its return (Shaw 2007: 68; 2005). As she emphasises, however, we should not be misled by this public silence into imagining that the scars of war had 'healed'. Her own research describes the deep layer of trauma that ran beneath the surface of everyday social interactions, as individuals privately 'struggled against insistent memories of death and violence, dreaming about it, anticipating its return' (Shaw 2007: 79).

If I asked about Tissana's recent history, people tended to publicly downplay the horror of Sierra Leone's war. 'It didn't *ohbohg* [bother] us too much here,' I was told repeatedly. 'The rebels never reached us. They were afraid of [being trapped by] the water.' So, it always came as something of a surprise when my neighbours slid into reminiscing about the relentless foreboding and intermittent terror that characterised that period in their lives. In these conversations, people would recall hungry nights spent trudging through the bush under thundering rain, or paddling frantically out to sea in the dark, in response to rumours that a rebel army was approaching Tissana. Fish traders recalled grisly, and sometimes terrifying, encounters with soldiers who flaunted their capacity for violence at checkpoints on the way to market towns.

On several occasions, I was taken aback to be informed, in the conspiratorial tones reserved for sharing dark public secrets, that one of my closest neighbours or best informants had 'toted gun', and had killed civilians, as a rebel fighter. These individuals, I was warned, were to be tolerated but never to be trusted. Such whispered accusations usually surfaced at moments of banal conflict, in response to the intense, routine frustrations of overcrowded housing and overstretched livelihoods. But the allegations also point to a level of anxiety and misgiving that continued to run as a discordant note beneath the surface of social life in post-war Tissana, however rarely it was expressed openly. In a context in which so many people have lived highly mobile lives, it was all but impossible to know which of one's neighbours had fabricated their own life history. As one elder told me, speaking of the young men who had come to Shenge to work on a construction site: 'Many are former rebels. It's hard to know the difference.'

An economy under pressure

When the war ended, Shenge's market rapidly dwindled, leaving in its wake a road destroyed from overuse. Meanwhile, even as fresh migrants continue to relocate to the coast, this relentless population growth has come at a cost. Long gone are the boom times of the 1980s: the fishing grounds upon which this population depends for its subsistence are showing visible signs of strain. Certainly, I never witnessed anything resembling the scene described by Thomas Aldridge a century previously, when it had apparently been 'no uncommon thing to see the Sherbro water . . . boiling over, as it were, with immense shoals of moving fish, and when it is the season for the *bonga* . . . the sight is indeed extraordinary' (1910: 249).

In common with other West African fisheries, Sierra Leone's once-abundant coastal waters appear to be teetering on the brink of ecological collapse. This is partly the result of overfishing by local fleets, including the use of unsustainable methods that target juvenile fish. Here, one of Patti's old-time Sherbro fishermen speaks with some bitterness of the fact that these newer fishing methods, which once seemed to promise such riches, have in fact contributed to the longer-term trend of creeping impoverishment:

The fish we caught first time, we don't catch anymore. We caught loads! But now . . . the types of fishing, the types of fishing are too many. It is not like it was before . . . now they draw these *sim*-boat nets [and] the fish have nowhere to hide. Before, when people went out to the sea to fish, the fish could come up by the land here, to hide, because nobody disturbed them. Now, with these bad-bad fishing methods, even where they breed, people catch them. (Pa Brima, Patti)

West Africa's rich coastal waters have also been an easy target for international poaching on an enormous scale (EJF 2012; Lucht 2011). Until recently, neither Sierra Leone nor its similarly under-resourced and conflict-damaged neighbours have had the capacity to effectively police their coastline, or to prevent illegal 'pirate' trawlers from pillaging their resources to satisfy European appetites (EJF 2012). Crews often encountered international trawlers at sea and witnessed the enormous catches they are able to haul, using vast nets that drag along the ocean bed, collecting everything in their path. Indeed, according to one of my informants, local fishermen learned their own more problematic fishing techniques by watching, and mimicking, the methods used by trawlers. However, as Ibrahim, a crewman, explained: 'Only, because we are poor, we heave the net by hand; trawlers have machines to do all the work.'

The biggest local boats can make 5, 6 million leones [£1,000] in one day! But it's trawlers who really cause the problem. They catch so much fish that they just throw away the ones that they don't want... [If] this man gathers fish and comes with them for everyone to eat; and that other man, he gathers them and throws them in the sea, which one is the problem? (Ibrahim, crewman)

Some people say the bad [local] methods of fishing... are destroying the fish in this sea. Yes, that's true. But from our own experience, if you could see those trawlers in the sea, you would condemn them more. (Moses, crewman)

According to international law, trawlers are forbidden from entering the Yawri Bay. In theory, if caught, they can be made to pay a hefty fine to the Sierra Leonean government. However, at the time of my research, there was no effective policing and trawlers frequently entered inshore waters with impunity, often ruining the nets and hooks of local fishermen – and sometimes even endangering their lives.

Sometimes, you can see the big international trawlers in the bay. No, no, we are not in favour of that... They catch tiny-tiny fish. It is illegal! Yes! It is completely illegal, but there is nothing we can do. All is left with the government, and they allow them to come, because they pay them money. There is nothing we can do. (Jacob, elder)

Jacob's fatalistic tone was typical. It is unclear whether the state would have the resources to stop this wholesale pillaging of Sierra Leone's fish, even if it were a political priority. However, most of my informants shared Jacob's assumption that government officials deliberately turned a blind eye to the pillaging in return for kickbacks from wealthy foreign boat owners:

If you are representative of the government, they bribe you! If the government is paying you 200,000 leones a month and then the trawler gives you more than that, you don't talk-oh! Because you think about your home. Your home is poor. (Ima, *banda* woman)

Fishermen emphasised the multiple different levels on which trawlers operated beyond the normal rules of accountability and transparency.[13]

If you capsize in the sea . . . they will never try and rescue your life! They will never rescue the life of we the African people . . . They decide that, to kill the people in the sea, they will just move away. They even cover their number plates so that, if they damage your nets in the sea, where will you report them with no number plate? (Moses, crewman)

A few hundred miles along the coast in Ghana, fish catches have begun to fail so dramatically and consistently that, according to Hans Lucht (2011: 180), the 'overwhelming majority' of young men can no longer imagine a future for themselves as fishermen. In Tissana, the situation is not yet so stark. In fact, many fisherfolk told me that, for all the hard work and deepening uncertainty, theirs was still a good life; it was even relatively prosperous by Sierra Leonean standards. Still, with the town's only real industry looking increasingly precarious, everyday social and economic life was often infused with a growing sense of anxiety. Fishing towns on this coast continue to attract fresh migrants from rural areas. However, suffocated by a transport network so dilapidated and dangerous that the peninsula is sometimes almost completely cut off from the outside world, population growth has not translated into any proliferation in livelihood opportunities.

Methods

I first arrived in Shenge-Tissana in March 2010, having spent a long, rather frustrating month travelling across southern Sierra Leone, searching for a suitable field site. I was curious to explore the tensions and opportunities that emerged for those people who navigated their livelihoods on the margins between the 'traditional' rural economy of 'wealth in people' and a more urban, market-based economy, governed by quite different moral rules and measures of 'profit'. However, finding a field site that enabled me to interrogate these questions proved rather more difficult than I had imagined. My original proposal had been to conduct a multisite ethnography, exploring the lives of the market women who shuttle back and forth between urban centres and rural villages, trading rice and palm oil. Bo Central Market, where I had initially thought I might base myself, turned out to be such a busy, densely woven labyrinth that there was barely space for a researcher to stand without getting in somebody's way. Meanwhile, my tentative enquiries about where I might

[13] Hans Lucht captures a similar sense of profound frustration among his informants in coastal Ghana at their inability to challenge the pirate trawlers that 'come like thieves in the night' (2011: 201), sometimes even colliding with local canoes that are night fishing.

find 'a village' in which to base myself were met with understandable bemusement.

It was at this point that I began to consider studying the economy of Sierra Leone's third major staple food: dried fish. Little has been written about the country's fishing industry, but, on the advice of my acquaintances in Bo, I made my way to Shenge. Arriving in town at the end of a long, dusty motorcycle ride, I was taken directly to the home of Kagboro's newly appointed Paramount Chief, Madame Eleanor Mano. By an extraordinary case of serendipity, 'Mammy Ela' had spent several years in my home city of Edinburgh while her late husband completed a PhD in African history. Perhaps in part because of these surprising parallels between us, she was as enthusiastic and welcoming as one could dream a host might be. Within a matter of hours, I had been found a language teacher, a home in Shenge's busy wharf town, Tissana, and, it seemed, the tentative beginnings of a research project.

No fewer than five languages are commonly spoken in Tissana: Sherbro, Krio, Temne, Mende, and Fula. For my first six months of fieldwork, I took Sherbro lessons most mornings with Pa Albert, who lived a couple of miles away in Dibia village and was respected across Kagboro Chiefdom as the greatest authority on 'Sherbro ways'. We worked our way through the colonial-era dictionary and grammar book that I had brought with me, and he taught me the hymns and prayers that he had translated into Sherbro for Shenge's church. I also took Krio lessons twice a week with Mr Carter, who was a teacher at Shenge's high school and a prominent member of the chiefdom's ruling family.[14] Although it doubtless helped to win me sympathy with my new neighbours when they saw how hard I was trying to master Sherbro, a language that nowadays only a few tens of thousands of Sierra Leoneans understand, in reality all my most interesting conversations were conducted in Krio. As the lingua franca in a highly polyglot community, Krio is far more widely spoken today than the indigenous language of the Sherbro Coast. Fortunately, it also happens to be by far the easiest of the local languages for an English speaker to master.

Both Mr Carter and, especially, Pa Albert also taught me a huge amount about the politics and social history of Sherbroland. As time went on, our lessons shifted from grammar and vocabulary into long, winding conversations about social life across Kagboro Chiefdom. I continued to visit Pa Albert regularly long after we had stopped formally studying Sherbro together. He would often tell me stories of life in his family village, or help me make sense of the dramas and disputes that had been taking place in Tissana. Although only a tiny fraction of this

---

[14] I paid Mr Carter directly for each lesson, whereas I gave Pa Albert more sporadic but larger gifts.

knowledge has made it directly into the chapters that follow, it provided much of the groundwork upon which this book is built.

As a second stroke of good fortune, the room I was given as a lodging was in a large and wonderfully dynamic household. The owner of the house, George Thomas, had long since retired to Freetown and his once-grand compound is now home to an eclectic, ever-fluctuating population of around 30 people – many of whom I came to count among my most valued informants. Jacob, who was Pa Thomas's nephew, was the caretaker of the compound and a well-respected elder. It was he who was officially recognised as my guardian for as long as I stayed in Tissana. In addition to Jacob's immediate family and foster children, Site was also home to three unrelated elders, all of whom had lived in the compound since it was built in the late 1970s: Pa Bimbola, Mama Koni, and Si Mary.

Around this core population, a steady flow of other people moved in and out of the large compound over the course of the 18 months when I lived there. Often these were relatives, foster children or strangers, freshly arrived from villages inland. Just as commonly, local Tissanan women sought temporary refuge there, sometimes with their children in tow, following the breakdown of a relationship with their parents or partner. As a result, many of the people whom I came to know best were living through an important moment of personal transition. They often reflected openly with one another, and with me, on what had caused their previous relationships to collapse, or had prompted them to relocate and start a new life on the coast. Although the voices you will hear quoted in this book include a far greater cross-section of Tissana's population, the residents of Site strongly coloured my impression of life in this coastal town.

As soon as I was less busy with language lessons, my most immediate problem – as for many ethnographers, I suspect – was how to pass the time. I sometimes went dragnet fishing in the morning, rising early to go down to the beach and join the teams of men, women, and children to wade, waist-deep, into the sea and spend the next couple of hours gradually drawing the long, arched fishing net up onto the shore. I went with the women in my compound to help in their gardens, and I followed them along the coast when they went foraging for oysters in the mangrove swamps. I tried my hand at basket weaving, fish processing, and fish packing. But, in fact, a huge amount of the material in this book was gathered simply by sitting on the busy back veranda of my own home, which ran like a corridor between the main building and the kitchen. It was here that everybody gathered if they were at home, to talk or to listen to the radio. The veranda also happened to straddle one of the busiest footpaths through town, so a near-constant trickle of pedestrians moved through the space each day, often pausing to rest for a while, to shelter from the weather and join the conversation.

Figure 2.6 Fish traders preparing to leave Tissana

Jacob's daughter, Buema, made laundry soap for a living, so every couple of weeks, after she had 'cooked' a new batch, I would be kept gratefully busy for a few days, perched on the floor grating kilos of soap into washing powder as the rolling drama of veranda life unfurled in front of me. When there was no soap left to grate, I devised another strategy for feigning busyness: crochet. Throughout my time in Tissana, I crocheted dozens of brightly coloured patchwork baby blankets, food covers, and children's clothes. This simple activity took the edge off the awkwardness I felt in simply 'hanging out' with no immediately evident purpose. There were a handful of other homes around Tissana where I learned to feel equally comfortable, and whose verandas were similarly busy with a passing traffic of garrulous neighbours. The 'vehicle park', where traders packed their dried fish into crates ready for transport, was another good place to intercept people with idle time to talk (see Figure 2.6); and, on most days, I spent an hour or so on the beach, sitting with one of the various clusters of women who were gathered there, looking out to sea, awaiting the fishermen's return.

Over the course of my fieldwork, I recorded about 40 semi-structured interviews – predominantly with older people. Initially, I relied on Jacob and Pa Albert to suggest people who were known for being particularly knowledgeable, or for having led especially interesting lives. In these

cases, Jacob accompanied me to interviewees' homes, to formally introduce me and explain my purpose. Although conversations very often
veered onto other subjects, we always began by asking people to talk us
through their life story – often with a particular focus on their story of
migration to the coast, and their personal experience of economic change.
Jacob is quadrilingual, so, in cases where people were not confident Krio
speakers (relatively common among the region's oldest residents), he also
translated back and forth between Sherbro, Krio, and Temne. A well-
respected and well-liked figure in coastal Kagboro, his presence went a
long way to making the elders feel at ease, and had the added advantage
of giving the interviews a relaxed, conversational flow.

Towards the end of my fieldwork I went back – alone this time –
and recorded conversations with many of the neighbours whom I had
grown to know best throughout my time in the town; I particularly chose
those people whom I knew would enjoy the opportunity to talk. In these
cases, I was already familiar with much of what was to emerge from the
conversations, but it was an opportunity to capture people's words and
their opinions a little more precisely. Although I generally found people
very happy to discuss their life experiences with me, I gave all interviewees
the same small gift of cash – or 'shakehand' – as a gesture of respect, and
to thank them for their time.

Ethics and positionality

Adamse: When you get back from Bo, we'll show you where the devils [spirits]
are, in the rivers . . . [so] you can come back to catch them.
Me: *Catch them*? No, I don't want to do that . . .
Adamse: Eh? Why not? Don't you want money? You can trap them in a jar, and
take them with you. Then you'll be rich! They've taken a lot of our devils
now, the white people . . .
Me: Why?
Kumba: Well, devils, they have ideas that you and I don't have. So,
when . . . [white people] want to make something, they ask their devil [how
to do it] . . . That's how your people can make so many things, like phones
and ships and guns. It is we who have the devils. They are here in our land,
but we can't catch them. And what can we make? Nothing.
Me: You made your boat!
Kumba: Ha! Just half-half things. We're just here, working in this fishing, nothing
more.

As has often been noted, ethnographers can never stand in a purely neutral position, outside the communities we set out to study: 'What we call
the outside position is a position within a larger political-historical complex' (Abu-Lughod 1991: 155). Across much of contemporary Africa,
people's sense of their own poverty is heightened by the ever-increasing

global flow of information and an awareness of the material prosperity enjoyed in other parts of the world (Ferguson 1999: 47).

For many in West Africa, encountering the world through the lens of a broader esoteric *episteme*, the disproportionate wealth of the 'white' world is assumed to derive from the power of Western 'secrets' (Bledsoe and Robey 1986: 217; cf. d'Azevedo 1962b: 30; Soares 2005: 133). In Tissana, people occasionally suggested that I might possess an innate ability to 'see' – and so to exploit – forces in the landscape that remained inaccessible to most of my neighbours. Similar powers of perception were credited to certain local people: among them, sorcerers, hunters, twins, and 'witches'. However, viewed in the context of Kagboro's long, deeply problematic history of interaction with Europeans, the association between white skin and ambiguous power seemed (to me) to carry a particular weight of moral disquiet. One of the most influential ideas to have emerged in Sierra Leonean scholarship in recent years has been Rosalind Shaw's (2002) suggestion that the more violent aspects of Temne spiritual beliefs contain within them an embedded 'memory' of Atlantic slavery. Certainly, although such an argument is difficult to substantiate, Kumba's claim that white people routinely seize Sierra Leonean spirits and transport them to Europe for profit would fit very neatly within Shaw's broader thesis.

Even if we limit our gaze to the more immediate historical moment, the more urgent problem for people in Tissana was that foreign-owned trawlers passed through Kagboro's waters covertly at night, illegally catching quantities of fish unimaginable to local fishermen. Perhaps it is hardly surprising, then, that many people assumed my research activities to be underpinned by a similarly extractive logic. When I travelled around Kagboro Chiefdom or visited fishing communities even further afield, I would often be approached by people who had already heard of me and had some sense of what I had come to do in Sherbroland: 'Oh, so you're the one who's come to steal our languages? When you take them home, they'll give you loads of money for them, is that not so?' The tone was always jovial, half-joking. Yet these encounters took place often enough for it to be clear that my activities had become the subject of considerable speculation around the chieftaincy.

I should stress that when my neighbours interrogated me about life in Europe, as they very often did, they were curious about far more than the reputedly lavish wealth of the Western world. Instead, they played with quite fine-grained models of how – they imagined – it might be possible for marriage, family life, and business relationships to operate differently. In these conversations, Europeans were often cast as a rather idealised 'other': fairer, more honest, and less prone to witchcraft than their African counterparts. As Ira Bashkow has demonstrated beautifully in a Papua New Guinean context, such morally bifurcated images of the Western world do far more than simply reflect the injustices of the postcolonial order:

What is striking is the extent to which Orokaiva have constructed the Whiteman within their vernacular culture as an Other that is morally charged and 'good to think with' about specifically local concerns ... The methodological point is that ... ultimately, we learn much more about the world of Orokaiva from their construction of Whiteman than we learn about white people. (Bashkow 2000: 322)

In this sense, my neighbours' reciprocal curiosity about 'white' society often proved a valuable methodological tool, for it led people to initiate conversations with me about the aspects of *their own* social order that they found most challenging or morally problematic. We were all of us involved in that very ethnographic process of trying to figure out how similar we were to one another, and how different.

Nonetheless, the fact that people sometimes likened my research to a form of theft brings into stark resolution the ethical cracks inherent in ethnographic research, and adds fresh weight to the problem of how I could 'fairly' reciprocate the considerable time, energy, and generosity of the many people who helped me live and work in Tissana. My day-to-day experience of fieldwork was heavily shaped by the assumption, shared by all but a few of my very closest friends, that I must have been extraordinarily wealthy. It holds true of most ethnographers working in contexts in which the people around them are very poor that 'perhaps more than any other object, money gives initial shape to fieldwork relationships' (Senders and Truitt 2007: 2). However, this rather uncomfortable dynamic becomes all the more salient for anthropologists like me, whose primary concern is to describe the 'morality' of everyday economic life.

The nature of ethnographic research is such that we learn what we know of other people's worlds only by entering into social relationships that are themselves inherently moral. What makes this experience most challenging – and, one might argue, most enlightening – is that anthropologists and their informants often begin with quite different expectations about what entails 'good' behaviour. In my own case, faced with an unfamiliar reality in which I could barely leave my room without being asked, very publicly and explicitly, for cash, I had no intuitive sense of what would be the 'correct' way of managing this barrage of requests.

Those myriad crocheted baby blankets that I distributed throughout Tissana were, in part, an attempt to 'moralise' my fieldwork relationships according to the logic of our own economic order. I wanted to demonstrate that I was willing and able to reciprocate the kindness shown to me, in a way that freed me of the uncomfortable sense that my friendships risked sliding into transactional relationships. However, as Bloch

and Parry noted over two decades ago, the assumption that money necessarily signifies relationships 'that are inherently impersonal, transitory,
amoral and calculating' (1989: 9) is a peculiarity of Western economic
thought. I came to accept only slowly that, for my neighbours in Tissana,
there was nothing contradictory about giving money as a gift to express
sincere gratitude or affection (cf. van der Geest 1997).

Still, the problem remained: the sheer volume of demands made upon
me each day far outstripped my resources. The anxiety this generated would have been familiar to almost all my neighbours. So, just
as Michael Carrithers described his experience of ethnographic learning
as one of allowing his 'whole person [to be] exposed and subjected to
the judgments and corrections of others' (2005: 457), in the end my own
unresolved dilemmas about money provided one of my most valuable
windows into the anxiety-ridden experience of inhabiting Tissana's
moral-economic order. If no one was able to give me definitive advice
about when I could materially afford to give, and whom I could morally
afford to refuse, it was because they were so often plagued by the same
question. As I explore in the following chapter, a near-ubiquitous characteristic of life on the Kagboro coast is for people to find their tight
resources pulled on by a seemingly impossible number of moral claims.

3   Economic runaways

I was sitting one Sunday with Hawa, in front of the house that she and her husband shared with the two fishermen who worked in their boat: Ishmael and Kumba. As Hawa and I chatted, I was aware, from the corner of my eye, of Ishmael strolling back and forth around the house, immersed in a long, animated telephone conversation.

This was a common scene in Tissana on Sundays. For most of the week telephone credit was a costly resource to be eked out frugally across functional, staccato conversations. At the weekend, however, that changed: the telephone company ran an offer in which a small amount of credit could buy a full day's worth of uninterrupted airtime. In a town of migrants, this was a precious opportunity for people to connect with friends and relatives left behind in distant parts of the country.

Hearing him repeating the same excited greetings and requests for news, it was clear that, at the other end of the line, the phone was being passed around between various members of Ishmael's family and former neighbours. After some time, Ishmael followed suit, handing his phone to Hawa: 'My sister wants to greet you!'

Hawa was a couple of minutes into her small-talk niceties with this woman she had never met – 'Yes, he is well. He is lodging with us ... Yes, we are all well ... Haha, it's true, we do eat a lot of fine fish here!' – when suddenly a flash of panic crossed Ishmael's face. He rushed over to her, having remembered something urgent, and mouthed the words, '*Tell her I'm in Tombo!*' Hawa didn't flinch. Nodding silently, she followed his instructions: 'Yes, we are all here *in Tombo*, fishing ... We are all very well here *in Tombo*.'

Afterwards, I asked why he had not wanted the caller to know where he was. 'It was my sister.'

I must have looked confused because, after a moment's pause, he elaborated. 'If they know where I am, they'll all come and find me!'

'Does this mean she's going to go to Tombo now to find you?'

'Yes. Maybe.'

This short anecdote hints at a deep tension that runs as an undercurrent through almost every aspect of social life in Tissana. On the one hand, there could be no doubting the depth of complexity and sincere affection that characterise family relationships here (just like anywhere else). Yet there is also a palpable sense in which the long-term grinding material poverty endured by Sierra Leoneans has taught people to be mistrustful of the material obligations that arise, inevitably, from any close social bond. While an important theme of this book[1] is that it explores the material ways in which people work to 'become' related, the flip side to this dynamic is that many people invest at least as much energy in attempting to *resist* absorption into onerous webs of relatedness.

Not only in Sierra Leone, but also across the world, fisherfolk are often associated with stereotypes of independence and unpredictability (Acheson 1981; Seeley 2009). In this respect and others, the Yawri Bay's maritime economy seems to conform rather neatly with popular imaginaries of frontier regions: often presented somewhat romantically as lawless spaces – the wild, unseen edges of the state that people retreat to in a conscious rejection of established authority (Scott 2009).[2] In later chapters, I describe the ways in which the Yawri Bay's established fishermen migrate fluidly across their maritime topography, pausing to settle – sometimes for a few hours, sometimes for several weeks or months – in one or other of the wharf towns that pepper the coasts of these fishing grounds.

My discussion in this chapter focuses on a quite different form of migration, and introduces a theme that will run as a thread throughout this entire book. Many fisherfolk I knew had taken significant risks to change their lives by moving to the coast. The rapid growth of Sierra Leone's fishing economy – like that of its diamond towns, city slums, and erstwhile rebel armies – has been fuelled by a steady stream of poor rural migrants who, for at least the past three generations, have been choosing to abandon their farming villages to seek a new kind of livelihood, often reporting that they were forced to do so by the violently exploitative micro-politics of village life. From the earliest colonial times, indentured farmers often opted to escape their family homes by moving to the city or seeking new livelihoods in the oases of youth that grew up in the diamond- and gold-mining regions (Dorjahn and Fyfe 1962). Some of the subtlest post-war research traces how, as the region's economy collapsed, fighting came to be understood as a viable form of migrant labour by the large pool of young men who saw no place for themselves in their villages – and ever fewer alternatives anywhere else (Hoffman 2007; cf. Utas 2008; Vigh 2006). This chapter adds texture to this post-war discussion by reminding us that, even at the height of Sierra Leone's implosion, not every young man who found village life intolerable was sucked into one or

---

[1] Especially in Chapter 5 on 'potato rope' families.
[2] As such, this chapter not only contributes to the (surprisingly small) anthropological literature on African fishing communities (Wyllie 1969; Jorion 1988; McGregor 2008; Nakayama 2008; Beuving 2010); it also sheds light on broader discussions about the economies of border zones and youthful 'boom towns' across the continent (Shipton 1989; Werthmann 2003; Walsh 2003; 2004).

other of the military factions (cf. Peters 2011). Some became fishermen instead.

James Scott has argued that many of the world's nomadic peoples, whose mobile lives skirt the fringes of national territories, could be described as 'maroon communities': runaways who had 'at one time or another, elected, as a political choice, to take their distance from the state' (2009: 8). Tissana offers an interesting slant on his argument. Most of the people I discuss in this chapter, who 'ran away' to become migratory fishermen in the Yawri Bay, did so from small farming communities in which they had already been living beyond the effective reach of the state.[3] For these runaways, the most salient and problematic political forces in their lives operated at a much more local level: in the fraught micro-politics of individual households, lineages, villages, and farms. Still, I argue in this chapter that the broader point holds true: there *are* deliberately political elements to fishermen's subsistence routines, which could meaningfully be read as designed to 'maximize dispersion, mobility, and resistance to appropriation' (Scott 2009: 329).

My suggestion is that commercial wharf towns such as Tissana evolved, in part, as a *refuge* from – and a conscious alternative to – the 'traditional' agrarian economy. As such, this discussion inverts one of the most familiar narratives of economic anthropology. For, far from being nostalgic for the lost morality of a pre-capitalist world, many people in Tissana entered this commercial world with the explicit hope of escaping a deeply embedded 'traditional' economic system.

In the first section of this chapter I sketch an impression of economic life in 'the village' (*fakai-ko*) as it appeared when viewed from the coast, refracted through the memories of the people who chose to leave that world behind. After discussing the material difficulties of eking out a subsistence from Kagboro's impoverished soils, I describe some of the ways in which landholding elders are able to control the labour of poorer client farmers. I end this section by reflecting on the depths of the tensions inherent within this patronage system, by narrating the stories of several fishermen who describe themselves as having 'fled' for safety to the Kagboro coast at different points in the past half-century.

In many cases, the greatest attraction of a life on the ocean was that it appeared to offer migrants a level of personal 'freedom' they could never have hoped to attain in their own home village. The emphasis in the second section of this chapter is on exploring the kinds of *economic* relationships people form in Tissana and how they appear to offer even the poorest young fishermen the hope of achieving personal independence. However, such dreams of economic 'freedom' are rarely more than

---

[3] See Ferme (2001: 20) and Richards (2005: 149) for an ethnographic account of the isolation experienced in some small inland communities.

fleetingly realised. The need for some semblance of material security, combined with familiar patterns of indebtedness and fosterage, consistently draw people back into binding networks of dependency relationships – relationships with a tendency to become both a burden on people's scant resources and a limit on their liberty.

Economic life in Tissana's hinterland

While it is common for households in Tissana to keep small kitchen gardens, attempts to farm on a more serious scale are rare.[4] The vast majority of households rely for their staple calorie intake on imported rice, hundreds of sack loads of which are brought each week by boat from Freetown and sold on by the cupful by petty traders whose customers' cash derives, by one route or another, from the commercial fishing economy. However, almost all Sherbro speakers along the Kagboro coast have close family ties in one of the subsistence villages of the hinterland, and an intimate knowledge of life there.

The people I knew often stressed the extreme hardship endured by their relatives in remoter parts of the region, who, unlike themselves, struggled to subsist without any regular source of cash income. During the rainy season, Tissana's Sherbro-speaking residents added a new stock phrase to their standard exchange of greetings on the wharf. After asking one another whether they had heard from their respective relatives in 'the village' (fakai-ko),[5] they would shake their head mournfully: 'There's hunger in the village-oh! They're hungry there now.'

Sometimes in the village, whatever you do, you will not be able to save enough to eat in the rainy season. You go half belly-full. If you are used to using ten cups [of rice] per day in the house, you have to cope on five cups, just to save enough to sow. (Pa Wilson, Tissana, formerly of Mompele Village)

The difficulty is not a shortage of land. Remoter parts of Sherbroland, in fact, are very sparsely populated. In Sierra Leone's hot, wet climate, wild vegetation grows fast, but this tropical luxuriance can be misleading. Sherbro farmers are quick to complain that the sandy soils of their low-lying coastal region make inhospitable terrain for cultivating food crops. Describing the years she spent in her mother's village (Moyibo), inland from Tissana, Buema recalled: 'Life there's hard, you know? They work and work and work and, with all that work, in the end, they can't grow enough food . . . because the soil's no good . . . People just can't grow enough food.'

---

[4] Pa Modu, whom I discuss below, is a rare exception.
[5] The same generic term is used, in the collective singular, to refer to any and all villages, rather as anthropologists might talk to one another about 'the field'.

Pa Modu and his wife Koni were among the few people in Shenge who even attempted to be self-sufficient in rice. The first time he took me to visit his new farm, I began to appreciate the truth of Buema's description of subsistence agriculture as a life of 'work and work and work'. The land was so completely engulfed in thick, mature growth that it resembled, to my untrained eye, a plot of virgin rainforest. Modu and Koni were hoping to plant three bushels of rice that year, but whether or not this would prove possible depended entirely on whether they were able to mobilise enough manpower to clear the dense bush.

Kagboro's soil can typically support two rice harvests in a row. After that, farmers are reluctant to plant again on the same area of land, anticipating that the earth will be so leached of nutrients that their harvest would drop below the amount of rice invested as seed. Common-sense farming wisdom decrees that land ought to be left fallow for at least 15 years to recover between planting cycles. Pa Modu had waited even longer: well over two decades had passed since this land had last been cleared. That long recovery period, he hoped, would be enough to ensure that the fragile soils yielded a healthy crop, but hacking through that dense bush would be an even more formidable task than usual. The amount of work was well beyond the physical limits of the ageing couple, their one tenant, and three adult children. If they were to clear this land, then they were reliant upon cajoling the help of the young male members of Koni's extended family,[6] fishermen who lived 8 kilometres along the coast in Bendu.

The route from Bendu to Shenge passed my compound, so I joined the 20 or so young men as they strode the last leg of the bush path to their aunt's village, machetes swinging jauntily at their sides: an impressive turnout. Every other day, these men worked in the sea, so they approached their short excursion into heavy farm labour with an almost festive air of novelty. Two of them had been identified as captains and, as soon as they arrived at the bush, they set about dividing the rest of their peers between them: each captain took turns to pick a team member, exactly as they might have done before a friendly football match. With everyone assigned a team, there was a flurry of competitive but good-natured posturing, a bet was laid as to which side would clear the most land before dinner, and then, to the soundtrack of thwacking machetes and friendly bickering, the real work began:

'I am not saying with paddling [a boat]; but with this work, I leave you way behind!'

'Ah! You hear his nonsense? I taught that boy to brush [clear land]!'

For all their initial high spirits, by the end of a day hacking through thick tropical foliage under the scorching dry season sun, the men were

---

[6] Pa Modu's family lived too far away to help.

exhausted. Koni and Modu paid their relatives the same small amount of pocket money, food, and cigarettes as would have been the going rate for day labourers inland. They could not have afforded to pay any more. But the truth is that these fishermen would never have agreed to work so hard, for so little, had it not been largely as a favour to two older relatives whom they held in high personal esteem. And there are limits to the amount of hard labour that affection alone can buy. Koni was unable to persuade her nephews to return the following week. In the end, she and Modu were forced to resign themselves to farm less than half the area they had hoped to sow.

Worse still – as if in fulfilment of the gloomy prophecy I had so often been told – even those virgin soils yielded an extremely disappointing crop that year. Pa Modu and Koni had other sources of income: they ran a bakery from their home. For a subsistence farmer in a small village, the compound failure of too small a farm and too low a yield would have been disastrous. It is against this material environment – in which a huge amount of tough physical labour is required simply to coax the most basic subsistence from the land – that the strong bodies of young people become among the most coveted, and contested, resource in farming economies. Full-time farmers cannot afford to risk relying on the willing help of their young relatives. Instead, more coercive methods are often used to obligate young people to work.

Inland, they make very, very big farms – not like our little ones here. At this time of year [rainy season], you won't see anyone in the village except for old people. All day long, from dawn, they are there in the farm. They aren't able to rest until night-time. Then they sleep. (Giatu, formerly of Mompele Village)

It is already evident that, when people in Tissana describe day-to-day life in small villages of the kind they or their immediate ancestors grew up in, these conversations rarely conjure up a sense of nostalgia for those close-knit subsistence communities. In the 18 months I spent living on the Kagboro coast, I became familiar with a rather dystopian image of life in a 'traditional' Sherbro village. As I explore in the following section, these representations do far more than simply recognise the poverty of Sherbro soil: they extend, too, to a moral commentary on the patterns of rural inequality and labour exploitation.

In one direction, a maze-like tangle of swamps and tributaries spread east around the Kagboro inlet. Then, westward, a full day's paddle across the wide mouth of the Sherbro Estuary, there lies the slender, sandy archipelago of Ndema Chiefdom.[7] Like the original population of the Kagboro coastline, the inhabitants of these regions are largely sedentary, Sherbro-speaking subsistence fisher-farmers. Yet, for all their important

---

[7] Although the waters around Ndema are at least as abundant as those of the Yawri Bay, the chiefdom is too remote to attract significant numbers of traders and has never developed the kind of commercial fishing economy that characterises the Kagboro coastline.

shared heritage, these places were often represented by my neighbours as a stark – and in some respects even frightening – counterpoint to their image of Tissana as a place of increasing openness and cosmopolitanism. Unreachable by road and untouched by mobile phone coverage, both Ndema and inner Kagboro are frequently mobilised in conversation as caricatures of 'backwardness': places where one still encounters barely disguised forms of domestic slavery and where cannibalism, witchcraft, and other covert forms of violence are a constant imminent threat.

Village runaways

I was planning to travel with my friend Buema to visit her mother's village, Moyibo, in one of the poorest, least accessible corners of inner Kagboro. The day before leaving, Pa Albert, who had himself grown up in a village nearby, told me something of what I could expect to see there. The image he painted – of the extortionate relationship between landholding elders and the labourers who enable them to manage their large farms – reproduced a pattern I was familiar with from ethnographic accounts of this region, in which elders set bridewealth at levels impossible for poorer young men to pay (cf. Peters 2011). The regular fining of poor men for adultery ('woman trouble') maintains them in a perpetual state of dependency, often obliged to work their entire lives for their in-laws or other lenders:

Wiser men, they use that trick: he may have five, eight, nine women, and maybe he doesn't have any boys to work for him on his farm. So, if a boy falls in love with his wife, he will say to the boy, 'The only thing you can do is work for me.' And the boy will do it. Whenever [the husband] has work, the young man will come. When you go to Moyibo, you will see it. (Pa Albert, elder)

Pa Albert's parting prediction proved uncannily accurate. On the very day we arrived in Moyibo, Buema and I walked straight into a 'woman trouble' case being heard on the veranda of the chief's house, overlooking the muddy banks of the Kagboro River. A middle-aged husband had summoned Baki, a handsome young man from his village, to accuse him of having flirted with his teenage wife. Baki admitted to being in love with the married woman and – although no one suggested that the two young people had actually touched one another – the elders agreed he should pay a fine of 300,000 leones (over £50): a sum that, everybody present must have realised, he had no hope of being able to afford.

Baki now had a choice. He could either stay in his village, slogging on the farm of his love's husband until such distant time as his debt was considered paid; or, as many have chosen to do before him, he could leave home for the uncertain prospects of life as a 'stranger' in an unknown town. I should stress here that a great many young people take the first option and remain where they are – embedded in tight networks of social relationships that, however riddled with ambivalence they may be, are also fundamental to their constitution as a social person. Indeed, perhaps the most surprising thing for me, watching that court case as it unfolded in Moyibo, was the anticlimactic way in which it ended. After the elders' harsh ruling, all three people – the young woman, her husband, and his lovestruck debtor – left with polite smiles and handshakes and climbed back into a single canoe to paddle back to their tiny village together.

However tempting it is to view Baki's hearing as nothing but a cynical strategy to extort his labour, Pa Albert reminded me that the personal tensions that riddle these tightly integrated rural communities are more real – and, potentially at least, more dangerous – than could be captured by such a straightforwardly functionalist model:

Other men [who are married to young girls], they will *hate* these boys. They will just hate that boy because he is trying to make something of himself. And any time there is a palaver, they will make sure he is penalised to the maximum. Sometimes, the boy will die. He might fall from a palm tree. Or get a snake bite.

With his allusions to snake bites and fatal accidents, the point Pa Albert is making is that a young man such as Baki would have good reason to fear being attacked by the jealous older man, using one of the various *ifohn wei* (bad medicines) that circulate through Kagboro's covert economy. Indeed, back in Tissana, one thing that struck me, as I began gathering the stories of men who had taken the second option and had chosen to sever their ties with their family village, was how many recalled the journey from home not as a cool-headed economic decision, but rather as a flight from physical danger.

Even Ba Kpana – who was, by most people's reckoning, the oldest living resident of the Kagboro coast – had first arrived on these shores an exhausted, isolated young man, fleeing a home in which he no longer felt safe. Like many subsequent generations of fishermen[8] in the towns around Shenge, Ba Kpana had grown up on one of the tiny, low-lying sandy islands of the Ndema archipelago. Over 60 years had passed since he first made that long, lonely canoe voyage, but now, sitting on the veranda of his Shenge home with Jacob and me, he had no difficulty conjuring the dramatic events that had prompted his younger self to flee his family's village.

Kpana's father had died when he was a teenager, which left him to live with his uncle. It was his uncle who had found a wife for him and who had paid the bridewealth on his behalf. After the couple were married, they continued to live in their patron's large household, as – or so Ba Kpana described it to me – his 'children' (*apuma*). The paternal relationship was

---

[8] This applied to almost none of the women.

not nearly as benign as that term might imply, however, as he explained
in a bit more detail:

When we were in Ndema, we would fish and farm for our parents (*ba hi*) for the
whole year . . . Our 'parents' would sell the fish and take it to Bo, Pujehum . . . But
we would never see the money. All they would give us was food . . . They arranged
everything for us . . . Even though we were fully grown, we were there under
'parental care'. You and your wife are just labourers (*noh haa mpanth*); just
workers under your parents. You don't know what happens to the money. That's
why they just go and find a wife for you. They choose the woman and pay the
bridewealth, and then you both work for them. You work and work and work and
you will not earn money. If they see any money with you – even one cent – they
will beat you and call you a thief.

Throughout this conversation, no one made any insulting reference to
slavery (*wono*), but the connection would have been obvious to anyone
listening. Domestic slavery was officially outlawed by the British colonial
regime only in 1928, following a period of several centuries during which
it had been integral to the ways in which families, marriages, farms, and
villages were organised. If ever I asked people directly what they knew
of the history of domestic slavery, one of the most common responses
was the claim that 'yes, in Ndema [or upriver], they still have that style
today'. From my own standpoint in Tissana, it was impossible to judge
the extent to which my neighbours were exaggerating when they suggested that nothing had changed in the remotest corners of Sherbroland.
Certainly, it has been suggested often enough by ethnographers focusing
on farming villages elsewhere in the region that, when domestic slavery
was formally abolished, the same models for understanding and mobilising social power did not disappear; rather, they became reframed within
expanded categories of kinship, clientship, and patronage (Ferme 2001:
171–2; Richards 2005; Fanthorpe 2006; Knörr and Filho 2010; Peters
2010).

   In either case, we are beginning to get a sense of the subtle ways in
which notions of paternal care, familial love, and exploitation were apt to
bleed into one another within the political economy of historical Sherbro
villages. At least in this respect, there have been clear continuities from
historical times up to the present day. In contexts where it seems to
come a little too close to the truth, likening a person to a 'slave' remains
one of the cruellest insults available, in either the Krio or the Sherbro
language. For example, as we got to know one another better, Jacob
would often confide in me his mounting private frustrations with his
lifelong client relationship with his 'uncle', George Thomas, the former
politician who owned the once-grand compound in which we all lived
and that Jacob worked hard to maintain. He had never been paid for
this work and, after long years spent waiting in vain to be rewarded
for his loyalty, he was finally beginning to lose patience. Increasingly,

he viewed his relationship with his uncle as one of exploitation, but he could see no way of extricating himself from it. So, when one of my fellow lodgers made the mistake of publicly calling Jacob 'a slave' in the heat of an argument, the slur was simply too offensive to be tolerated. With the Paramount Chief's consultation and full approval, the lodger – a policeman stationed in Tissana from elsewhere in Sierra Leone – was evicted from the house the very next day, along with his entire family.

This complex blend of affection, exploitation, dependence, and power goes some way to explaining why, despite the extreme conditions in which he and his wife were living in Ndema, Ba Kpana stressed that he had not ever *chosen* to sever the ties with his patron. Rather, his position as a dependent member of his household had suddenly become untenable when one of his uncle's sons had died and Kpana fell under suspicion:

My uncle summoned me in secret and said, 'Look. For me, I have no problem with you. But my wife is cooking for us [and she believes you killed her son], so I don't know what intentions she has for you [she might poison you . . .] Go! Go and hide yourself!'
    I didn't stop. I went straight to my canoe, and paddled all night, until I came to Shenge. When I got here, I met with the elders in Shenge. The Ndema people who were here already introduced me as their guest.

Ba Kpana's story resonated strongly with Jacob's. The latter's father had run away from his own village some 30 years later, and – according to family history – under a similar threat of imminent danger:

He found his cousin's canoe – a boy he used to go to sea with – abandoned, all covered in blood. He grew very afraid! He just paddled, paddled, paddled all the way to Shenge, in the dark. He never went back there until he died. Even when his family called him, he'd just say, 'Yes, I'm coming, I'm coming!' But he never went.

Nowadays, there is a weekly *pampa* (a slow, motorised passenger canoe) between Ndema and Kagboro, but, at the time when these two young fishermen each made their night-time getaway, there was almost no direct communication between the two chiefdoms. 'When we were young, we did not know that such a place as Ndema existed,' Mr Dumont, a middle-aged schoolteacher once told me. And yet, as Ba Kpana's account makes clear, when he arrived in the 1940s he met a community of émigré fishermen already established on the foreign coastline; these were part of a steady trickle of young men, all of whom had been desperate enough to escape close family relationships, which they came to view as so hostile that they were prepared to risk a long journey into the complete unknown.

Sometimes, Ndema men would arrive, paddling. But they seemed to come from a very, very distant place, with their strange [dialect of] Sherbro. Maybe a young man would run away from his village. Even now, this is happening. Sometimes young men will be killed for woman trouble. And most of these Ndema boys who are coming here, it is for this: either for women or [for fear they will become the victim of] cannibalism. Even now, they are coming. (Mr Dumont, Shenge)

The marine migration route from Ndema to the Kagboro coast is travelled almost exclusively by men, but Tissana is far from being a predominantly 'male' space. Although it is also common for women to leave their landlocked villages in search of an alternative livelihood on the sea, this narrative of liberation through migration is an overwhelmingly male one. In my experience, female migrants are far less likely to describe their move as one of radical rupture, and far more likely to emphasise their continuing connectedness with family networks left behind. These rhetorical differences map onto wider gendered expectations about how young people in Sierra Leone 'come of age'.

Narratives of 'running away from home' have come to occupy a central place in constructions of rural masculinity, and reappear in various guises throughout the ethnohistorical record. For decades, commentators have been reporting that the poorest young men were choosing to leave their villages, hoping to escape the harsh physical labour and sexual constraints that characterised their lives there, and pursuing the promise of freedom and social mobility in cities and diamond-mining towns (Dorjahn and Fyfe 1962; Little 1967 [1951]; Utas 2008). As we saw in Chapter 1, the theme of 'intergenerational'[9] tension between young men and male elders has been revisited in recent years with added urgency. Since the civil war, it has become common to argue that many young fighters were first driven from their home villages, and into one or other of the armed factions, by their anger at the ways in which local landholders were able to control their labour (Richards 2005; 2004; Knörr and Filho 2010; Peters 2010). The narratives that these authors gathered from retired rebel fighters bear striking resemblance to the stories I encountered among émigré fishermen, circulating around themes of poverty, forced labour, and 'woman trouble'.

Viewed against this existing literature, perhaps the most surprising story I encountered from any village runaway was that of Moses Bundu, who had made the seemingly unusual decision of exiling himself from a home village in which he had been one of the wealthiest patrons:

Any bush you could see [around the village], it was my father who owned all that land. So I used to farm. I'd prepare two farms – big farms! I'd plant ten to 15 bushels [of rice] in each. I'd grow groundnuts. I'd plant pepper . . .

Clearing an area of land that size is a massive undertaking and would have required him to mobilise a serious amount of labour in his village.

---

[9] While societies in this region are often described as 'gerontocratic', this is rather too literal an interpretation of a local idiom that obfuscates patronage relationships behind the language of 'parental care' (cf. Murphy 1980: 202).

You might recall that, back in Shenge, Pa Modu and Koni had failed to recruit enough workers to clear a farm one-tenth that size. Yet, for all his evident social power, Moses recalls the experience of being a local big man as one of unbearable anxiety:

The way conditions were with me in my village, it was so bad . . . My people fought me, together, as a family. You know, on our native side, we have that – how do you say it? – that *hateness*, that hateful jealous mind. They use that bad-bad business [*ifohn wei*], so that they can spoil your life.

When Moses became seriously ill, he was certain that it was as a result of an attempt by members of his own family to destroy him. 'I scatter-scattered all my seven children to live with different brothers and sisters . . . [then] I left, without saying goodbye to anyone. That was 1984. I've never been back.'

The fact that migrants should emphasise so often the imminent physical danger of the moment in which they opted to leave home is important for several reasons. Firstly, as we will continue to see throughout this chapter, there is nothing unusual in the way in which émigrés conflate overt economic tensions – over labour, land, and debt – with more embodied, if more covert, forms of violence: poisoning, witchcraft, fetish medicine or 'cannibalistic' murder. The easy way in which people's explanations slide back and forth between these two apparently distinct spheres of material life points to a much broader characteristic of social life in this region. Here, the human body is not (only) fertile ground for constructing metaphors and moral narratives *about* economics. The various strategies through which people set out to influence one another's bodies are themselves a constituent element of the everyday economic order.

Secondly, it is striking that not only former tenant farmers but also their former patrons should remember village economic life as riddled with potentially fearful animosity. In this sense, my data appears to support William Murphy's suggestion that the moral economy of patronage and dependency is also inherently 'a moral economy of violence and punishment (or rebellion), as dependants can be accused of failures in loyalty and gratitude to patrimonial dispensation, and rulers can be faulted for failures in protection and support – as well as excessive extraction of tribute and labour' (2010: 42). Although the details of their accounts differ, both Ba Kpana and Moses found that their closest personal relationships rapidly transformed into their greatest source of fear. In both men's stories, what is taken for granted is that intimacy, animosity, exploitation, and risk are often facets of the same relationship. Discussions in the post-war period have (quite rightly) focused on working to understand the anger of the marginalised young men who eventually became fighters. The broader point to stress is that, when an economy is stretched to breaking point, the tensions inherent within households and dependency relationships often become the clearest focal point for these frustrations (Schoepf and Schoepf 1988; Bolten 2008).

Still, by narrating their departure from their ancestral village as a flight from mortal danger, émigrés are also emphasising the fact that they would not have left under any normal circumstances. For people growing up in such tightly integrated sedentary villages, it is a radical move to sever the familial ties that, up to that point, had been the very basis of their social identity. It is not without good reason that rural Sierra Leoneans might be extremely wary of the prospect of beginning a new life alone, a 'stranger' in another land.

One of the most intriguing things about the high level of immigration into the fishing economy is that, throughout rural Sierra Leone, 'strangers' have long been structured as the archetype of poverty and vulnerability – closely associated, in fact, to the historical figure of the domestic slave (d'Azevedo 1962b; Dorjahn and Fyfe 1962). In Sherbro farming villages, as elsewhere in Sierra Leone, access to land is controlled by a few key members of important local lineages: those people, in short, who are able to claim the longest ancestry in the region. In subsistence communities, where land is the very basis of every person's basic liveli-hood, this structures immigrants in a permanent state of dependency, wholly reliant for their subsistence upon the goodwill of the landlord and 'father figure' who agrees to grant them the means to grow food.

As we have already seen, wherever one encounters idioms of 'parental care' used to describe a relationship between two adults, it suggests a situation in which patrons have the potential (at least) to exert extraordinary control over their dependants' lives. Hardly surprising, then, that people might feel wary about leaving even the most difficult circumstances in their family homes, if the alternative they imagine for themselves is a life in which being a 'stranger' guarantees rapid reintegration into new kinship structures: once more under 'parental care', but this time more vulnerable to exploitation than before. As I explore in the following sec-tion, however, there are various reasons why a young migrant arriving in Tissana might feel rather more optimistic than this model suggests.

Seeking 'freedom' on the sea

If we return to Ba Kpana's story, we will see that – even back in the 1940s – his experience of settling on the Kagboro coast was not characterised by a move into new forms of dependency:

When I reached Kagboro, I found the same system – because the people in Ndema and the people here are the same people. We are all Sherbros. There were no vehicles in Shenge at that time, and not many Temnes yet. But for me, here, life was better, because I was not under parental care. I could fish for myself! (Ba Kpana)

By Ba Kpana's own account, social life on his adoptive Kagboro coast had not been inherently very different from life on the Ndema archipelago he had left behind. Indeed, here is another of Tissana's oldest living residents, Mi Yoki, remembering her own youth in Tissana, when it, too, had been a tiny, near-subsistence fisher-farmer hamlet:

> You had to work for your *ba hi* ['parents']. You would never dare ask for money. You wouldn't even dream it. The only thing you could ask for – and, in fact, you would not even ask for it – is food. They would not even give you clothes. You might be 20 before you have anything to wear.

Yet, Ba Kpana's personal experience was that, *as a stranger* in Tissana, unburdened by the debts and obligations of family life, he was far more independent than he could ever have hoped to be in his ancestral home. For the first time in his life, he was able to sell his own catch to his own customers and do exactly what he pleased with his small profit.

As I explore throughout the remaining part of this chapter, Ba Kpana's seemingly simple observation captures a tension that has continued in Tissana, through all the radical socio-economic changes of the intervening decades. Even today, much of the town's social life is played out at the interface between two quite different models of moral economy. Firstly, as we will see, there are various reasons why newcomers arrive in Tissana, hoping that the maritime economy might offer the kind of personal freedom that would have been unthinkable in a subsistence farming village. Yet, when people have been in Tissana for a longer period, this initial impression of the town as a place of 'freedom' has a tendency to wear thin. In an economy as tight as Tissana's, networks of social relationships (*subabu*) remain the only viable form of material security.

The old, land-based models of patrimonial power fail to translate smoothly into the Yawri Bay's commercial fishing economy. For generations now, the real source of wealth and prestige in a town such as Tissana has not been land rights but boat ownership, and, unlike land, there are no customary regulations or patterns of inheritance to keep this kind of property restricted within certain high-ranking lineages. As the commercial fish trade has steadily intensified over the last few decades, Tissana's economy is now so squarely oriented towards the sea that an individual's ability to claim deep ancestral roots on the Kagboro coast is of ever-diminishing material relevance to their ability to become a wealthy or respected person.

This dramatic shift in patterns of regional power appears to have contributed to an equally radical shift in people's understanding of the relationship between history and place. So, whereas classic accounts of social life on the Upper Guinea Coast describe a people preoccupied with accessing and manipulating powerful, half-hidden knowledge of the past (d'Azevedo 1962b; Ferme 2001), my experience in Tissana was that ancestors appeared to be losing their position at the centre of social life (see Chapter 7).[10]

One result of this truncation of historical memory is that the distinction between locals and strangers has been radically eroded. Certain kinds of immigrants are able to thrive perfectly well in Tissana, without even the most nominal patronage of a local big man. Following in Ba Kpana's wake, a steady stream of young fishermen continue to make their way, by canoe, across the Sherbro Estuary from Ndema to settle on the Kagboro coast. Nowadays, a whole section of Tissana is dominated by these Ndema migrants:

Yes, they still come! It is only men who come: they meet Kagboro women here. [They come] because they want to change their environment. When they are over there, they are in a hole. It is something like a hole. Here in Kagboro, it is more advanced. You are closer to Moyamba and Freetown and other places. You gain experiences. (Pa Brima, Tissana)

In common with fishing towns elsewhere in Africa, Tissana is at once remote and surprisingly 'urban' in its social character (cf. Beuving 2010: 243). For a start, its population – like that of larger urban centres – is visibly dominated by young migrants. Immersed, often for the first time, in a diverse multi-ethnic peer group, newcomers from small villages relish the vibrancy, camaraderie, and open flirtation that characterise social life on the wharf, far from the familiar watchful gaze of village elders.

Here, there is cinema, there are bars, there are jams [dance parties]. They meet interesting people. Here, people know how to speak Krio, they know how to dress well. Those things do not exist in the village. Those things change people's lives! (Timbo, town chief and boat owner)

So, aside from its location at the edge of a fragile state's territory, Tissana is a 'frontier town' in the sense described by De Boeck. It sits on a socio-cultural frontier, at the interface between two quite different ways of life: '"rural" and "urban" . . . "traditions" and "modern" categories, practices, mentalities, relationships and belief systems' (De Boeck 2001: 559). The porosity and fluidity of Tissana's social networks often bear a striking resemblance to those described in the informal economies of African cities (Simone 2005). This is a world in which marriages are typically informal and unstable; friends and customers are apt to leave town with little warning; even children move between households with surprising frequency.

---

[10] I am not in a position to comment on the rituals that take place within secret society bushes, which may involve ancestors.

And yet, for all the potential insecurity of their new life surrounded by strangers, I am not the first ethnographer to note that, for many rural migrants in frontier towns, the greatest appeal of their adoptive home is precisely this metropolitan promise: of a life liberated from stifling kinship structures (Beuving 2010; Walsh 2003).

Freedom, the market, and 'living in the moment'

Although he was writing well over a century ago, Georg Simmel's reflections on *The Philosophy of Money* (1978 [1900]) capture a moral ambivalence that still runs deep in the Western world view today. He argued that, whereas the gift of a specific object creates an ongoing reciprocal bond between giver and receiver, the empty and indifferent character of money acts instead to create a sense of neutrality and distance between exchange partners. Until the 1980s, the prevailing tendency among anthropologists was to focus on the purely negative aspects of that shift: lamenting the corrosive force of the market, as it eroded the specificity of local economic arrangements.

We saw in Chapter 1 that, since the 1980s, repeated moves have been made to complicate a set of rather moralised binary models of economic life that had become hackneyed through overuse (Bloch and Parry 1989; Browne 2009). It is now well documented that so-called 'amoral' market economies are invariably permeated with 'gift-like' relations (Rajak 2011; Dolan and Rajak 2011). West Africanists have been particularly vocal in the move to 'rehabilitate' money's reputation, illustrating that cash need not necessarily corrode social relations, but, on the contrary, is often regarded as inseparable from, and constitutive of, love, respect, and social personhood (e.g. Cornwall 2002; van der Geest 1997; Barber 1995).

Less often acknowledged is the possibility that, for some people in some contexts, severing social relations might be exactly what they want, and that herein lies the greatest appeal of an economic life characterised by transactability. Simmel himself was well aware that economic alienation was not entirely without its attractions:

In as much as interests are focused on money...the individual will develop the tendency and feeling of independent importance in relation to the social whole...since he is free to take up business relations and co-operation wherever he likes; modern man is free – free because he can sell everything, and free because he can buy everything. (Simmel 1978 [1900]: 343, 404)

Now, as in Ba Kpana's times, Tissana's newest arrivals still revel in the freedom that comes from their newly disembedded status. Removed from the debts and family obligations that had characterised their lives at home, here they are able to sell their catch to whomsoever they please, and spend (or indeed waste) their small cash exactly as they like.

Ha! Those Ndema fishermen – they *enjoy* their catch-oh! If they catch plenty fish one day, the next day they just blow [relax]! They don't go to sea again until they run out of fish. (Fatti, petty trader, Tissana)

Such an apparently wilful lack of interest in pursuing material profit was regarded with something between admiration and frustration by their neighbours, who were more established on the coast. The Krio verb 'enjoy' is a loaded one and tends to be used in Tissana in a way that implies immaturity, selfishness or lack of foresight. Those connotations are made more explicit by Marie in the following quote, as she jokingly explains why she would never want her relationship with her Ndema fisherman boyfriend, Asana, to evolve into anything more than a casual love affair:

Argh, that man! You see how he bluffs [swaggers]! That boyfriend of mine: when he gets a good catch, he just kicks back and bluffs! You see how he walks. He struts! He bounces! He eats fine fish. He enjoys himself till all his fish is done. Only then, he goes back to sea. Tissana men are different. Tissana men work! They'd even sell their fine fish and eat those cheap-cheap ones, just to make money.

Marie had a point. I would often bump into Asana strolling unhurriedly around town; the two of us were conspicuous, in the busy throng of Tissana's economy, for the unreasonable amount of leisure time we appeared to have. And, while I spent much of my time guiltily feigning busyness, Asana did nothing of the kind. If ever I asked what he was doing, he would reply, with a sparkle in his eye: 'Nothing!'

Ndema fishermen's seemingly deliberate disinterest in accumulating material wealth can be viewed as one element of the broader 'frontier' mentality with which many new migrants approach their adoptive life in Tissana. If dominant, sedentary notions of economic responsibility typically require people to manage their resources carefully and plan for their future, Day, Papataxiarchis, and Stewart (1999) observed that marginalised groups, living on the edges of society, often take exactly the opposite approach: opting instead to live defiantly 'in the moment' – even when to do so may come at a cost to their already tenuous material security. By eschewing institutions such as the household that 'organise long-term social reproduction and, simultaneously, produce hierarchical relationships', the argument goes that marginal people's *aspirations* to freedom and autonomy come to be 'defined precisely by their monetary characteristics – which refuse to be caught in any framework outside their fleeting performance' (ibid.: 2).

Applying this argument to another 'frontier' economy – this time a Malagasy sapphire-mining town – Andrew Walsh emphasises the creative performativity with which the miners enact their disdain for money. By visibly 'daring' to consume their earnings on fleeting pleasures, with little regard for their uncertain future, these marginal young men, he argues, are taking part in a wider public performance of defiance against a world in which they otherwise have negligible power: 'establishing for themselves and, in some cases, for others around them, their mastery of those things that might master them' (Walsh 2003: 292). Here, we see clear echoes of Richard Wilk's survey of the 'binge' economies that emerge in towns frequented by male gang labourers. He, too, emphasises the theatrical machismo of economies in which, for the limited periods when they had access to money or opportunities to spend it, these poor men often 'competed to get rid of it in elaborate ways' (Wilk 2007: 19).

In fishing economies, like mining ones, wealth arrives in staccato, unpredictable bursts – and here, too, fishermen often describe themselves as incapable of or resistant to saving money for the future (cf. Astuti 1999). However, while Walsh emphasises the creative performativity of 'daring' economic lives, this boat owner reminds us that there is more at stake as a result of a person's economic choices than the language of 'performance' suggests:

He [a single man] will make a lot of money and spend it! But the women don't. They are thinking about the problems of educating their children – medical problems are there... So women don't spend money like that. They are very, very careful. But men just burn their money! They think, 'Tomorrow, I will go to sea and get a good catch and come again.' But the women see [that] this money needs to be controlled. (Sumana, boat owner)

Far from exhibiting any disdain for money per se, the people I knew in Tissana were wary of the expensive relationships in which one tends to become embroiled the moment one sets out to accumulate cash.[11] In Tissana, money was neither made nor squandered with sufficient fervour to be labelled a 'binge economy' in the sense described by Wilk and Walsh. And yet there is an important respect in which the town's economy is located far more squarely 'in the present moment' than we have come to expect of communities elsewhere on the Upper Guinea Coast. Looking backwards, a creeping disinterest in genealogy is made evident by the gradual disappearance of ancestors from the lived landscape of the Kagboro coast. Thus freed 'from the burden of the past' (Astuti 1999: 84), there is an equally widespread acceptance that the marriages and households of today will rarely turn out to be more than a provisional arrangement.

[11] The discussion I develop here could be read as a critique of Parker Shipton's argument that neophyte goldminers were driven to spend their cash with seemingly reckless speed because gold (and the money associated with it) was tainted with cultural associations of pollution that rendered it dangerous for long-term investment (1989; Werthmann 2003).

When we allow for the possibility that there might be an element of deliberate political resistance in young men's decisions to 'live in the moment', this adds a quite different perspective from the clichés I often heard repeated about fishermen: that, even if they make a lot of money, they will prefer to invest their windfall in a new boat than in an improved home; and that they are always half-ready to up-anchor and relocate to a different wharf (and a different wife). Just as Day, Papataxiarchis, and Stewart might have predicted, both expressions of 'timelessness' are concerned with sidelining once-powerful institutions for organising long-term social reproduction. So when fishermen opt to 'enjoy their catch' rather than thinking of the future, this is a deeply ambivalent assertion of independence: at once a statement of autonomy and an abandonment of responsibility.

In fact, for all the relative freedom experienced by newcomers to this coast, this is a world in which even the slightest perceived accumulation of material wealth is apt to transform itself rapidly into a sticky web of material demands from one's neighbours and relatives. As a lifelong res-ident of Tissana, and the head of a large, complex household, Jacob's experience of the town was completely different from that of the newly arrived, seemingly carefree Asana. With a network of relatives spread wide throughout the entire town, Jacob was well known and well respected. However, as this excerpt from my field notes demonstrates, none of this 'prestige' gave him any particular comfort when faced with the con-stant barrage of demands made upon him each day by his extended family:

Jacob's great-aunt, Mi Yoki, came to the back veranda looking for him. A couple of moments later, as I walked towards my room, I heard an urgent whisper: 'Jenny. Ssss! Jenny! Lock the door. Lock this door, please!' Jacob was pressed against the wall, around the front of the house. 'Problems, problems, problems! Is Mi Yoki there? She is coming to ask me for money...'

'Well,' he told me later, after the coast was clear, 'that's what we're like here. They know I have nothing, but they will find a reason to ask. Especially now, because they see you [a white and, presumably, wealthy person] here with me.'

'Konima left today, to go to her sister's Bundu ceremony,' the next conversation began, innocuously enough. 'You see that? *More* problems! Problems, problems, problems... She knocked on my door saying, "OK, I am going now!," so I just had to dig into that money and give her something. That is how we are here. The only reason you would say goodbye to someone is to let them give you something.'

So many of his neighbours felt entitled to make these kinds of small, daily claims upon him that Jacob experienced his life as a constant losing battle to retain some limited personal control over his scant material resources. He would have sympathised, then, with Ishmael, whom we met in the introductory paragraphs of this chapter, giving a false address to his sister.

Not being in the position to employ any such radical evasion technique, Jacob nonetheless invested much of his energy in the ultimately futile work of attempting to avoid his many suppliants.

It is hard to imagine a sharper contrast to the situation described by Melissa Leach in the Gola Forest 20 years previously, where, although 'wealth differentials now exist only within generalised poverty' (1994: 185), anyone with spare cash tended to be very eager to lend it to their neighbours. As one man explained to her, 'I would not want you to have more money than me; instead, I want to have more money than you so that you are always coming to me and asking for things' (ibid.: 187). It remains the case in Tissana, as in farming regions, that we would expect financial debt to translate into ties of social dependency and political loyalty. What is much more debatable is whether non-farming households have much to gain from accumulating large numbers of people. In a town where everything costs money, dependants are expensive.

Yet, even while struggling to live up to the impossible expectations placed upon him by his kin and neighbours, Jacob was equally frustrated that his own *subabu* (social network) failed, in a similar way, to provide for him (cf. Bolten 2008). His sister, Sento, happened to own one of Tissana's largest boats, and to run one of its busiest *bandas*. It was a cause of considerable bitterness among the members of our household that she had not done more to help her immediate family. For her part, Sento spent her days fielding her own inexhaustible barrage of suppliants from every corner of town; but this did nothing to prevent her name being cited, in conversations around our compound, as an arch-villain of sorts. Here, Buema is speaking in the immediate aftermath of her latest failed attempt to beg money from her aunt:

As I was sitting there, another woman came along, who is not even family . . . and asked her for 350,000 leones to buy [produce to sell]. And, I swear to God, Sento went inside and counted that money and came out and gave it to the woman. In front of me! This is how she treats me, Jenny . . . she will help this other woman and she won't help me, her own family. And she won't help her brother, Jacob, either.

When my sister died, when you were in England just now, I went to their compound to tell my auntie she had died. Do you know what Frank [her husband] told me? Straight away? I didn't ask her for anything . . . He said, 'Every man has his load to carry! That's your problem! That's not our problem!' You see that? I didn't ask her for anything, I didn't go to her for help. I just went to tell her, nothing more. Those people – their hearts are black.

Without wanting to undermine the importance of a post-war project that has sought, as its first priority, to understand the anger of the young farmers who became fighters, what Buema's, Jacob's, and Sento's stories reveal is that models of peacetime life that emphasise *only* top-down exploitation by patrons of their clients fail to do justice to the multiple material tensions that riddle communities in which even the so-called 'wealthy elders' are often struggling at the very edge of subsistence.

Even while criticising the irresponsibility of men such as Asana, Tissana's more established residents also recognised – and possibly even envied – the assertion of personal liberty these newly arrived young migrant fishermen were able to make in their defiantly short-term livelihood patterns. As streams of migrants arrived in Tissana from their villages each year, Jacob would occasionally tell me, wistfully, that he dreamed of making the journey in the opposite direction, and relocating to Ndema: away from Pa Thomas's ever-disappointing patronage; away from the unrelenting stream of needy relatives, begging him for help; away from the sinister presence of his successful but seemingly ungenerous sister.

We will see in more detail in Chapters 4 and 5 that, if they remain longer in town, migrant fishermen invariably marry local women, develop long-term customer relationships, take loans that need to be repaid, and generally find themselves re-entangled in lattices of responsibility that belie any aspiration for complete, unattached independence. If he stays in the town long enough, then, whether he wants it or not, it is likely to be only a matter of time before Asana will also find himself attempting to dodge a steady flow of neighbours, knocking hopefully on his door. In the meantime, however, his deliberate avoidance of family commitments, and his defiantly relaxed labour rhythm, could hardly have stood in more stark opposition to the patterns of familial obligation that shaped his labour when at home under 'parental care'.

The tenacity of exploitative power relations

As we are beginning to see, this is a town in which successive waves of immigrants have worked to create an alternative economic order to the one they left behind: an alternative to the lived experience of stifling 'parental care' and the half-remembered history of domestic slavery. However, if one looks more closely at the individual life stories of the most vulnerable people in Tissana, it becomes evident how very contested this ideology of 'freedom' remains. Men such as Asana and Ba Kpana were already skilful fishermen and navigators when they arrived in Kagboro, equipped with their own canoes and a detailed understanding of the sea. Migrants from landlocked villages, arriving for the first time on the coast, are much less equipped to make a life for themselves in the maritime economy – less still one characterised by the kind of autonomy enjoyed by solo canoe fishermen. These migrants often find themselves drawn rapidly back into exploitative labour relations with boat owners who are already established on the coast.

Although it is true that the old agricultural models of dependence have been deeply challenged in Tissana's fluid, maritime economy, it is certainly not the case that they have disappeared altogether. The same syntax of power we saw operating in the village – in which love, 'parental care' and labour exploitation often appear as different facets of the same relationship – persists in Tissana as one model through which vulnerable people are integrated into the social world. The alternative – of managing without a patron – comes with its own significant risks.

To illustrate this tension, let me introduce the stories of two fishermen, Cho and Abu. Both men had migrated to Tissana in the second half of the 1990s from small farming villages, arriving on the coast with no friends, no family and no knowledge of the sea. In other respects, though, as we will see, their experience of integration followed two quite radically different paths.

Abu's story

Abu had grown up near Port Loko, a full day's travel by public transport from Kagboro Chiefdom. When he was 15 years old, however, his step-mother suggested sending him to live with her brother, a fisherman who owned a boat in Tissana. Abu described how, when he first arrived on the coast to live with his new *boss-man*-cum-foster father, 'I just took that Pa as my daddy, no more. And he took me now, like his child.' How-ever, from the start there was a clear difference between Abu's treatment within the household and that of 'the Pa's' own birth children. Whereas the other boys went to school, Abu spent his days working on the family boat. Speaking to me 20 years later, he vividly recalled how frightening and isolating those first months had been for him as a young farming boy, suddenly thrust into a life on the sea.

You know what people are like. If you send them your son, he's not their son. They don't feel sorry for him. He used to tie a rope around my waist – I was small! He'd tie a rope around my waist and throw me in the water. He'd say, 'Dive!' When I didn't dive, he'd take the rope and beat me with it, to force me to learn to swim! At that time there, my daddy wasn't there, my mama wasn't there. My family were all far away... He used to tie the rope around my waist, and say 'Sink!' until I sank for some time, then he'd draw me back out.

Abu remained living in his foster father's home, and working in his boat, for many years. Long after he was a fully grown adult and a skilful fish-erman in his own right, both 'the Pa' and his fellow crewmen continued to treat Abu as a junior within the boat. 'They saw me as a boy... But I worked! Ah, I worked *well*! They used me, that's all, just to show that power there; to say I was just a boy.'

Just as we saw taking place in the more 'traditional' farming vil-lages of the region, Abu's subordinate relationship with his foster father was cemented when the older man found a wife for him and paid the bridewealth on his behalf. Now heavily indebted – and still being 'cared for' as a foster child rather than earning any money of his own – Abu was unable to contemplate moving to another boat. Even as he grew increasingly frustrated, Abu understood that the older man was going to such lengths to tie him to his boat because he had grown to rely upon the young fisherman whom he had trained from a child:

> He can find other fishermen, but to get my kind again, it's not easy. Because, me: he trained me himself. He trained me. He overworked me. And now I am strong. It's something like mental slavery. It's not slavery but it seems like slavery. Once you're married, he can treat you how he likes in that boat there. He can treat you any way he wants. How are you going to leave that boat? You have to pay him, is that not so?... Sometimes you can feel really ashamed. You want to leave now, with your woman, but if you want to go, he'll say, 'Where's the money?' It happens in Africa here. Right now, as we are sitting here, it's happening. This is Africa-oh!

Abu's quote reveals to us, again, something of Tissana's 'frontier' mentality, 'in which local and global imaginaries meet and, eventually, merge' (De Boeck 2001: 559). On the one hand, we saw in the previous section that when people in Tissana mobilise metaphors of 'enslavement', the associations they are drawing refer not only to a half-remembered past but also to a half-imagined rural hinterland. The memory – albeit a distant and perhaps distorted one – of a hinterland in which 'slaves' occupy the lowest and most denigrated rung on the social ladder continues to inform the ways in which people on this coast contemplate and negotiate their own unequal power relationships. However, in his throwaway comment, 'This is Africa!', Abu also draws comparisons in a completely different direction. For all the continuing force of inherited models of reckoning power, the people whom I knew in Tissana were highly conscious of the existence – or, at the very least, the possibility – of other, quite different ways of organising wealth, power, and obligation.

If, as Keith Hart has claimed, 'economic anthropology at its best has always been the search for an alternative to capitalism' (2012: 179), the fisherfolk of the Yawri Bay are engaged in a parallel search of their own: in their case, for an alternative to the economic model of patronage.

> One of anthropology's most cherished promises is to show us our lives afresh through the defamiliarising insight afforded by cross-cultural comparison. Usually it is we who are doing the comparing, but in principle we should be open to the insight that is gained by the others when they are drawing the comparisons themselves. (Bashkow 2006: 1)

Just as previous generations of anthropologists turned to Africa for evidence of working economic systems more 'moral' than our own, my neighbours in Tissana often referred to their own constructed 'others' as a foil against which to contemplate the virtues and vices they saw in their

Figure 3.1 Fisherman weaving a new fishing net

own economy. Here is Abu again, for example, describing his relation-ship with the foster father-cum-*boss-man*, whom he was still referring to as 'the Pa' even years after their relationship finally disintegrated:

I worked for the Pa for 18 years! Eighteen years! Now, with you white people, if somebody worked for you for 18 years, you have to pay them, is that not so? But we now, we don't pay.

Abu did eventually manage to extricate himself from his 18-year depen-dency relationship with his foster father, but it was not easy. He made himself a small fishing net, and – whenever he was not working in 'the Pa's' boat – went alone to fish for mullet directly from the beach. Gradu-ally, secretly, over the course of three years, he managed to save enough money to make a full-sized fishing net of his own.

I strained-oh! I'd hide! To not let him know that I wanted to make a boat for myself. I hid! Because, if he knew . . . it was he who controlled me. Whatever he wanted to do to me, he could do! At that time, I was small-small. All I had was an idea, a dream. So I hid. This is where I kept the net. In this house, here . . . I made it inside my bedroom.[12] Finally, after three years, I pulled it outside, and everyone saw it! Now, there is a grudge there. Yes. He has a grudge for me.

---

[12] Usually, men make fishing nets in the open, either on their veranda or on the beach (see Figure 3.1).

Because he just wants me to work for him...I know [how to fish] and I have decided to get my own boat; to work for my own family.

However, if Abu's experience reveals the extreme lengths some young men are prepared to go to in order to break free of the stifling patronage economy, Cho's story gives us some insight into the dangerous isolation experienced by poor young migrants at the other end of the spectrum, as they attempt to navigate the stark insecurity of Tissana's open labour market alone.

Cho's story

Cho had moved to the coast in the late 1990s, having grown up in a Sherbro-speaking farming village so small and isolated that it has since disappeared entirely, abandoned by all the people who once lived there. In his home village, life for Cho had been tough: 'I worked under my father. Ah! The work was just too much. Strain! We strained, no more.' When Cho found himself the focus of targeted aggression from one of his neighbours over a case of 'woman trouble', he decided, finally, that it was time to leave.

Arriving with no sense of how the fishing industry worked, nor any established friends or relatives to help him navigate the unfamiliar world, Cho had struggled in his new home. The very largest vessels on Tissana's wharf can go to sea with crews of up to 20 fishermen. Representing an investment of around 35 million leones (£6,000 to £7,000), and with nets that sometimes reach a kilometre in length, these are impressive pieces of property by any standard – and particularly so when one considers the general level of poverty in a town such as Tissana. Most are significantly smaller than this, but even in the smallest crew-boat, there can be a fairly complex hierarchy of labour, with different fishermen working on quite different terms, depending in part on their of level of skill, and in part on the kind of relationship they have with their *boss-man*.

It's just like education. There, you have primary, secondary, university. Is that not so? Well, so it is with fishing: by stage. How well you understand fish, that's how they pay you. (Sana, crewman, Tissana)

As a novice in the fishing industry, Cho found work as a '*job-man*'. Working by the day or by the week, for any captain prepared to give them work, these floating labourers are always on the fringes of the crew, and are treated as such. Cho spent years shifting between different fishing boats, always working as the most low-skilled, low-paid, least respected man in the boat. And yet, for all the hardship he endured in his new role, there was one important respect in which Cho considered his life to have improved dramatically since moving to the coast:

Here, I am free. Anything that I want to do now, I'm free. Sometimes, if you are working with someone, he may try to work-work-work-work you and you will not get any benefit from them. But you can leave the place. I don't have anybody telling me, 'Don't do this, don't do this . . .' So [for that] I tell God thank you. When I wanted to leave a boat, no problem – I went to a different boat.

It would be difficult to overstate the importance – or the novelty – of this kind of freedom for a young man arriving directly from a farming village. So, despite their undeniable vulnerability, the very 'outsiderness' of floating *job-men* stands them in sharp contrast to the kind of family-bonded labour in which Abu had found himself embroiled. When boat owners want to demonstrate that they treat their crewmen 'fairly', the first thing they are likely to emphasise is that their employees are free to leave at any moment.

Paying crewmen with 'time'

One of the most interesting things about the evolving economic relation-ships within crew-boats is that, over the past 15 years, it has become rare for boat owners to pay their fishermen directly, either in cash or fish, or in any other obviously material form of wealth. Instead, every boat I knew of now operates a system of payment in 'days'. This means that, on the first four days of the working week, the crew do not expect to be given anything other than a small 'gift' of fish; this is rarely any more than their own family will consume that evening for dinner. The remaining two working days are 'given' in payment to the crew. On these days, they can use their boss's boat as though it were their own. They club together to pay for their own fuel and, when they return to land, they divide the catch among themselves, each selling his own share to his own customers.

This system can be seen as a pragmatic response to the gradual deple-tion of the Yawri Bay's fish stocks. In contrast to the initial 'boom years' of commercial fishing from the 1960s to the 1980s – when, to hear fisher-men reminisce now, the fish in the Yawri Bay had seemed inexhaustible – progressive overfishing during the intervening decades means that fish catches today are increasingly unpredictable. Over recent years, Tissana's fishermen have come into line with fishermen in 'virtually every area of the world', negotiating payment structures flexible enough to absorb these extreme fluctuations (Acheson 1981: 278).

However, these patterns of risk sharing have a very particular sig-nificance in the Sierra Leonean context, for it is difficult to imagine a system better designed to destabilise the old moral model of patron-age and dependence. Rather than being cared for, and controlled by, a patron of the kind that dominates folk memories of power in this region, crewmen are offered instead a window of opportunity through which to operate as entrepreneurs in their own right, albeit a narrow and increasingly uncertain window. One important result of this shift is that it allows poor crewmen a period of time in which to experience some sense (or perhaps only the illusion) of the independence we saw among solo canoe fishermen. *Boss-men* do not fail to note the importance of working to give the men in their boat the strongest possible impression of economic independence, at least on those two days when their work time is their own. Here is Abu again – describing his efforts to ensure that his own crew are treated more fairly than he was in 'the Pa's' boat:

Me, I'm a *dreg-man* [lowly labourer] at heart. I suffered for a long time before I got my own boat. So I know, when you work under a person, I know what you go through... On my fishermen's days... I don't even look at how much they have. As soon as they start counting, I just leave – so they know that I don't know. I just take whatever they give me.

For their part, by 'giving' their crew the same fixed, reliable amount of time each week, boat owners are absolved of direct personal responsibility for the reality that, for almost every crewman on Tissana Wharf, the fish they catch is barely enough to subsist on. Here, Kumba, a boat owner, explains why he considers 'time' to be the fairest possible way of paying his crewmen:

The new system – of days – is better. Because, now, if you go to sea on your day and you don't get anything, you know that God has not given you. But if you go and you get a fine catch, then anything that you bring home is yours. No boss can interfere again to say, 'I gave you these days but now I want to take some of this fish.' No! You'll offend them. So everyone keeps to his own satisfaction.

Even by local standards, Kumba was not a rich man, and he worked hard, going to sea with his crew every day. Like many small-scale *boss-men*, caught in the slipstream of global forces bigger than themselves, he was struggling to manage the increasingly narrow margin between declining fish stocks and the dramatically rising price of fuel, nylon thread (for making nets), and imported rice. Sitting for long hours together in the tight isolation of his tiny boat, paddling for miles under scorching dry season sun and battered by rainy season downpours, it is hardly surprising that these men developed a deep and sincere sense of solidarity.

Nonetheless, even with all these caveats, any discourse that enables boat owners to claim that their crewmen's poverty is evidence that 'God has not given them' can be a dangerous one. This is especially problematic in the largest boats, in which crew must divide their day's catch between as many as 20 people:

Before I got my boat, I was working as the captain in my brother's boat. There were so many of us in that crew!... At times we would be 14 or 15. So just imagine: maybe you get a good catch. You take the petrol money out, what's left there? Maybe 400,000 or 500,000 leones. There's not much money there, when you have to share it between 15 people – let me say 30,000 or 35,000 each [£6 to

£7]. So you're holding 35,000 leones. You've got a woman. You've got children. You have to eat. You understand? So I think it's not fair. You aren't able to satisfy your needs. (Moses, boat owner)

In theory, at least, it is true that, if a *boss-man* treats his crew unfairly, 'then the following morning, you will not see any of them! They will go to another boat!', as Akin Mama, a boat owner, explained. Yet, there is a clear sense in which the very 'freedom' village émigrés crave is often what leaves them most exposed to exploitation in their adoptive home. Experienced fishermen are in a much stronger position, but, given the rate of migration into the Yawri Bay, the unskilled labour of newly arrived rural migrants is never in short supply. Indeed, Cho's experience suggests that some *boss-men* are fairly indifferent to a high turnover of unskilled fishermen in their boat:

There are some *boss-men* who embrace their fishermen – who hold them fine, take care of them. If the fisherman has a problem, it's just as though it was their [the *boss-man*'s] own problem. Because if you've got a person [dependant], that's how it should be; if he has a problem, it is you who has that problem. Yes. But there are others who don't look after their fishermen. Sometimes, even if the fisherman who is there with him is sick, the boss doesn't care! That sickness can sit down [fester] for a long time, and the *boss-man* just doesn't even have time [to care]. Even up to the last, and they die. Yes. (Cho, crewman)

Cho's testimony draws us back, once more to that now-familiar tension. However relieved he might have been to escape the suffocating insularity of his home village, the fact remains that Cho had lived his entire life in a world structured by the basic moral principle of patrimonial kinship: that patrons have a fundamental duty of material care towards the people 'beneath' them. It was disorienting – and frightening – to find this safety net removed.

Conclusions

This chapter has sought to introduce Tissana through the narratives of some of those young men who, for at least the past 60 years, have been arriving on the Kagboro coast hoping to build a different kind of life for themselves there: an alternative to the stifling patrimonial authority of 'traditional' economic life. Presenting themselves, as they so often do, not just as economic migrants but rather as outcasts and fugitives, Tissana's village émigrés appear, inadvertently, to align themselves with 'the stock figures of many frontiers' (Scott 2009: 132). In this regard, their stories resonate rather neatly with James Scott's (ibid.) image of inaccessible frontier regions as spaces of political *resistance*, where people are able to retreat in a conscious bid to reject the dominant political order.

One thing I have been interested in exploring in this chapter is the extent to which Scott's argument remains salient in contexts where the state is conspicuous only by its absence, such as rural Sherbroland. When economies come close to collapse, it is not uncommon for these frustrations to be experienced most powerfully by individuals at the level of their most immediate personal relationships; even when, as is often the case, these micro-political tensions divert attention from the wider structural roots of their poverty (cf. Booth, Leach, and Tierney 1999: 23; Whitehead 1990; Schoepf and Schoepf 1988).

In rural Sherbroland, the most salient focus of oppression and resistance in people's lives is not the missing authority of an invisible central government but the subtle forms of coercion that weave through kinship networks, households, and close, interdependent personal relationships. Tissana – with its highly fluid population, its informal marriages, porous households, and often casual patterns of employment – appears, at first glance, the perfect antithesis to the tightly integrated mono-ethnic villages of the kind Pa Kpana, Moses, and Cho had each decided to flee as young men.

And yet, an argument that recurs in various guises throughout this book is that the memory of that moral economy of the village continues to play a powerful role in shaping the complexities and ambivalences of the moral economy in Tissana. Whenever large numbers of young rural migrants converge in boom-town economies, in places at once remote and cosmopolitan, the social worlds created in these 'frontier' spaces are marked by a complex 'potpourri between . . . "traditions" and "modern" categories, practices, mentalities, relationships and belief systems' (De Boeck 2001: 559).

Much of the anxiety in circulation in Tissana derives from the fact that, in the wake of this massive social upheaval, people find themselves navigating between two quite different models of reckoning economic value. For the individuals steering a course through these economic transitions, it is rarely self-evident where their social responsibilities, or even their social aspirations, ought to lie. On the one hand, most of Tissana's residents shared the ideal that theirs is the kind of town where a person *ought* to be able to aspire to personal economic 'freedom' – an ideal strongly held if only ever fleetingly realised. On the other hand, Tissana's most vulnerable people live so close to the edge of subsistence that it is typically only a matter of time before they find themselves in need of financial help. However much crewmen might dread the proposition of falling into the 'mental slavery' of indebted labour, the alternative – attempting to manage with no patron at all – can be an even more frightening proposition.

This chapter has been almost exclusively about men, and the relationships I have focused on have tended to be clearly hierarchical. In

Chapter 4, I complicate this image by turning my attention to the daily negotiations between boat owners, crewmen, and the women who buy their fish on the wharf. Through the lens of these gendered trading partnerships, I continue to explore the uneasy intersection between the apparent 'freedom' offered by the market, and the tenacity of other, more socially binding ways of relating.

4   Plantain Island sirens

Loads of men I've known, they left Tissana to go to Plantain Island –
just for a few days, just to make a bit of money – but you never see
them back in Tissana again! Loads of men I've known, they're never
coming back here again... That's why I never sleep on Plantain. The
women there will say, 'Why don't you just stay here for one night? In the
morning, I'll find you some bait...' No! If I ever land my boat there,
I just sell my fish and come straight home! The women who are there,
they know how to catch a man.

(Kumba, boat owner)

Tissana's boat captains often exchange cautionary tales like this, in which
the *banda* women in neighbouring wharf towns are represented as powerful seductresses and dangerous economic predators. Although these tales
are usually recounted playfully, I argue in this chapter that they express a
genuine concern among fishermen, who fear finding themselves ensnared
against their will in unequal and binding gendered relationships. In the
context of a deepening ecological crisis, these tales of entrapment offer a
window into the increasingly fraught gendered negotiations that characterise economic life on the fringes of the Yawri Bay.

Similar anxieties have a long genealogy in Sierra Leone. We saw in
Chapter 3 that, in conversations about their life experiences and ambitions, fisherfolk often express a deep preoccupation with the importance –
but also the fragility – of their aspiration to personal 'freedom'. The direct
association drawn by fishermen between their sexuality and the potential
loss of personal autonomy forms part of an enduring model of social
power. In agricultural economies, one of the most deeply resented mech-
anisms by which elders are able to manipulate the labour of their poorer
male neighbours is to accuse them of adultery and fine them for 'women
trouble'. However, the tensions that characterise heterosexual relationships around the fringes of the Yawri Bay need to be viewed as arising
within a very particular material environment, and at the intersection of
specific tensions within the maritime economy.

'Freedom' is a notoriously slippery concept: one whose meaning, as
Isaiah Berlin once noted, 'is so porous that there is little interpretation
that it seems able to resist' (1969 [1958]: 121). Still, if they are to hold

any real emotional resonance, ideologies of freedom must be consti-
tuted against a particular, historically grounded, knowledge of oppression. Within Europe and American political philosophy, debates about
liberty have tended to reflect anxieties about the potential for *state* oppression. At one end of the spectrum, political libertarians conceptualise
liberty in its 'negative' sense, as the *absence* of, or freedom *from*, state-
imposed constraints or interference. This argument gained particular
force in the post-war period, against the immediate memory of fascism
and a backdrop of totalitarian socialist regimes. Arguments made by
liberal economists, that unfettered 'free markets' were an essential pre-
requisite for political freedom, reflect a similar moral suspicion of 'big
government' (Friedman 1962: 289; Hayek 1944). On the other side of
the ideological divide, advocates of a more 'positive' conception of liberty
have argued that state interventions are sometimes essential in order to
create the conditions under which vulnerable individuals are free to take
control of their own lives, or realise their full potential (Sen 1988).

In Tissana, people's aspirations to 'freedom' are equally layered and
contested, but they take as their starting point an entirely different, and
far more *intimate*, model of oppression – one grounded in a recent history
in which domestic slavery was a widespread social institution. As we have
seen, one result of this legacy is that it is fairly common for people's experiences of familial love to be interwoven with anxieties about exploitation
and entrapment (see also Argenti 2010). Within the fishing economy,
these tensions play out against a backdrop of considerable economic and
social uncertainty. As I argued in Chapter 3, part of the appeal of the
maritime economy is that it appears to promise a radical alternative to
the strict hierarchies, tight communities, and harsh working conditions
of a 'traditional' agrarian village. And yet, within just a few decades of its
initial boom, this newly emergent economy is already under enormous
pressure, as fish stocks have suffered a noticeable decline and catches
have become dramatically smaller and more erratic. The decimation of
West African fisheries is well documented in the marine ecology literature
(Ukwe, Ibe, and Sherman 2006); what is much less well understood is
how these new pressures are being refracted through the social fabric of
coastal communities.

In Western accounts, fishing has historically been associated with
stereotypes of tough, independent men. This long-standing aesthetic,
linking the romance of the sea to images of rugged masculinity (Phelan
2007), has often led researchers to take a curiously androcentric perspective on life in fishing towns. When they were visible at all, women
have often been represented as secondary or subordinate actors: 'always
marginal to the maritime enterprise and culture they entered almost as if
by mistake' (Creighton and Norling 1996: 10; cf. Davis and Nadel-Klein
1992). Such an approach would be impossible to sustain in a town such

as Tissana, where daily economic life is powered, to a very large degree, by exchange relationships that are explicitly and richly gendered: almost every woman in Tissana works, at one scale or another, as a fish processor (*banda* woman), procuring fish from boats on the wharf and drying them on behalf of the urban traders who congregate here from every city in Sierra Leone.

What interests me in this chapter is how understandings of gendered intimacy and interdependence are being strained in new ways, and how they are being reconfigured in a context of deepening economic uncertainty. As such, I hope to offer a window into the ways in which people readjust their expectations and renegotiate their intimate relationships in the face of economic precarity, when 'it appears that a boom that once gave them hope is now a thing of the past' (Walsh 2012: 237; cf. Ferguson 1999). Elsewhere in post-war Sierra Leone, Catherine Bolten has described a situation in which deepening poverty forced people to neglect the webs of patronage and mutual obligation that, under 'normal' circumstances, would have provided the foundation of social life (2008: 3). Material scarcity had led to the emergence of a kind of desperate 'individualism' that was experienced by almost everyone as deeply threatening to the moral order. In Tissana, everyday life is saturated with similar anxieties around individuals' inability – or perceived unwillingness – to share their meagre resources with family and neighbours (see Chapter 5). However, this suspicion of 'greediness' is matched by an equally deep ambivalence towards the 'traditional' Sierra Leonean values of patronage and dependence. And, as I explore in this chapter, many people in Tissana have responded to the increasing precariousness of the marine economy, not by retreating into ever more atomised survival strategies, but by working to re-embed themselves in exactly these ties of ambivalent obligation.

The chapter unfolds over four sections. After a general discussion of the relationship between intimacy, exchange, and gendered power, I briefly sketch my neighbours' nostalgic memories of their town's economic 'boom' in the 1970s and 1980s. These years now appear, in the narratives of my informants, as a period of rapid economic liberalisation in which fish changed hands on the wharf according to the simple, impersonal logic of supply and demand. In the third section, I discuss how the declining size and reliability of catches has dramatically reconfigured these relationships, putting particular pressure on women's livelihoods, and forcing them to learn to be far more strategic in how they work to create, manage, and sustain relationships with fishermen. Finally, I discuss the patterns of male migration that create these highly charged encounters between fishermen and the women they meet on foreign wharfs. My overarching suggestion is that the men's cautionary tales of predatory economic seductresses in other wharf towns can be understood as playful expressions of deep gendered tensions in the Yawri Bay's econ-omy, where people continue to aspire to economic 'freedom' but the 'free market' is already part of the receding memory of a historic 'boom'.

Intimacy, exchange, and gendered power

The idea that feelings of love might be entangled with and formed by economic transactions runs contrary to Western folk ideology. But, as Viviana Zelizer has demonstrated, the 'grip of intimacy affects the way we organise economic life' (2005: 2) more than most people would like to admit. From the late 1970s, feminist ethnographers in Africa began doc-umenting the agency of women in their everyday interactions with men, often emphasising how women were able to use sex to negotiate access to material resources (Bledsoe 1980; 1990b; Leach 1994; Whitehead 1990). While these studies provided an important counterpoint to ear-lier representations of women as the passive property of their husbands, they also formed part of a broader trend in social scientific literature, to '[reduce] African intimacy to sex' (Thomas and Cole 2009: 3).

This focus on sex, at the expense of other aspects of gendered inti-macy, became more pronounced in the wake of Africa's HIV epidemic (ibid.). Since the 1990s, a vast body of literature has been produced, analysing how patterns of sexual behaviour enabled the spread of the virus in different parts of the continent. Often, these studies emphasise the role of economic insecurity and gender inequality, as women are forced to navigate an increasingly unstable field of transactional relation-ships in order to make a living.[1] While much of this work is nuanced and important, en masse it exacerbates a constricted view of love in Africa: one that downplays the importance of both romantic passions and emo-tional attachment (ibid.: 9). As Thomas and Cole have noted, such a narrow focus on sex – and, in particular, on sex as a vector of disease and pollution – is especially problematic when viewed against a colonial history in which racial stereotypes of hyper-sexuality were often used to dehumanise African populations (ibid.: 3).

Of particular relevance here is the literature describing the economy of 'fish for sex' in fishing communities across Southern and Eastern Africa. Responding to evidence that rates of HIV are consistently higher among fisherfolk than in the surrounding farming communities, researchers have pointed to the high rates of transactional sex that reportedly characterise wharf-side life in this region (Allison and Janet 2001; Seeley 2009; West-away, Seeley, and Allison 2007). In keeping with a much broader set

---

[1] In a sophisticated example, Mark Hunter (2010) has traced how chronic unemployment transformed the political economy of intimacy in poor urban communities in South Africa, creating an environment in which 'provider love' has come to play an increasingly important, and complex, role in men's and women's struggles to make a living.

of assumptions, which run as a powerful thread throughout gender and development discourse (Cornwall, Harrison, and Whitehead 2007), this literature tends to present women as victims: forced, as a consequence of their extreme economic impoverishment, to 'prostitute themselves' to exploitative fishermen, so as to secure access to a shrinking supply of fish (Geheb and Binns 1997, cited in Béné 2007: 884).

At the time of my research, levels of HIV were far lower in Sierra Leone[2] than in many other parts of Africa, making it easier to discuss patterns of sexual relationship without pathologising them. And there are two key respects in which my ethnography suggests a more nuanced story. Firstly, the purely transactional term, 'fish for sex', cannot do justice to the liaisons that develop between Tissana's fishermen and the women who buy their fish. While these relationships may sometimes involve sex, they are characterised by far more complex entanglements of material exchange, indebtedness, and moral notions of patronage and loyalty, as well as deliberate strategies to manipulate 'the purchase of intimacy' (Zelizer 2005) through elicit substances that nurture feelings of desire.

Secondly, the balance of gendered power between fishermen and their female business partners is complex and variable. While it is generally the case in Sierra Leone that women are 'less educated, make less money, and are legally and politically subordinate to men' (Coulter 2009: 71), there are other, equally important, axes of difference – along lines of age, generation, and wealth (see Moore 1993; Oyewumi 1997). Despite the fact that Sierra Leone remains a largely patriarchal society, there have always been examples of resourceful, ingenious women becoming successful entrepreneurs and wealthy patrons. Tissana is no exception, and there are huge differences in the range of resources that individual *banda* women are able to wield in their relationships with men.

'Her man' (*in man*) and 'his woman' (*in uman*) are the terms most often used to describe the partners in any socially recognised heterosexual relationship. In Tissana's fluid world, these are malleable categories and can apply regardless of whether the two people are legally married, have had children together, or cohabit; indeed, they apply regardless of whether they even live in the same town. Spanning this diverse range of relationships, the one thing that is relatively certain is that, wherever these terms are used, there will be an important economic dimension to the partnership.[3] As a result, most of the largest smokehouses (*bandas*) in town belong to the wives of the men who own the biggest boats. Even so, it would be rare for their conjugal finances to merge completely. Here, as in rural parts of Sierra Leone, 'husbands and wives have always

---

[2] According to UNAIDS, 1.3 per cent of the adult population in Sierra Leone were living with HIV in 2015 (www.unaids.org).

[3] This is in contrast to more illicit heterosexual relations, where gifts are made more secretively.

maintained separate income streams and expenditures, whether in cash or kind' (Leach 1994: 189). What this means is that many women buy fish from their husbands then sell it on to their trader-*kustoments* at a small profit.

It is not uncommon for a woman to co-own a fishing boat with her male partner, if the initial investment came from her or her family. However, boats are inherently male spaces – just as *bandas* are almost always female ones – and, in everyday speech, most couples tend to slide towards referring to the man as the *boss-man* of 'his' boat. Only rarely does one come across women like my neighbour, Sento, who not only owned a boat, but also wielded, seemingly uncontested, all the management powers usually associated with *boss-men*. Sento's husband had his own boat, but it was hers – *Defender* – that lent its name to the cluster of houses and *bandas* where they and their dependants lived: Defender Compound.

Sento was exceptional – not for nothing was she known throughout Tissana as a particularly formidable figure – but, even in a more typical partnership, the rhetorical slide towards recognising the man as '*boss-man*' refers only to one quite specific form of power, explicitly located within the delimited male space of the boat and the sea. In fact, as a wealthy boat owner was keen to stress to me at length, there are important respects in which women are recognised as more powerful than their fishermen counterparts.

Women are the stakeholders in fishing communities...Even if a man has ten boats, he cannot manage the affairs of the home! We really rely on women. We just bring in the finances, but to control those finances is a problem for us...The women, they bargain on a certain price [with traders]...If you want to lead a better life in a fishing community as a man, you *must* have a strong woman. You *must* have a strong woman in the home who can manage the finances. For you the husband, all alone by yourself, it is not easy...You will make a lot of money and spend it! But the women don't do that. (Ben, boat owner)

His use of that tell-tale development term, 'stakeholders', suggests that he might perhaps have been performing, if only subtly, to the white woman's sensibilities he projected upon me: Ben is a worldly man, and no stranger to NGO discourse. Nonetheless, while his tone differs from that of most men I knew in Tissana, the main point he is making here – that women are, if anything, the more canny and business-minded of the sexes – is something that few of my friends would have disputed. The following section traces how patterns of gendered power have altered in recent decades, in response to broader shifts in the maritime economy.

The substance of fish and recollections of a 'free' market

We were waiting for Asana's wife to be 'pulled', finally, from the women's secret society bush. This was the public culmination of an initiation process that, for

Mary, had spanned over a decade – although you would hardly have guessed it was such a momentous day if you had seen the men sitting there, sipping tea, chain-smoking, bemoaning the state of the world.

Ibrahim, fresh from a long, hard day at sea, was slumped at the end of Asana's veranda: a bulky mass of aching muscle and briny disappointment. 'Don't take my photo today – I'm so dirty!' he warned me when he saw I had my camera with me. Seeing him so crestfallen, I assumed at first that he had had a disappointing day at sea. I was mistaken. In fact, he and his crewmates had landed an unusually good catch that day. Things had only begun to look bad for them when, returning to town triumphant, they discovered that several other large boats, equally successful at sea, had made it back to shore ahead of them. 'The fish is there – loads!' he recounted, wearily, 'but there's no profit.'

Such was the influx of fish onto the wharf that afternoon that, even as Mary and the other initiates completed the final stages of their long transition into adulthood, their fellow Bundu women had little chance to show an interest. Rather than passing the day as they might have anticipated – singing and dancing for their friends in the society bush – almost all Tissana's women were here, in town, crouched in groups of two or three at the doors of their *bandas*, industriously washing, gutting, and scraping the scales from bumper *baff*-fulls of glittering fish: fish that glittered all the brighter for having been bought so cheaply.

This scene from my field notes highlights two very simple facts about life on Tissana Wharf. Firstly, it serves to illustrate the absolute centrality of fish to Tissana's social life: even on a day of ritual celebration that the women had been anticipating for months, all their previous plans were immediately relegated when the unexpected opportunity arose to buy cheap fish. Secondly, it begins to suggest something of the fluctuating power relations played out between men and women on the wharf each day – sometimes the fishermen's loss can be the *banda* women's gain.

To understand gendered economic relations in this coastal economy it helps to begin by considering the particular material substance of raw fish. In Sierra Leone's hot, humid climate, raw fish rot fast. Fishermen have no choice but to sell their catch the moment they return to land. On the other hand, every *banda* woman has a limit on the amount of fish she is able to dry. This depends on her capital, the size of her *banda*, and her supply of dry wood. Combine this with the unpredictability of fishing – on a day when 25 boats go to sea, it is impossible to forecast whether one or seven or none at all will return to land with a substantial catch – and you can begin to imagine how these extreme fluctuations in fish supply might translate into equally extreme fluctuations in the price women are prepared to pay for the fish.

In what appears to be a very neat description of an economy regulated by morally neutral market forces, the captain of one large boat explained to me: 'When loads of fish come...if two, three, four boats catch together, it's stiff [there's pressure] to make the price come down. If the fish shorten again, it rises up.' In extreme cases, on days when there is a bumper catch, those fishermen returning to land late in the day can find themselves in Ibrahim's frustrating situation where, as he put it, 'The fish is there – loads! – but there's no profit.'

According to my informants' recollections, days like these had once been common in Tissana. The latter decades of the twentieth century are remembered with nostalgia as a period of seemingly inexorable economic growth, as local fishermen adopted a series of increasingly efficient fishing methods, each imported from elsewhere on the West African coast. Whenever I asked non-fishermen to recall this recent history, they would almost always emphasise, as Pa Bimbola does here, that '[s]ometimes, there were so many fish they had to just throw them away. If you went to the wharf, they'd give you fish – sometimes even a *baff*-pan full!' Here, one of Tissana's experienced fish processors paints an evocative image of the wharf-side economy at the time when Kagboro's seas seemed to contain inexhaustible riches:

At that time, if you stood on the land, you could see *bonga*...If we stood right here, you'd see them; it looked like the water was boiling...with the fish jump, jumping...We women, we'd stand on the land; we'd see the fish and we'd call to the men, 'Come! Come, look at the fish!' Then they'd take their net and come and cast it – catch so many fish! (Sina, *banda* woman)

What is striking, as Sina continues her account, is that for fishermen there had been a limit on the value of these enormous catches, which often exceeded the amount local women were prepared to buy. The closest urban fish market is well over a day's journey away, so any fish that were not dried immediately would rapidly decay from a valued source of wealth to a stinking liability:

If they'd caught a lot of fish then, at dawn, the chief would walk around all the *bandas* and, if he smelled rotten fish, he'd summon that person [to court]. Because rotten fish attracts flies, and flies spread diseases...[He'd check] every house; every house...So, eventually, the boat owners – they'd just dig a hole in the sand and cover them up, so as not to let them smell. We couldn't finish them all. There wasn't enough wood to dry them. We *banda* women, we'd dry teeeeee...we'd dry from morning, till night, till dawn. (Sina, *banda* woman)

Looking back to this time, men and women remember patterns of bargaining on the wharf as having been driven by the simple mechanics of supply and demand. Provided she had enough money, any woman who came to the wharf could buy as much fish as she was capable of drying. If several boats landed a good catch on the same day, the cost of the fish would fall until, eventually, their value bottomed out entirely:

If you had money, you'd dry; you'd fill your *banda* full – pim! At first, they'd sell for 5,000 leones [per *baff*]. Then the price would drop; 4,000, 3,000...But, if they saw that no one else was coming...They'd just leave the fish on the wharf and call, 'You who have *bandas*, who have wood, come and gather! Don't let the fish rot!' And they'd just give you! (Hawa, *banda* woman).

As Hawa goes on to describe, experienced *banda* women like herself knew very well how to exploit such unpredictable surges in the fish supply:

They'd just give the fish to any person who was able to dry! Because there are some people: they have wood, they have a *banda*, but they don't have money. So, if you've got wood, you've got a *banda*, they'd *tross* you [give you fish on credit]. You know, my *banda* takes five or six *baffs*. So, if you've *tross'd* me four *baffs*, now I'll wait until the laaaaast minute, when they just decide to give the fish away. Those last two *baffs* are for me! So, after I've sold my fish, I'll only pay the fishermen for the four pans...I've made a profit!

By the time I arrived in Tissana in 2010, the dynamics of the wharf had shifted dramatically. Although the volume of the catch on the wharf fluctuated sharply on a day-to-day basis, the longer-term narrative I was repeatedly presented with was one of gradual but dramatic decline. Certainly, in the 18 months I spent there, I remember less than a handful of isolated occasions when the supply of fish outstripped demand. These were notable events, becoming the subject of conversation around town for several days or even weeks. This excerpt from my field notes captures some of the excitement generated by one such catch at Tissana Point, about a mile along the coast from where I lived:

Buema came into my room last night, excited. 'Those fishermen from Delken caught nasty [so much] fish! There's not enough wood to dry it all. If you could see the population there, at the wharf, the place was full up – pim!...They're begging people to take the fish. There's no wood left!'
    When Fatti arrived this morning, she was full of the same story. Playing the role of a fisherman, she bounded around our veranda, clutching her hands in mock desperation, begging each person in turn, 'Please, please, I beg you, take this fish from me!...Fine-fine fish, big as your arm; they were measuring by the *baff*!'[4]

So, however routine it may once have been for fishermen to auction their surplus catch down to extreme bargain prices, such occurrences are now seen as exceptional. To understand the depths of Ibrahim's disappointment at being forced to sell off his fish cheaply, it has to be viewed within a contemporary context in which *banda* women rarely wield such direct haggling power on the wharf as they once did. In fact, the most urgent problem nowadays concerning *banda* women is not what

[4] Usually only small, cheap fish are sold by volume in this way. Under usual circumstances, larger 'fine' fish are priced individually.

Figure 4.1 Women waiting on the wharf

price they are able to bargain for the fish, but whether they are able to buy any fish at all.

Sell-gi *transactions and declining fish stocks*

I was often struck by the fact that, just as men must use all their skill and strategy to hunt fish on the open water, the same is equally true of women hunting fish on land. Many *banda* women pass a large part of each day meandering up and down Tissana's two-mile wharf, attempting to match their movements to coincide with the (only very loosely predictable) arrival times of the different boats. Where they assemble at the landing sites of particularly large boats, *banda* women form the kernel of a vital, but transient, gendered social space within Tissana. As they sit waiting, sometimes for hours – watching the sea, chatting, braiding one another's hair – these would-be buyers are joined by other women; sometimes with pans full of fruit to barter, sometimes with cakes or cooked food to sell; sometimes hoping that their friendship alone might be currency enough to elicit a few fish when the boat finally arrives (see Figure 4.1).

My early field notes are littered with often quite confused accounts of the scenes that unfolded on the wharf immediately after one of these larger boats returned to land, as I attempted to untangle the unspoken logic by which some people were able to buy fish and others returned home empty-handed. This breathless excerpt from early in my field notes captures some of my initial bewilderment at the scene of an unusually good catch:

We were already 'down wharf' when Buema received an urgent call from Jacob, telling her to rush to Patti: Tito's boat had landed the most enormous catch! By the time we arrived, that entire stretch of beach was crowded with hundreds of people, all focused in an orderly jostle for fish. Steady strings of women were wading back and forth, chest-deep into the sea, to huddle around Tito's boat where it sat, heavy in the water, piled impossibly high with its shimmering load. So full was the boat with fish that Tito's crew had to balance on its edges as they sorted and counted the fish, helping the women to fill their heavy pans to be toted back and turned out on the beach, and counted and sorted and redistributed again; hundreds of hands, industriously, methodically redistributing the fish according to patterns that remained, to me, unreadable.

Some women had a few fine fish laid out beside them; some were picking through *baff*-loads of small fry, removing the jellyfish; others still were standing over heaps of *bonga*, turned out on the sand...Jacob, for his part, had been bouncing up and down on the balls of his feet when we arrived: 'I heard a great commotion on the beach and came to see what was happening!' But, as the fish were gradually distributed, his excitement began to wane. It became clear that he was not getting anything that day.

Contrast that with the following excerpt, describing the scene on the wharf following a more typical catch (see Figure 4.2):

By the time Brima's crew drew close to land, there must have been over 50 of us awaiting them on the beach. But despite the large number of women who'd come to the wharf... only a small fraction stirred from their seats when the fish began to be carried ashore. A handful leaned over the heaps of fish where they were turned out onto the sand and began picking through to decide which they would take. Other women were displaying varying degrees of half-interest in this measuring and sorting but most, seeing the disappointing size of the catch... began to drift off in different directions or, for lack of anything more urgent to do, simply finished their mango and their conversation...

When I asked Marriama whether she was planning to buy anything, she had laughed at the silliness of my question: 'If they *sell-gi* [sell–give] me, I'll buy!'

This expression, *sell-gi*, captures an important quality of the transactions that take place on the wharf each day. Regardless of the fact that Marriama had come to the wharf with cash, fully expecting to pay for any fish she managed to procure, her words have embedded within them the implication that, *if* any transaction transpired, the fisherman or boat owner would have been doing her a personal favour.

After some time in Tissana I began to realise that, for all their seemingly opportunistic movements up and down the wharf, *banda* women know very well which men are likely to *sell-gi* them fish, and under what circumstances. Put simply, the only way to secure a reliable supply of

Figure 4.2 A disappointing *sim*-boat catch

fish is to establish a '*kustoment*' (trading partner) relationship with a fisherman, who is then obligated to give you first refusal on his catch. Although they will buy opportunistically whenever they can, many *banda* women have only a single regular *kustoment*. Usually this will be her 'man', and their business relationship is closely interwoven with their personal one.

Unfortunately, if a *banda* woman's partner is a poor crew member, his custom alone does not go very far towards securing a steady supply of fish. Crewmen are typically 'given' two days each week to divide the boat's catch among themselves, each channelling his share directly to his own *kustoment*. For the rest of the working week, the catch belongs to the boat owner, and it is his decision to whom to *sell-gi*. Yet, even on these days, one can expect to see the entire crew's wives waiting at the wharf for their husbands' boat. Their personal connection to the *boss-man* gives them good reason to hope that they may be offered the opportunity to buy some of the surplus – after the owner's wife's *banda* is full. This is by no means guaranteed, however, and they will be competing with various other women – relatives, friends, perhaps girlfriends of the boat owner – each of whom has her own special social claim to buy a share of the catch.

This straining of rather too sparse resources across rather too stretched social networks is a common feature of life in Tissana, and one that stands in sharp contrast to a not-so-distant past in which fish were in plentiful supply. As these two elders explain, reminiscing about life in the 1970s:

Everyone would sell to everybody... There was no discrimination. (Pa Kwashie)

Yes... before, there were no regular *kustoments* at that time. Whoever had money could buy. This fish was plentiful. We'd get a good catch! I think the people who were here before were more lively than now. There was more happiness. The money was flowing. (Pa Yannie)

What I want to emphasise here is that the elders are not just expressing nostalgia for the lost *material* bounty of this era, but also for what they remember as a simpler, more impersonal market economy. This forms an interesting counterpoint to the substantial body of classic ethnographic literature that describes the anxiety people experience when previously complex and multi-layered economic systems are eroded by the depersonalising forces of market economics (e.g. Bohannan 1959; Burkhalter and Murphy 1989). Whereas it had once been possible to buy and sell fish with little thought for anything other than the simple calculation of profit, the wharf-side economy today is increasingly 'permeated with [the] ... atmosphere of the gift, where obligation and liberty intermingle' (Mauss 1990 [1925]: 65).

In their conversations with me, boat owners were explicit that, whenever they sold fish on the wharf, these commercial transactions had a strongly moral dimension. Sitting outside her cavernous smokehouse, my wealthy neighbour Sento explained that:

Myself, I have my own boat. But on some days, I don't dry. I *sell-gi* to my companions. [For example] you and me, we know one another; I'd help you. I'd *sell-gi* to you... I'm not just going to say, 'Only I can dry, no one else.' If I *sell-gi* to you, God must add to my own money, because you'll be grateful to me.

On another occasion, when I asked Tito whether it was the same women who came to meet his boat every day, he answered, 'Yes, I have my regular *kustoments*. But sometimes another person can come and *ask me to help them*. I *sell-gi* them' (emphasis added).

We should be careful not to read this moralising language as evidence that the transformations in Tissana's tightening economy are in any way benign. In more industrial contexts, for example, ethnographers have described the ways in which the language of corporate benevolence can work to obfuscate new forms of labour exploitation (Sanchez 2012). The very fact that boat owners are able to talk convincingly about selling their fish as though these transactions were acts of munificence only serves to highlight the extent to which economic power has slid away from the women who buy and dry fish. However sincere boat owners might be in imagining their sales on the wharf as acts of 'helping' the women who buy their fish, the reality is that they tend to make a far greater profit from these transactions than their buyers could ever hope to. What is being 'given' is not wealth, but only the coveted crevice of an opportunity through which, perhaps, to make some money.

Unsurprisingly, to hear a poor fish processor describing the same trans-action, one comes away with rather less of an impression that she consid-ers herself the recipient of a generous gift. The tone of Leagbe's quote, here, is typical: 'Even the fish that we buy on the wharf, with all the suffering... I get so little profit. If I had any other work to do, I'd leave this fish business straight away... The fishermen still earn but we *banda* women; nothing!' The steady slide in the balance of supply and demand on the wharf had eroded women's bargaining power to such an extent that, as Ima explains here, women often found themselves struggling to work within a stiflingly narrow profit margin:

For each *baff*, you need two bunches of wood – those two bunches are 10,000 leones! Then two pints of kerosene, which is 4,000 leones. It's reached 14,000 now, you see?... Some days you pay 60,000 [for a *baff* of fresh fish]; some days, 55,000; some days, 40,000. If you buy them for 40,000, then you sell them for 55,000. There's no profit! We're just trying, that's all, to get what we need to live – for our family. Perhaps you might get 5,000 leones there [approximately £1].

The following conversation gives some sense of the mundane drudgery endured by small-scale *banda* women such as Leagbe and Ima, who simply coax the most basic subsistence from the fish economy. I had met Alimatu on the wharf, sitting in the sand, cleaning a half-*baff* full of tiny, juvenile fish. The little fish were all mixed up with silt and leaves from the seabed, so I sat down to join her, absent-mindedly cleaning them. 'Let's go,' Alimatu said, tossing me a cloth, so that I could tote one of her *baff*-pans back to her *banda*. When we arrived, I perched on a piece of firewood beside her, as she rapidly processed the fish – efficiently scraping scales, cutting off tendrils, removing tiny guts. She let out a deep sigh: 'This work! This work is *mona* [hard, tedious]!'

Alimatu: When traders give me money, I go down [to the] wharf to buy fish... If I get fish, I scrape them, wash them, lay them on my *banda*... I go and buy wood, then I carry it back here and lay the fire, buy kerosene. I watch the fire through the night then, at daybreak, I turn [the fish] and go and buy more wood, to make a new fire – new, fresh fire. I watch that fire now, till afternoon.
Me: Wow – when do you sleep?
Alimatu: If the boats land... in the afternoon, sometimes you won't sleep. Some-times you can sleep a little in the smokehouse.

Tissana's women routinely stay up all through the night and spend many hours each day in their swelteringly hot, dark, densely smoke-filled *ban-das*. Because her day is structured by the movements of the fishing boats, and mechanics of fish drying, Alimatu's punishing working rhythm continues unabated, regardless of whether she managed to secure a decent load of fish on the wharf, or whether, as on the day described above, she had only a tiny quantity of low-value fish. For all her labour, it is unlikely Alimatu would have made more than 2,000 leones (£0.40) profit that day.

In short, although the current context of ecological decline is affecting everyone in the fishing economy, it has proved particularly damaging for *banda* women, who now find it increasingly difficult to secure fish on the wharf. As Sento's emphasis on 'knowing one another' suggests, it is almost impossible to buy fish nowadays without having an active personal network upon which to draw. As I explore in the following section, women have responded to the economic crisis by learning to be increasingly strategic in working to build and sustain relationships with fishermen that will enable them to access a supply of fish. The level of skill this involves should not be underestimated.

Kustoment relationships

Throughout my stay in Tissana, I watched as my good friend and host, Jacob – a respected elder – struggled and repeatedly failed to establish himself as a small-scale fish processor and trader. More often than not, I saw him return home dejected and empty-handed, complaining, 'This scramble for fish is just too much.' Eventually, I asked Hawa, one of Tissana's most successful businesswomen, why it was that Jacob experienced such difficulty, even on days when he had plenty of money to spend. She answered: 'Even if you don't have a *kustoment*, you can still buy fish, but you have to talk to the fishermen fine; greet them fine; *turn-turn* [cajole/coax] them fine! If you just stand there on the wharf with your money, you won't get anything!'

As Hawa notes, a bit of strategic flirtation can go a long way to persuading boat owners to sell you their surplus fish; and it may be largely for this reason that Jacob was experiencing such difficulties in what is, after all, a highly gendered role. To repeat a point already made, the emphasis on working to create an atmosphere of intimacy and charm in wharf-side transactions stands in direct contrast to Hawa's own recollection of a not-so-distant past when, as she put it, 'If you had money, you'd dry; you'd fill your *banda* full – pim!' Her response also hints at the moral tensions that so often riddle these gendered transactions of the wharf. While she is perfectly open about the fact that her feminine charm is part of what makes her good at her job, the Krio term she uses here – *turn-turn* – is hardly an unambiguously positive one. In fact, it is often used by people to describe situations where they consider themselves to have been manipulated or conned.

But, in the current ecological context, it takes a lot more than charm to become a successful *banda* woman. To illustrate this, I introduce another of Tissana's most respected *banda* women – Ami. Ami was constantly on the move: all day, back and forth, meeting one boat after another and shuttling fish, often in small, piecemeal lots, back to her *banda* to be dried. Unable to rely on her husband (who was a heavy drinker and had long since stopped going to sea), over the years she had managed to accumulate over a dozen small-scale *kustoment*s. They were mostly young crew members who, having arrived in Tissana as strangers, had found a valuable ally in Ami.

When I asked Mohammed why it was that he chose to work with Ami rather than any of the other *banda* women in town, he immediately emphasised that he valued the mentoring aspect of their relationship:

Sometimes she'll call me; advise me. When I first came here and she didn't know me, she saw that my eyes were red [like a person who has been smoking marijuana] so she took me aside and said, 'Please, you've come from far away to come here; don't get involved in that nonsense!' . . . We've been *kustoment*s for years now.

Like many of Tissana's Temne fishermen, this was not a life Mohammed had grown up imagining for himself. It was only in adulthood, when the war destroyed his small-town petty trading business, that he had decided to relocate to the fishing town and try his luck at this radically different livelihood. 'They taught me how to paddle, how to sail, but I was afraid at first, because people die at sea!' However gleefully macho the male fishing culture can sometimes appear, Mohammed's candidness here reminds us that – even for a virile young man – such radical relocation can be as frightening as it is lonely. Thrust into such an unfamiliar new world, it is hardly surprising that he felt comforted by Abi's mentoring and concern for his welfare.

But Ami's importance to her *kustoment*s went far beyond simple moral support. One evening in the rainy season, I stopped by her *banda* and found her serving up rice from a pot that was cavernous – even by Sierra Leonean standards. Just as I was wondering what she could possibly be doing with such a vast quantity of food, Mohammed arrived with a pan to collect his own serving. Mohammed lived at least half an hour's walk away, at the other end of town, but, not having gone to sea for several weeks, he was more than prepared to make the journey to collect his dinner.

As we have already seen, fishing is, at best, a highly unpredictable business. Even a relatively successful fisherman can never be certain on a day-to-day basis whether he will catch enough to meet his basic household needs. For those who opt to work with a *banda* woman other than his own wife, receiving this steady food supply from outside his own household can go a long way towards evening out these fluctuating everyday insecurities. Gift relations are so embedded within these commercial economic exchanges that the two are mutually dependent and inseparable.

What gives these gifts an added salience is that, in other contexts, people often stress the danger inherent in accepting gifts of food; that, by doing so, you expose yourself to the mercy of your benefactor. 'Bad medicines' (*ifohn wei*) are assumed to circulate widely through Kagboro's covert economy, and in a bewildering array of forms. At one extreme are rare and dangerously potent substances said to be made from the body parts of human victims. But, at the other end of the spectrum, 'half-half *ifohn*' – which are used to influence people or secure their loyalty – are considered a fairly mundane element of day-to-day economic life. Viewed within such an atmosphere of widespread mistrust, the customers' small, daily, taken-for-granted acts of giving and receiving take on an added significance, and play an important role in transforming economic interactions into social ones. By publicly receiving and eating her food each day, the fisherman implicitly resigns himself to the fact that, if she wanted to, his customer could and would use this power to 'influence him' – but he trusts her not to exploit this power. Even in the absence of any sexual element to their relationship, the result is that not only the economies but also the identities of their two households begin to blur at their boundaries.

Perhaps it is precisely because the flow of food serves so vividly to illustrate – and at once reinforce – the level of faith and mutual dependency which must necessarily develop between them that such gifts remain conceptually important between *kustoments*, even in cases where the fisherman does not appear to be in any particular 'need' of help. As the reluctant head of a large all-female household,[5] for example, my neighbour Leagbe was struggling financially in a way that her boat-owning *kustoment* almost certainly was not. Yet, almost every evening she would send one of the girls from her compound to take a pan of rice to Pa Ali, an ex-husband who lived some two miles along the coast with his current wife and family.

While it might appear surprising that Pa Ali should have chosen an 'ex'-wife to be his main business partner, rather than his current one (whom Leagbe dismissed in private as 'not serious about business'), marital relations in Tissana – in common with most forms of social relations, in fact – were characterised by a structural potential for extreme flexibility. It was not at all uncommon for people to use the terms 'ex-husband' and 'husband', or 'ex-wife' and 'wife', rather interchangeably; in many cases, these relationships did not so much 'end' as fall

---

[5] Encompassing her elderly mother, a daughter, two granddaughters, a cousin, niece, and recently married daughter-in-law.

dormant, always with the capacity to be reconfigured on a different basis at a later date. So, although Leagbe had remarried and divorced three times since first separating from Pa Ali some 25 years previously, the reciprocal stream of small gifts between them serves to highlight a continuing ambiguity in their relationship; as *kustoments*, there was a sense in which the pair continued to be conceptually linked – if not as a marital unit per se, then nonetheless as a 'couple' in some broader sense of the word.

Debt and fish: gendered patronage

Returning to Mohammed, these 'gifts' of food were, for him – as they were for many of Abi's *kustoments* – far more than a symbolic gesture of goodwill or trust. As not only a poor crew member, but also a 'stranger' in Tissana, Mohammed was in a doubly vulnerable position. He worked as a 'regular crewman' within a large boat, a position that was considered slightly more prestigious and, in general, more secure than being one of the floating 'day workers' who touted their labour to any *boss-man* in need of an extra pair of hands. However, if they want to retain their jobs, crewmen are obliged to remain loyal to their boat at all times, even when torn nets or dangerous weather conditions prevent them from going to sea at all. During these periods, in which the crew spend their days mending their nets, some *boss-men* might choose to feed them and give some token amount of 'cigarette money'. Some might, but Mohammed was not so lucky.

Throughout the long, rainy season of 2011, Mohammed's boat was plagued with technical problems. Each time I saw him, he would return my greeting with the same stoical sigh and an ever-mounting tally of his days without earnings: 'Manageable! Things are only just manageable! But even now, we are still on maintenance; today makes 35 days.' Very few crewmen can afford the luxury of saving money, so these periods of enforced economic inactivity put them under enormous strain; this is particularly the case for strangers such as Mohammed, with no local network of kin to whom they can turn in time of need. That 'things were manageable' at all came down, in large part, to his relationship with Ami:

If we don't go to sea then we don't get anything, even if we are working on mending the fishing nets. We have stable *kustoments*. So, if you're my *kustoment*, any time that I'm broke, I'd come to you and say, 'Jennifer, I don't have any money.' You'd lend me something. I don't pay it back bulk-oh! Small-small, small-small [very gradually]. Even last year, when my woman was pregnant – at that time, I didn't have any money, so Ami lent me 100,000 leones. I paid it back small-small, until I've paid her back now. She never once shouted at me. Me, I like to be secret. I don't want to expose my business. So that was the thing that made me like her more.

Given that many *banda* women find it increasingly difficult to secure access to a regular supply of fish, it is easy to see the benefit to Ami of keeping her suppliers in debt. However effectively fish sales may be channelled by love, friendship, or habit, it is only when a fisherman owes you *money* that you have the legal right to summon him to court if he sells to another woman. This puts rather a different light on Mohammed's gratitude that, as he was so keen to stress, Ami has never pressured him to repay her anything other than 'small-small, small-small'. Although she never charges her *kustoments* interest on these loans, Ami nonetheless profits directly from their indebtedness to her, for it buys her the loyalty she needs to secure a reliable supply of fish for her *banda*.

One could easily imagine that this situation – someone as vulnerable as Mohammed being so routinely indebted to his far more prosperous and better-connected trading partner – might foster a potentially exploitative power dynamic. Yet, however 'unequal' he and Ami may be in terms of their social and material capital, it is clear from Mohammed's own account that he considers Ami to have liberated him from an altogether less appealing possibility:

Like, you see this problem that I have at the moment in court? If I went to my *boss-man* and told him, he'd help me. But I don't want that. I don't want to be in debt to my boss. I prefer to borrow from my *kustoment* ... [because] even if I decided to switch to a different boat, I'd keep my *kustoment*.

For a poor crewman such as Mohammed, it would be hard to overstate the importance of this freedom – to 'decide to switch to a different boat'. The examples Mohammed gives – of medical costs and court cases – are typical of the kind of unexpected expenses that occur now and then in the life of every crewman, and that few are able to afford without turning to someone more prosperous for help. Put in a similar situation, some would opt to borrow from their *boss-man*. But, as Mohammed went on to explain, 'If I borrowed money from [my boss], I'd be frightened to leave him in case he took me to court.' In conversation, people often described these indebted crewmen as resembling the one thing young men most fear becoming: 'like slaves'.

Tissana's economy is one in which elements of 'the market' exist alongside – and often in explicit tension with – more personalised and socially binding modes of economic relationship. There is a substantial body of gender and development literature singling out informal West African markets as the paradigmatic example of how poor women, despite all their disadvantages, are able to use commerce 'as an instrument of social and political emancipation' (House-Midamba and Ekechi 1995: xvi; cf. Solomon 2005: 12). The assumption running through much of this literature is that economic 'empowerment' necessarily entails a heightened sense of individualism. But, far from exercising 'economic autonomy in ways that would free them from the shackles of men' (Cornwall 2007: 150), the most successful businesswomen in Tissana are those who are most effective in *accumulating* close, durable, economic partnerships with fishermen. In what appears to be an echo of an older, agricultural economy of 'wealth in people', large-scale *banda* women such as Ami are the only actors in Tissana's economy who continue to invest a substantial amount of their creative energy and material resources in work to accumulate 'people'. For Mohammed, forging a relationship with a strong *banda* woman is a compromise: one that affords him the basic social security than comes from having a patron, without structuring him (too explicitly) in the role of an indentured dependant. However, as we will see in the following section, it is an uneasy compromise.

Alehn relationships

It should be clear by now that the one thing all successful *banda* women have in common is that they have learned to be highly strategic in creating and managing their relationships with fishermen in order to secure access to a resource that seems to be increasingly scarce and precious. The fact is that, under 'normal' circumstances, the myriad small negotiations that go into 'making' any relationship as durable and intimate as that between a fisherman and his long-term customer are simply too many and too subtle to be easily summarised. Emerging as they do from far longer stories of emotional and economic entanglement between two individuals, these relationships extend well beyond the wharf, into kitchens, bedrooms, and imaginations around Tissana.

However, there is one context on the wharf in which customer relationships are forged with a special urgency and a stripped-down simplicity. That is when, as is often the case, fishermen take their boats and go 'on *alehn*' to base themselves briefly in another fishing town along the coast (see Chapter 2). Although they worked hard throughout the day, the houses in Tissana where groups of visiting fishermen were temporarily lodged tended to have a special kind of festive atmosphere about them. Given that *alehning* crews were not enmeshed in any long-term networks of social obligation, a large catch from one of these visiting boats tended to generate even greater commotion on the wharf than a similar catch by a local crew. On such a pristine social playing field, everyone had an equal hope of negotiating a sale of fish. Unsurprisingly, the level of friendly attention they receive is well appreciated by visiting crewmen. If one took a stroll down to Atia Base, Tissana's main social hub in the evening, and met some *alehning* fishermen there, one could almost guarantee that they would be drinking more heavily and flirting with more exuberance than the local men. When I asked this fisherman, visiting from Bonthe, how he was enjoying his stay in town, his effusive response was typical:

'Yes! Ah! Yes, we like it here! Clearly! This fine, fine *alehn*? They look after us well. Don't you see how we're enjoying ourselves here?'

Whatever pay arrangements they may have been used to with their *boss-man* in their home town, crewmen on *alehn* can expect to be lodged together and fed throughout their entire stay away from home, whether that be for a few days or, as is sometimes the case, it stretches to a period of several months. Crewmen were therefore very conscious that, in theory, these periods away from home ought to provide them with a rare opportunity to save money; but they were equally conscious – as they would often joke when comparing their experiences in Tombo and Plantain – that, for all but the most uncommonly disciplined crewmen, exactly the opposite was likely to be the case. With so much fun to be had, Mohammed told me, 'In Plantain, money won't stay steady in your hand! You make money fast; but you spend it faster! Most men, when they go on *alehn*, they just spend all their money on women and enjoyment!'

Alehning fishermen are able to rapidly form new relationships on unfamiliar wharfs, but the flip side of this dynamic is predictable. Many women live with a palpable sense of insecurity, knowing that their partner is perfectly liable to relocate at a moment's notice, moving to a different wharf town and taking up a new life with a different wife and business partner. In their conversations with me, *banda* women often discussed their anxieties about abandonment in very material terms – as the severing of an economic partnership, which left them far more vulnerable in the aftermath. In some cases, as with my friend Sungao, we recited the same optimistic conversation almost every time I saw her for 18 months, and as I watched her baby grow into a toddler; her man, she would always tell me, was just about to come back to fetch her.

And here, I think, we have uncovered a fairly fundamental difference between the way in which men and women experience their social worlds. For me, as for Sungao, it was the town itself that formed the nexus of the social landscape as I recognised it. That sprawling jumble of houses and *bandas*, woven through with intricate, long-standing networks of obligation and friendship, appeared so substantial. Viewed from this angle, it would have been easy to imagine that such a solid world must surely have occupied a similarly paramount space in fishermen's emotional landscape. Surely the town came first? Surely it remained their key point of reference when they were adrift at sea each day? Indeed, it is true that I did know some fishermen who, on any day when they went to sea, would return home without fail to Tissana. My friend Abas was one such fisherman. In the 18 months during which he was my neighbour, I never once heard of him landing his canoe anywhere other than directly in front of his wife's own *banda*. Yet Abas was not typical, and, in any case, even he had *alehned* extensively in his younger years. So, the same place that appears to a woman, on the land, to be so very solid, so permanent, is sometimes no more than an *alehn* to the fishermen who visit it – a location etymologically defined by movement, fluidity, impermanence, uncertainty.

Elsewhere in West Africa, scholars have tended to agree that, beneath the official narrative – that mobility is necessary in order to track the seasonal movements of fish – many fishermen share a less explicit motive for keeping on the move: that is, it enables men to eschew expensive moral entanglements at home. By choosing to constantly shift back and forth between neighbouring wharf towns, fishermen are able to establish fruitful temporary relationships while limiting their exposure to the wives and sisters who 'make demands that the fishermen can hardly refuse, such as paying the children's school fees or medical bills' (Lucht 2011: 196).[6]

In this sense, the Yawri Bay's fishermen exemplify the 'intensified movement' (Simone 2003) that has become a defining characteristic of social life in many contexts across postcolonial Africa (cf. De Boeck 2015; Hoffman 2007; Vigh 2006). In a broader context of chronic economic instability, social navigation, for many Africans, has come to be defined by movement as 'a process without foreseeable end... an ongoing career of sometimes incessant shifts in places of residence and work' (Simone 2003: 8). For Tissana's fishermen, as for the urban residents described by Simone, one appeal of such restless, open-ended motion is that it offers an escape from expensive and morally complex webs of obligation: 'a means of effacing specific constraints in both [or, indeed, all] places' (ibid.: 9).

But the freedom and mobility that fishermen claim to value so dearly is often experienced as a source of considerable anxiety by the women whose lives and livelihoods are entangled with theirs. Early on in my time at Site, for example, there was a great commotion in my compound when it emerged that one of the young girls I lived with had a boyfriend: Alfred, a young crewman from Tombo, who had joined one of Tissana's larger fishing crews. Aisha was only 15 years old, and her family were concerned that she might be pregnant. Had her boyfriend been a local man, the families of the two young people would have met together to arrange a formal marriage and negotiate the payment of bridewealth; as it was, Aisha's grandfather, Pa Dulai, was worried that this young stranger would too easily avoid taking responsibility for Aisha's 'belly':

The thing is, this boy, he didn't come from here. Let me say he is just... passing. So what I predict is that, if we try to take him to court, he'll just disappear.

---

[6] Describing a similar pattern of migration in Ghana, Overå has argued that, 'above all, fishermen migrate in order to accumulate material wealth... Long-term stays away from social and economic obligations towards the extended family at home make saving possible' (2001: 1; cf. Marquette et al. 2002: 333).

Because we don't know his family. We don't know his people. That's what they [visiting fishermen] do. They come here and cause trouble and then they leave.

Similar anxieties are not new for women in the Upper Guinea region, nor unique to fishing contexts. Over 20 years ago, Caroline Bledsoe discussed the shifting micro-politics of fatherhood in 'modernising' farming communities in which the high cost of Western-style education had destabilised older models of wealth in people. Her male informants were left ambivalent as to whether young children should be cherished as a valuable asset, or eschewed as a risky and expensive burden. Despite this new ambivalence towards fathering children, the men Bledsoe interviewed made no effort to avoid impregnating their girlfriends:

The main risk lies not in preventing the birth of children but in definitely claiming fatherhood to them. Claiming fatherhood adds expenses that might be spared by leaving paternity ambiguous until children reach an age at which they may be useful. (Bledsoe 1980: 40)

Young women sometimes hoped that, by getting pregnant, they might succeed in cementing their relationship with a new lover. But such tactics were risky, and met with mixed success: 'If a relationship deteriorates, this child can become an economic burden as well as a social hindrance for a woman trying to initiate a new union' (Bledsoe 1995: 136). If the social and economic risks of pregnancy are high for vulnerable women in sedentary communities,[7] these risks are multiplied in a fishing town where, as Pa Dulai had learned through decades of experience, visiting fishermen 'come here and cause trouble and then they leave'.

Yet, despite their real – and justified – anxieties of abandonment, it would be rather too simplistic to view *banda* women as the guileless victims of their menfolk. Rather, the difference between these two phenomenologies of space serves to highlight the tensions inherent in a social world as mutable as Tissana's, in which the momentum towards establishing relationships and the desire to disentangle oneself from them are often held in dynamic opposition.

Plantain Island sirens

The image that is beginning to emerge, then, is one in which men and women inhabit quite different landscapes. There are interesting parallels here between the ways in which gender has come to be mapped onto the coastal topography through everyday practices associated with commercial fishing, and other, much older patterns of gendered segregation.

---

[7] Not to mention the enormous health risks – Sierra Leone has the highest recorded maternal mortality rate in the world. It is estimated that one out of every 21 women die of childbirth-related complications (WHO 2014).

For as long as we have ethnographic records about Sierra Leone, it has always been the case that people experienced their landscape as powerfully gendered. Young people become unambiguously male or female only following time spent in ritual seclusion in their respective initiation sodalities' bush. Throughout their adult lives, it remains the case that certain important decisions and pivotal life events can only take place safely in gendered seclusion, in the Poro or Bundu society 'bush'.

Bundu and Poro ideology has historically cast any boundary space in which men and women come into contact outside the careful regulation of sodality laws as potentially dangerous, but also as powerfully productive. In various contexts, Bundu symbolism also emphasises the mingling and integration of male and female elements, rather than their simple separation (Lamp 1985).[8] Indeed, powerful society elders derive part of their mystique precisely from their ability to flaunt the dangers inherent in these liminal spaces (Bledsoe 1984).[9] In the maritime economy, heightened patterns of male mobility, combined with the importance of heterosexual trading partnerships, create a coastal topography in which men and women routinely find themselves operating across highly charged gendered boundary zones. When *alehning* fishing crews land their boats on the shore of an unfamiliar wharf town, they enter straight into potentially complex economic relationships with women about whom they know almost nothing.

A tiny piece of land just two miles off the coast of the Shenge Peninsula, Plantain Island is Tissana's closest *alehn*. It also happens to be the busiest and most profitable fishing centre in Sierra Leone. In theory, then, a short stay on Plantain ought to be as profitable as it is convenient for Tissana's boat owners. Yet, many of the more experienced captains I knew claimed to view the island with considerable trepidation. Here, Sumaila is describing the ease with which he would expect his boat to be welcomed into an unfamiliar fishing town:

There are so many *alehns*! You can go anywhere you want. If you hear fish are dying in Bauma, you go to Bauma; if you hear fish are dying in Katta, you go to Katta... Even if I have never once been there before, I can go; the only thing is, on the day that I arrive, I should come with fish... That fish there – it is that which will open all my *subabu*. Yes! That fish: it will make them lodge me fine – in a fine place. It will let me live there well, make them give me respect.

---

[8] In Tissana, both boys' and girls' period of ritual seclusion was punctuated by key moments in which neophytes paraded publicly through town dressed in the clothes of members of the opposite sex.
[9] As in other Sierra Leonean language groups, a small number of exceptional Sherbro women, particularly female chiefs, are permitted to join the Poro society and to enter its sacred grove. Such a move carries considerable prestige, but it also comes at a cost: after initiation into Poro, a woman will never be able to bear children again.

Subabu is a Krio word describing a person's network of useful relationships. It is striking that, in the absence of any pre-existing *subabu*, it is the catch – not the men themselves – that Sumaila credits as having the power to forge these new relationships. Whereas crewmen tend to experience new *alehn* relationships as emerging naturally out of fisherfolk's mutual camaraderie and rules of good hospitality, Sumaila (as the person responsible for the fish and the money) interprets any social interaction in this strange environment as underpinned by strategic negotiations of a more material kind. And, viewed in this light, it is the feminine attentions of *banda* women that, in particular, come to be viewed with a new suspicion.

Whereas locally based fishermen are almost always tied into long-standing relationships with their female buyers in town, these visiting boats, full of (locally) unattached men, offer a rare opportunity for *banda* women to establish new – if temporary – *kustoment* relationships. But competition is fierce, and women have to act very quickly to claim a new boat when it arrives. Sumaila's account of what happens when he *alehns* to Plantain Island is typical of the way in which captains and boat owners describe these encounters, with something between attraction and misgiving:

They want your fish, but they want you too! Like myself, I have a boat, so . . . the moment my boat lands, the women all come around! They come around and talk to me like they already know me; they'll bring me fine food . . . She'll come and lean her head on me; she'll just linger on me now; she'll talk to me closely now . . . that's how they do it. (Sumaila, boat owner)

One day in the rainy season, I spent an afternoon sheltering from a storm in my friend Kumba's parlour, watching as he and another boat owner, Ibrahim, swapped ever-inflating accounts of their encounters with the women on Plantain Island. I had rarely seen the two men so animated, as they described the extent (they claimed!) to which these women were prepared to go in their attempt to entice guileless boat captains into entering a *kustoment* relationship. As I wrote in my field notes:

Ibrahim and Kumba loved recounting these stories, wide-eyed with a theatrical emotion somewhere between delight and fear. As the rain thundered down outside, they were on their feet moving around Kumba's tiny parlour, taking turns to role-play the different characters. First Kumba was the fearsome seductress, Ibrahim the gormless young fisherman. Now it was Ibrahim's turn to play the Plantain Island siren, sashaying over to where Kumba sat, pretending to laugh coquettishly at his jokes, stroking his arm fawningly. Striking a comedy feminine pose he mimed peeling his skirt up to his waist to seductively remove a stack of cash from the pocket of his tiny skin-tight shorts. Soon, the roles had switched again. Ibrahim lay on the floor in his imagined bed, half-cowering, half-laughing as Kumba tap-tap-tapped gently on his bedroom door, asking in a husky whisper, 'Are you that fisherman who just landed today . . . ?'

One thing that is particularly striking about these tales is that they seem to compress, into a single, highly charged encounter on a foreign wharf, many of the material layers that, as we have seen, characterise the longer-term negotiation of gendered economic relations at home. An undercurrent of sexual tension is certainly one facet of that encounter – and the one the men most enjoyed recounting – but it is no coincidence, for example, that both Kumba and Ibrahim also mention being given gifts of food and offered loans of cash by the women hoping to secure their custom:

> If you say that you're there to earn money – that you don't want a girlfriend – they'll say, 'Let me lend you money for petrol.' They have their little handbags, where they keep their money and their half-half *ifohn* [fetish medicines], which they put in your food. (Kumba, boat owner)

As we have already seen, there is a good reason why, under normal circumstances, people are extremely wary about from whom exactly they agree to accept gifts of food. Whereas back home, the flow of rice between a *banda* woman and her long-term customer can be read as evidence of the implicit trust between them, on these foreign shores the gifts are experienced with a heightened sense of anxiety. In this conversation, Fatti reinforces the widely held assumption that women on Plantain Island make generous use of *ifohn wei* (bad medicines) in their attempts to nurture relationships with visiting fishermen:

> Fatti: Women come to Plantain from all over the country. They come from Port Loko, Makeni – to work, to make money. When they want to get medicine, they go to those fetish people, up Temne-line. Those fetish people, they know how to make *dozag*. So they go there; they pay money.
>
> Me: What's *dozag*?
>
> Fatti: It's a medicine! For turning people's heads [influencing people]. When they want to catch fishermen, that's the one they use. They grind it up, fine – put it in their rice.

Early studies of 'traditional' medicine in Africa often pointed to the frequent use of 'love potions' and 'love magic'. However, as Thomas and Cole have noted, these observations rarely prompted anthropologists to reflect on local conceptions of love 'as an omnipresent health concern, an occult force, and an involuntary state of being' (2009: 7). The Yawri Bay is a world in which it is impossible to disaggregate the strategies by which people set out to influence one another's bodies from their broader efforts to build the intimate relationships that enable them to navigate Tissana's tight economy. The complex ways in which movements of cash, food, sex, and 'fetish' medicines are implicated in one another in the men's stories speaks powerfully to the intimacy and interdependence that characterise many gendered economic relationships across the Yawri Bay, but also to the deep-seated ambivalences men so often feel, finding themselves drawn into relationships that are as binding as they are transactional.

Here, my ethnography diverges from many accounts of sexual economies in fishing communities elsewhere in Africa. While exchanges of 'fish for sex' are usually analysed as evidence of women's desperation and exploitation (Allison and Janet 2001; Seeley 2009; Westaway, Seeley, and Allison 2007), my experience on the Kagboro coast is that people were more likely to make exactly the opposite assumption. You may remember that, back on Tissana Wharf, Hawa admitted quite openly that, in the current economic climate, manipulating men – or '*turn-turning*' them – is an essential skill for any hopeful fish processor. Faced with a wharf full of unfamiliar *banda* women, all vying to secure his custom, it was Sumaila who described himself feeling open to predation.

The women who are over there – their eyes are open [they're shrewd]! They know how to catch a man! That's their work right there, Jenny! As soon as you land and they see that you are strangers, the women come over, dressed fine ... They ask, 'Who owns this boat? Who owns this boat?' And, if Kumba owns the boat, he's the one with the problem now! And, when it comes to sleep, she'll tell the boat's owner, 'You're sleeping in my room!' And *then* what's going to happen? Hey? Men, we're fools, we're easy to confuse. You know we're easy to confuse. How are you going to be able to sit in that room, while a woman's pull-pulling all her clothes off? (Sumaila, boat owner)

Of course, there need not be a direct conflict between emphasising women's profound and deepening material vulnerability, as I have tried to do in this chapter, and also the tactics and strategies they employ to survive in these difficult economic conditions (cf. De Certeau 1984; Cornwall 2003). In Tissana, as elsewhere, the interplay between gendered livelihoods, love, and moral discourses on sexual intimacy are constantly shifting in response to the broader political, social, and economic landscape. While informal 'loving' relationships had existed in Sierra Leone before the war, new patterns of transactional relationships emerged in response to the particular challenges of displacement, violence, and war-time shortage (Gale 2007). Life, for many women during the war, was experienced as a 'constant battle for protection' (Utas 2003: 179; 2005) in which their sexuality was often the only resource they were able to trade for their safety.[10]

In a less extreme context, Groes-Green (2013) recently described the tactics used by young women in urban Mozambique as they set out to seduce foreign men in order to gain access to money and material gifts. These intimate exchanges are entwined within a broader realm of

---

[10] Emphasising the extreme insecurity and abuse experienced by young women associated with the rebel army, Denov and Gervais (2007) explore the ingenuity with which 'camp wives' learned to mobilise their sexuality, forming relationships with powerful men in order to secure their survival.

esoteric feminine knowledge and power, in which senior women educate girls in the skills – including tabooed forms of magic[11] – for seducing and manipulating men. Without implying that eroticism can overthrow deeper structures of inequality, his ethnography reveals how, even in highly patriarchal societies, sexuality can sometimes become a 'space for female assertiveness' (ibid.: 103).

Conclusions

It is striking that these highly caricatured images of *banda* women – as powerful sexual-cum-economic predators – are only ever used to describe the women in other *alehns*. I heard men talking in similar ways about their experiences of visiting Delken, Tombo, and Funkea, but always with the same caveat: 'Here in Tissana, our own women's style is different. Our women would be ashamed.' My intention is not, therefore, to suggest that these stories are an impartial reflection of ethnographic fact, but rather to view them as a playful form of commentary through which fishermen reflect on their experience of the shifting coastal economy.

In small-town Nigeria, Andrea Cornwall observed the emergence of a parallel set of narratives about 'voracious temptresses' (2002: 964), who, like the Plantain Island sirens, were described as exploiting a string of guileless men. In both cases, the gossip could be interpreted as pointing to a widespread anxiety about the increasing commodification of love. However, Cornwall highlights the important ways in which love and money have always been intertwined in West African ideals of gendered relations. The perceived 'moral crisis', therefore, did not emerge from any new interweaving of economics and intimacy. In the Nigerian case, she argues, 'the image of the wayward woman' (ibid.: 971) served to mask a deeper set of anxieties about a perceived shift in the economic power of men and women. At a time when growing unemployment had left many men unable to contribute to household economies, successful independent women exacerbated an existing crisis in masculine identity.

In Tissana, as we have seen, there is a huge variation in the amount of social and economic power that individual women are able to hold in their economic relationships with fishermen. In a broader context of patriarchy, it has always been the case in coastal Sierra Leone that a minority of 'especially adept women' have been able to control 'land, labor, and something we might call capital in both a Firthian sense and a classical economic sense' (MacCormack 2000: 37; cf. Hoffer 1972). So,

---

[11] Francis Nyamnjoh describes similar fears in Senegal. Here, too, men are advised to think twice before eating food prepared for them: 'For if [women] really want to keep men, in everything they cook, there are likely to be charms specially packaged by marabouts – whom Senegalese visit . . . to capture and cage love' (2005: 304).

without taking the fishermen's salacious stories too literally, or allowing them to distract us from the real hardship and vulnerability that shape most women's lives in the Yawri Bay, these tales remind us of the complexity of cultural understandings of gendered power in this region.

In other contexts, people in Tissana did express concern about the vulnerability of young girls to sexual exploitation, but images of women as powerful predators also form part of a wider cultural discourse. During Sierra Leone's war, stories proliferated both locally and in the international media about the extreme brutality of female fighters, often described as more vicious than their male counterparts. For outside observers, the fascination of these women was that their violence was implicitly taken to contravene some 'natural' womanly role, as peacemakers and nurturers. However, Chris Coulter found that her Kuranko informants held a quite different image of femininity: far from being inherently peaceful, women were perceived as being 'by nature raw, wild, and dangerous', so that the image of violent fighters 'did not necessarily transcend, but rather reinforced, certain aspects of femininity in Kuranko thought' (Coulter 2009: 240).[12]

The stories that men share about these Plantain Island sirens draw at least part of their emotional energy from the ways in which they both echo and resonate with broader tropes about freedom and, in particular, the risks inherent in boundary spaces, and the fine line between seduction and predation. In Tissana, as across West Africa, people are familiar with stories of Mami Wata – a seductive, fearsome spirit, often described as enticing her devotees into a watery prison with false promises of lavish wealth. Seemingly modelled on the mermaid figureheads that adorned European slaving ships, folktales about Mami Wata remain a powerful motif for reflecting on contemporary experiences of economic violence (Argenti 2010). Plantain Island had once been the site of one of the busiest slave forts on the Upper Guinea Coast, so it is striking that this liminal space continues to be imagined as a site where the lure of economic riches, and the fear of personal entrapment, come together in the figure of a powerful female seductress.

You want to come home, but they don't allow it. They talk to you fine, they wrap-wrap themselves around you, kiss you ... Or, the ones who have money, they take money and lend it to you! They're bad-oh! So that, when the time comes that you're ready to leave, then they'll ask you about the money. They say, 'Eh! You want to go? What about my money? Why don't you just stay in this water here first? The fish are dying so ... ' You sit down. (Kumba, boat owner)

---

[12] Across the border in Guinea, Mike McGovern describes adult women regarding their daughters with trepidation, 'as agents whose strong desires and fantasies could wreak havoc in their communities and needed to be domesticated' (2015: 255).

Anthropologists have often returned over the years to the classic argument – made by both Marx (2000 [1946]) and Simmel (1978 [1900]) – that by enabling people to imagine material transactions as devoid of any moral specificity, liberalised markets are corrosive of social relations. We are by now used to hearing that, for many people in newly capitalised societies, this desocialisation of economic relations is experienced as a source of extreme moral anxiety (e.g. Taussig 1980). However, in Tissana, fishermen's most clearly expressed anxieties seem to be focused in exactly the opposite direction. To understand the trepidation my neighbours expressed – as they watched their economic lives become increasingly determined by patterns of intimacy, debt, and social obligation – these changes need to be viewed against a recent historical trajectory in which the rapid growth of the commercial fishing industry appeared to be ushering in a period of unprecedented personal independence. According to the wistful recollections of my informants, there had been a period on Tissana Wharf, however fleeting, when they seemed to have achieved something close to Simmel's vision of a monetary system in which 'man is free – free because he can sell everything, and free because he can buy everything' (1978 [1900]: 404).

Nowadays, both fishermen and *banda* women look back with nostalgia to their town's 'boom' period through the lens of a present in which the maritime economy is coming under ever greater pressure. As competition for fish steadily accelerates, the day-to-day labour of an increasing number of women involves working to create ties of intimacy or obligation with fishermen simply in order to win the opportunity to buy fish. For many fishermen, their greatest concern is that, when faced with women more wily than themselves, they might inadvertently find themselves entangled in sticky webs of obligation that they had no intention of entering.

5   'Potato rope' families

When I asked whether Jo Kebbe was Jacob's brother, everyone on the veranda looked baffled, as though they had no idea why I would ask such a question.

'Well,' I tried to explain, 'Sento is Jacob's sister, and you just said that she's Jo Kebbe's sister so I thought...?'

'No!'

'They're *family*!' Aminata explained, as though this blanket term ought to iron out any remaining confusion as to how, exactly, the three people were related. But Buema was not prepared to accept such a facile explanation: 'They are not family! What family? Jo Kebbe is a Kebbe! Jacob is a Yannie! What family is that?'

'So...?' It was my turn to look baffled now. 'Why would he go to Sento for help?'

Inspired, Buema leapt to her feet, 'Have you heard of a potato rope family?' Without pausing to wait for an answer, she took two potato stems from the bench beside her and began to mime planting them in the concrete ground of the veranda. 'This one; you plant it here. You see? And the other one; the other one is all the way over...' She was bending double now, holding the two bundles as far apart as her stretched arms would allow: 'Here! But this rope, it grows like so. And the other one, it grows like...so...until...'

Slowly, she drew the two stems towards one another along the ground, revelling in her own performance. 'They meet and join and look like one rope! Do you see?' She straightened up, triumphant. 'That is what we call a potato rope family!'

The 'potato rope' would be a particularly resonant metaphor for anyone in Tissana. Although only a small minority of households in this fishing town find the time or labour to farm on any significant scale, almost all keep at least a small kitchen garden in which they grow vegetables for their own domestic use. By far the most widespread and lowest maintenance of all garden plants are the cassava and the sweet potato; each one is grown not only for their starchy tubers, but also for the leaves that form that basis of '*plassas*', the staple, daily accompaniment to rice and fish. In the dry season, potatoes are planted in gardens near watering holes a short walk from town, but during the rainy season small potato patches spring up on every scrap of spare land around town: on the edges of compounds, between houses, and at the sides of paths. 'Picking *plassas*' is one of the most basic daily household chores, and might be entrusted to a child as young as five. There is no one, in other words, who is unfamiliar with the way a potato rope grows.

Sweet potato vines are cut in short lengths with no leaves or tubers attached, and planted in small bunches, each a foot or two away from their nearest neighbour across the bare earth. Yet, in contrast to cassava stems, which maintain their integrity as individual plants when they grow, potato ropes have altogether less respect for personal boundaries. Within a couple of months of being planted, those fragile, isolated stems have grown into such a luscious tangle of roots, leaves, and tubers that – as Buema mimed so effectively to us on the veranda – 'they look like one rope'.

Writing over 20 years ago, Liisa Malkki criticised a tendency among social scientists at the time to naturalise people's relationship to places through metaphors of 'rootedness'. Her concern had been that, when people's identities are defined as arising naturally from an ancestral history embedded in the land, this fosters a vision of population movement as inherently pathological (Malkki 1992: 27). But Buema's botanical image achieves something quite different: it provides a template for imagining how, in this highly volatile maritime world, two strangers might become as entangled with one another as if they had been related all their lives.

Set against Tissana's context of widespread population movement, household instability, and deepening material insecurity, this chapter traces how vital webs of affect and intimacy are woven through gifts of fish and rice. In a town where hunger is an all too familiar aspect of mundane experience, there are few more fertile material expressions of the relationship between two people than the ways in which they choose to share and exchange – or withhold – food. As Shepler describes in her discussion of food in wartime Sierra Leone:

Food is material, but also symbolic, and literally everyday. Our experience of food is a physical, sensual, shared human experience. Food is embodied, mundane, often gendered in its preparation and consumption. It allows the physical reproduction of bodies, but is part of social reproduction. (Shepler 2011: 45)

Because of these urgent visceral qualities, food is an apt vehicle for what David Graeber calls a 'social' currency, the circulation of which concerns 'the creation and mutual fashioning of human beings' (2012: 412).

These patterns of gift exchange offer a window onto the social energy and creativity people invest in creating some sense of permanence in the face of radical insecurity. A recurring theme in recent African ethnography is the extent to which uncertainty has been taken for granted as the context within which people weave their lives: the 'inevitable force' (Johnson-Hanks 2005: 366) that shapes day-to-day experience. Unsurprisingly, chronic instability – and the anxieties it generates – is usually described in ethnographic literature as a negative state: the absence of knowledge, security, and control. In a recent intervention, however, Cooper and Pratten sought to emphasise that uncertainty can itself become a 'productive resource' (2015: 3) and an experience that stimulates people's imaginations and actions in potentially creative ways.

It is no coincidence that the best-known examples of 'creative' kinship patterns tend to be found in studies of populations living in unpredictable conditions. From refugees to boom-town migrants (Walsh 2003), one way of navigating the narrow line between material scarcity and population fluidity is to develop strategies for forging vital social relationships 'on the fly' (McGovern 2012: 748). This struggle, to balance social belonging with economic survival, is a familiar aspect of precarious livelihoods across post-war Sierra Leone. As intimate social structures were disrupted by war and its aftermath, people were quick to respond to the violent upheaval by 'creatively resuscitating' (Gale 2006: 78) new kinds of kinship network. Lacey Andrews Gale has demonstrated, for example, that even in the stressful environment of a refugee camp, the work of forging and maintaining family relations through fostering, marriage, and reciprocity remained 'the life goals around which all else [turned]' (ibid.). It was these new webs of kin that, ultimately, enabled people to navigate an unfamiliar camp system and meet their basic material needs.

In fact, even in the most 'traditional' and seemingly stable communities in the Upper Guinea region, family lineages have rarely been quite as 'arboreal' as public genealogical histories purport them to be. Across this region, it was – and remains – common for 'strangers' to be absorbed, first as fostered children or tenant farmers and eventually (in the manner of a potato rope, if you like) as in-laws or 'nephews' within the lineages of established local families (Dorjahn and Fyfe 1962; d'Azevedo 1962a).[1] These patterns of 'aspirational kinship' – which evolved in the context of many centuries of endemic warfare, displacement, and slavery – became vital once more in recent decades as millions were forced to flee their homes and seek refuge with strangers under conditions of real danger or precarity (McGovern 2012).

In the fishing context, vital social relationships must be forged, abandoned, and reforged so frequently that it undermines even a *discursive* commitment to values of intergenerational continuity.[2] But, despite

[1] In this classic landlord–stranger model, a person's ability to *claim* genealogical 'roots' in the land continued to determine their social, political, or economic belonging – even if everyone knew that these histories were often fictionalised (Sarró 2010; Berliner 2010).
[2] The 'canoe houses' that flourished in the Niger Delta from the eighteenth century are a historical example of a domestic institution in coastal West Africa in which social and

all this restless population movement, a strong social network remains the only available form of protection against overstretched, precarious livelihoods (cf. Alber, Häberlein, and Martin 2010: 44). People in Tissana therefore invest a huge amount of their daily energy and material resources in working to forge webs of affect and social belonging (*subabu*) that defy any neat classification between friendship, 'fictive' kinship, and biological relatedness.

So, as the chapter progresses, a more ambivalent picture begins to emerge beneath this image of munificence and mutual generosity. In a broader regional context in which patronage relationships have often been experienced as deeply exploitative (cf. Richards 1986), gifts of food are not only the substance of survival but also have the potential to become a potent gesture of control. These anxieties are given explicit material form in an economy in which 'fetish' medicines are commonly understood to be widely in circulation, and where complex expressions of power may sometimes be smuggled within the most innocuous-seeming gift of rice. Beyond this, there is a basic level of chronic anxiety built into a system of reckoning belonging that requires people to work – and work hard – simply to sustain the kinship relationships they depend upon for material survival and social identity. In recent years, this experience of insecurity has been compounded by the ecological crisis in West African fisheries, which has made it increasingly hard for vulnerable people to find the resources needed to prevent their most intimate family relationships from atrophying and collapsing.

Metaphors of movement and belonging: roots, flows, and potato ropes

The prevailing tone of anthropological writing has shifted significantly since Malkki highlighted the ubiquitous use of language 'rooting' particular peoples in particular places. She had been at the vanguard of an important move to refocus ethnographic attention away from neatly compartmentalised 'indigenous cultures' towards those things – refugees, migrants, knowledge, contraband – that challenge cartographic boundaries by 'flowing' across them (cf. Nordstrom 2007; Mol and Law 1994). Over the past couple of decades, watery idioms rather than botanical ones have come to dominate scholarly discussions on how social lives play out across physical topographies (Appadurai 1990; Tsing 2000).

Viewed from the perspective of seagoing fishermen, the Yawri Bay conforms rather neatly to this image of waterscapes and spaces of movement and connectivity. We have seen in Chapters 3 and 4 that Tissana's

political belonging were decoupled from ideals of shared lineage and descent (Wariboko 1998: 143).

fishermen often place a strong rhetorical emphasis on the aspiration to personal 'freedom'. Perhaps the most vivid expression of this claim is the way in which they explicitly valorise their fluid migratory patterns.

Just as the fish migrate, so, too, the fishermen migrate... The fish go, the fishermen go. The fish stop, fishermen themselves stop. Anywhere they go, the fishermen will go there too. (Ben, boat owner, Plantain Island)

It was common for fishermen to make this analogy between their own fluid, unpredictable migrations and the equally unsettled movements of their fishy quarry, unseen beneath the water's surface. In this sense, one sees surprising analogies, not only to the imagery, but also even to the ideological overtones of certain post-structuralist literature, the writers of which (rather optimistically, perhaps) projected the emergence of new kinds of subjects: people who might '[relinquish] all idea, desire, nostalgia for fixity' (Braidotti 1994: 22).

However, for academics and fishermen alike, these images of unbounded fluidity are the projection of an ideal as much as they are descriptions of a lived reality. When Deleuze and Guattari refer to their 'nomadic subject', for example, the figure they describe – who 'can be called the Deterritorialised *par excellence*... precisely because there is no reterritorialisation *afterwards*' (2004 [1987]: 421) – was not based on any ethnographically observed nomadic population (Cresswell 2006: 54), but rather *against* their own experience of life in a modern nation state. Similarly, we saw in Chapter 3 that the fishermen's romanticisation of movement needs to be understood – in part at least – as an attempt to assert their rejection of another more explicitly 'arboreal' model for reckoning power, in which kinship, social belonging, and personhood are all heavily predetermined by a person's roots in the land.

As Anna Tsing has warned, such imagery brings with it the risk that we overlook or undervalue the experience of those 'local folks who are still stuck inside [local situations]' (2000: 346). There are a couple of senses in which Tsing's caveat is important in the case of Tissana, both of which I have already touched on in previous chapters. Firstly, the surface of the Yawri Bay is far from being a 'friction-free' (Wigen 2006: 721) boundary blurring substance, for it is only fishermen who are able to move across it. Secondly, however much men might claim to value the promise of 'liberation' that comes from their seemingly rootless mobility, in a marine environment as stretched as the Yawri Bay, all people depend for their most basic daily material security on being enmeshed in strong networks of social ties (*subabu*). It is at this juncture – between heightened forms of mobility on the one hand, and the urgent material need for social connectedness on the other – that we can begin to imagine the importance of the kind of kinship structures Buema was describing when she told me about 'potato rope' families.

A place defined by movement?

Migrants from Ghana first introduced the practice of '*alehning*' to this coastline in the 1960s (see Chapter 2). Within the anthropology of fishing, the pattern is familiar. Earlier ethnographies of fishermen further south along the Guinea Coast described them following regular annual circuits in synchrony with the predictable seasonal movements of shoaling fish (Jorion 1988; Wyllie 1969; Marquette et al. 2002); when I first began asking fishermen in Tissana to explain where and how they decide to migrate, they often began by recounting a similarly neat pattern. Abas expressed a commonly expressed wisdom, for example, when he told me:

Well, fish swim against the wind. So, during the harmattan, when the winds blow from the land [December to March], the fish come up close to the coast. At that time, we really catch a lot of fish here! That is the time when this place really fills up. (Abas, boat owner)

However, my own experience in Tissana is that neither the fish nor the men who attempt to track their movements were nearly as predictable as these models suggest. Indeed, there were long periods during the harmattan season when people in Tissana were consistently frustrated by the small size of the catches that were being landed on their wharf. If ever fishermen had followed such a regular pattern in the past, nowadays a combination of outboard engines and mobile phone technology has made it possible for captains to move much more intuitively, relying on hearsay to judge, day by day, whether it might be worth trying their luck in a different fishing town:

There are so many *alehns*. My own boat has just gone to Tombo – we hear the fish are dying there just now. They will go and lodge for one week; they will look at how the fishing conditions are there. If they see the catch is poor, then they'll come back here ... Or perhaps I'll call them, and say, 'Come! Come over here! Fish are here!' (Timbo, boat owner, Tissana)

This one word, *alehn*, captures much of what is distinct not only about the lifestyle but also about the position from which the Yawri Bay's fishermen view their world. As we have seen, it has two slightly different meanings. In one sense, to *alehn* is a verb: to move, to migrate fluidly through the water, often not knowing with any certainty where one might settle, or for how long. In its other usage, an *alehn* is also a place. It is the generic name that migratory fishermen give to 'other' coastal towns viewed from the sea: a location etymologically defined by movement and impermanence.

In this second sense, Plantain Island stood in the imaginations of my neighbours in Tissana as the 'purest' example of an *alehn* they knew: a dynamic, unstable town, through which every cliché of fishing life could be illustrated. Having been established as a makeshift camp in the late 1950s, this 'temporary' outpost rapidly burgeoned into the most

Figure 5.1 The ever-busy wharf on Plantain Island

frenetically busy fishing centre in Sierra Leone. Today, Plantain's beach is incessantly busy with boats being hauled into the sea or back up onto the sand (see Figure 5.1). As fishermen jostle directly with traders on the beach, everywhere one looks people are pulling fish from nets, packing dried fish, negotiating a deal:

This is the area, here, where money *flows*! We have fishermen here from as far as Senegal. Yes! And we have traders coming from Bo, from Kenema, Moyamba, all over the country... You can't sit down and idle here – just sit down and relax. Oh no! Those who go to sea, go to sea. Those who sell, sell. Those who buy, buy. That's it! That's the way we move here! (Sufyan, boat owner, Plantain)

The language Sufyan uses here to describe his island home as a node in wider oceanic currents of migrant fishermen, cash, and trade goods calls to mind Hau'ofa's (1993) description of the Pacific Ocean as a 'sea of islands'. Rather than being separated by the expanses of water between them, Sierra Leone's *alehns* appear, from this perspective, as points in a social universe that is inherently liquid. The most experienced captains are highly tuned to the shifting dynamics of their watery region: not only where other boats are experiencing fishing success, but also how the prices are fluctuating at different points around the coast:

Mohammed (boat owner): In every *alehn*, the price can change. Like here in Tissana, for now, they buy *bonga* for 700 leones per dozen... But right now in Plantain, they're buying them for 1,500 leones per dozen. Now-now-now! The difference is too much! So people decide to leave here and go to Plantain.

Me: How do you come to know the price in another *alehn*?

Mohammed: The communication now is very close now we have mobile phones. But even without telephones, there are many, so many fishermen here in Tissana. Maybe one fisherman will go and land in Plantain, then come home and say, 'Eh man! In Plantain they are buying fish [at] 1,500 – we waste our fish here! Let us go and land in Plantain.'

Viewed from the sea, then, the first impression one gets of the Yawri Bay is of a world of incessant, restless movement. In this vision of the bay's social universe, not only the ocean itself but also the settlements that surround it are defined by flux: by the constant, shifting streams of people, fish, and money that flow through them.

However, there is another sense in which Plantain seems to epitomise fishermen's ideological commitment to fluidity over stasis. For despite the fact that, according to Tom, an elder in Shenge, 'no town in Kagboro booms like Plantain', the settlement retains a certain sense of imper-manence, even all these decades after it was first established. Despite all the evidence of people making and circulating money, my neighbours in Tissana often commented on how visibly dilapidated Plantain is. In Tissana, my neighbours understood this juxtaposition – of profit and decay – through the logic that Plantain Islanders are *archetypical* fisherfolk. Always half-ready to up-anchor and set sail for a new wharf town, they would prefer to spend money on a new boat than invest their resources in the buildings and infrastructure of a place to which they had limited commitment. We already began to see in Chapter 4 that for the women, children and non-seafaring men who make up the majority of Tissana's population, this chronic lack of stability is more likely to be experienced as a source of anxiety than of liberation. In the following section, I trace some of the most visible ways in which people seek to overcome this sense of social precariousness, through the strategic use of material exchange.

Two fish economies

Within moments of landing on Tissana Wharf, a successful fishing boat will already be surrounded by a crowd. In a sometimes bewildering clam-our of flirtation, begging, and bullying, a tangled web of negotiations is played out on the sand between the fishermen in the boat, their cus-tomers, girlfriends, neighbours, and debtors, as each person attempts to cajole for themselves a portion of the catch. Prominent among these crowds are the professional fish processors (*banda* women) discussed in Chapter 4. These women are marked out by the distinctive, brightly coloured rubber tubs (*baffs*) that broadcast their desire to buy fish in bulk, and – to adopt the phrase local people often use to emphasise the difference between these monetary transactions and the plethora of other exchanges that crowd the wharf – to buy them 'for physical money'. As I have already suggested, however, *banda* women are by no means the only people who gather on the wharf each day in search of fish.

Invariably, for example, at the landing sites of the largest fishing vessels, one can expect to meet at least a dozen or so women sitting on the sand with baskets of fruit, coconuts, and fresh vegetables gathered from the bush or cultivated in gardens around town. This loose knot of petty traders spends much of the day wandering up and down the wharf, ensuring that their long pauses on the sand coincide with the arrival of Tissana's largest crew-boats. For there is only one currency accepted in this mobile market – and it is not cash, but fish. Each item has a certain fixed price, counted in the small 'measure fish'[3] that dominate the catch of every *sim*-boat net.[4] In 2011, the going rate for a small bunch of bananas was six of these measure fish, for example; a mango cost three; a pawpaw, 12.

Aside from the bartering of fish for fruit and vegetables on the wharf, one of the things that struck me most when I first arrived in Tissana was the frequency with which both fishermen and *banda* women agreed to give some of their hard-earned fish away, apparently free of charge, to the people who came to beg from them on the wharf.

There are two basic opposing principles that combine to make the strategic pursuit of '*plassas*' fish such a constant preoccupation in Tissana. On the one hand – and perhaps this is hardly surprising in a place where one sees baskets, *bandas*, and glittering *baff*-fulls of fish almost everywhere one turns – people expect to eat fish every day. A central theme in the myth Tissana's residents narrate about their town is that, whoever you are, you will 'eat loads of fine fish'. People who have migrated from towns and villages inland remember with pity the impoverished diet 'up-country', where people are forced to make do for their meagre protein on the small, dried, bony fish (*bonga*) that provide the staple source of protein for all but the most prosperous of Sierra Leoneans inland. These 'poor fish' – as they are sometimes referred to dismissively in Tissana – may have been the foundation of the town's trade economy, but they are only eaten here as a last resort.

Yet, in apparently perfect contradiction to this attitude, the surprising reality is that, for all their seemingly glorious abundance, it is almost impossible to buy fish for one's own household consumption. Here,

[3] These are so-named because they are too small to be counted by the dozen and, wherever they are bought, sold, or given in payment to crew members, they are instead measured in one of several standard-sized pans.

[4] These are more tight-meshed than the nets of other boats.

Marriama is trying to explain what initially appeared to me a rather baffling contradiction:

> It's not every fisherman who will agree to sell you one or two fish. If you were to go and ask, '*Sell-gi* [sell–give] me fish, I want to cook,' there aren't many who would agree to sell you them. If you want *plassas* fish, you have to beg.

Although it is a fairly large town by Sierra Leonean standards, neither Tissana nor any of its immediately neighbouring towns has a physical marketplace. If one has money, it is easy enough to buy a wide range of household essentials from the stream of petty traders who weave through the town each day. However, the one staple food almost never sold to household customers is fish.

Over time, I came to realise that it is not simply that fishermen and *banda* women do not *want* to sell their catch piecemeal to their neighbours in town; rather, important structural dynamics within Tissana's fish trade often prevent them from doing so. As we have seen, fishermen are typically tied into a more or less exclusive customer relationship with a single *banda* woman who has first claim to buy and dry as much of the catch as she is able. She, in turn, will usually be tied into similarly binding relationships with her trade customers from the city. Anything sold on the wharf is therefore destined to be passed through a predetermined chain of business relationships until it arrives, wholesale, in a distant urban marketplace. The result is that a parallel and equally vibrant economy runs alongside the commercial market trade – one in which fish are gifted according to an altogether different set of rules.

The Krio word to describe this commonplace act of fish gifting is to *wap*. It would be difficult to overstate the real, material urgency of this vast gift economy, which provides the only source of protein for many of Tissana's residents. I was often taken aback by the heights of anxiety my friends experienced on the days when they had been unable to procure fish. Regardless of how much other food they might have, a cooking pot devoid of fish is a source of great stigma in Tissana, and is generally taken as evidence of a social unit failing to provide the most basic necessities for its members. During the rainy season in particular, these days occur far more frequently than one might imagine from listening to the common, optimistic assertions that, 'Here, we eat like gentry.'

Begging for fish

A constant preoccupation within all non-fishing households, including my own, was how to secure gifts of fish. As a woman, it is taken for granted that the best way to secure a reliable supply of *plassas* fish is to 'love' with a fisherman. The flow of fine fish into our own cooking pot fluctuated wildly depending on the ups and downs of Buema's relationship with our neighbour – a married man who lived nearby with his family. I recorded this conversation on a day when Buema was particularly buoyant, having just received a visit from her lover:

When I got home, Buema was glowing. 'Did you see my fish? Over there, by the well – go and look.' I went over to inspect the two beautiful red snappers, and gasped my appreciation. 'Fine, eh? Wilson brought them for me! He went to sea today, and he didn't get anything at all. Just those two fish. And he gave them to me!'
   'Sarah [his wife] must be angry . . . ' I said, which delighted her.
   'Hahaha! Yeah, Sarah's *mad*! But they're Wilson's fish and he gave them to me. So let Sarah be angry!'

As Buema's easy dismissal of Sarah's anger suggests, she expected her affair with the other woman's husband to be tolerated, however begrudgingly. Although men in Sierra Leone are permitted, by custom, to marry multiple wives (Crosby 1937; Little 1967 [1951]), fully polygamous households are rare in Tissana. On the other hand, separation, remarriage, and a whole spectrum of extramarital 'love' relationships are extremely common for both men and women. Many of these ostensibly 'illicit' affairs – like Buema's relationship with Wilson – were veiled with only the faintest token gestures towards secrecy; in fact, more often than not, they were broadcast perfectly publicly in the daylight movements of large fish from the boats of fishermen to the kitchens of their lovers. Not without good reason, married women typically work a lot harder than their husbands to keep their extramarital romances secret. One of the most disturbing moments of my entire spell in Sierra Leone took place when another member of my compound returned home earlier than expected from visiting his family in another town, and found his wife gutting an impressive fish. Taken by surprise, and unable to improvise a quick explanation for the fish's provenance, Gilo's infidelity was self-evident. Although no one was seriously hurt, the scene of violence that followed was quite terrifying.
   To a keen observer, the movements of gifts of fish around town could be read as a map of the ever-shifting patterns of 'love' in Tissana. People often asked me quite openly, for example, whether I was having an affair with my married friend, Kumba, because he was so often seen walking through town carrying large fish in the direction of our compound. In fact, his gifts were not motivated by love, but by debt (but that is a different story).
   We saw in the Chapter 4 that, in discussions of fishing communities elsewhere in Africa, similar patterns of gift-giving are often pathologised under the term 'fish for sex' and read as evidence of sexual exploitation (Allison and Janet 2001; Béné 2007; Seeley 2009; Westaway, Seeley, and Allison 2007). Such language fails to do justice to the kinds of

romances characteristic of Tissana's social life; in my own experience, these were usually underpinned by a very real thread of attraction and sentiment. That said, it is undeniable that single women (and sometimes married ones, too) have an important material incentive to initiate these kinds of 'love' relationships, which become a key element of their basic livelihood strategies (cf. Leach 1994: 198–9). Here, as anthropologists have discussed elsewhere in sub-Saharan Africa, 'affect and exchange are entangled rather than opposed...material provision and emotional attachment [are] mutually constitutive' (Thomas and Cole 2009: 20).

When Buema finally called off her affair with Wilson, her daily work-load increased dramatically, as our household joined the many other households for whom 'begging' on the wharf was a constant daily chore; indeed, it stands as testimony to Marriama's claim: 'If you want *plassas* fish, you have to beg.' Even the presence of a Western visitor in the house – cash-rich by any local standard – did almost nothing to diminish the amount of work Buema was forced to invest in finding fish for our cooking pot each day.

Disgruntled that most of this substantial new responsibility had fallen directly on her shoulders, she attempted to cajole her 15-year-old sister, Alimatu, into taking on some of the work:

Buema: Alimatu's a young girl! But she never goes down wharf [to beg]. She's lazy!
Alimatu: [Laughing] Eh! You know what people'd say, if I went down wharf to beg, even twice in a week...D'you know what they'd say, Jenny? They'd say I had a boyfriend!

Young girls' sexuality was the subject of much closer moral scrutiny than that of mature divorcées such as Buema. This short exchange reveals the difficult balance that young women are asked to navigate: half-expected – even obligated – to exploit their sexuality to cajole fish for their house-hold's cooking pot, but risking stigmatisation if they do so with too much enthusiasm.

However, if the word 'beg' appears to suggest images of deferential supplication, in Tissana it has quite different connotations. 'Begging' is viewed instead as a form of labour, and one that requires a considerable level of skill. This excerpt from my field notes was written on a day when I had gone fishing with the *sim*-boat crew. The scene it describes took place just after the large crew of men, women, and children had spent several long hours wading waist-deep through the shallows, in order to guide the long fishing net in an arc around the beach:

Buema's own performance was remarkable. She arrived at the shore just as the net was finally being dragged ashore, involved herself in someone else's argument, gossiped for a bit, and then turned to me expectantly: 'So where are your own fish, Jenny?' I explained that they hadn't paid me yet, but when they did, I wanted to use the fish to barter for a pawpaw. Immediately, she was on her feet and in action: picking through, helping herself to small fish in the net; wandering around the various *banda* women's *baffs* scattered around the sand; taking one fish here, one there; until, within minutes, she had gathered the two dozen fish needed to buy a pawpaw.

I left her to go back along the wharf in search of my flip-flops, and, by the time I returned 20 minutes later, her plastic bag was bulging with fine fish – far more than any junior member of the fishing crew had been paid for their hours of hard work. 'How did you manage to get all those?' I asked, incredulous, as we walked home. 'You really know how to beg!' Buema laughed. 'I beg, and I *barranta* [bully]. I begged them by force!' She paused on the path to lean over, mimicking herself. 'I take them from people's *baff*-pans. I say, "Aren't you going to give me this one? And this one? Come on, I beg you! I have my stranger to cook for!"' Her expression was cheeky and she threw her head back and laughed at herself. 'People tell me, "Stop! Buema! You're more shameless than your daughter, Abi!"'

On other days, when fish are less plentiful, begging is no easy job. However committed fishermen might be to the ideal of giving generously on the wharf, the reality is that they only do so on days when they land a bountiful catch. During the rainy season, in particular, there were days when almost every woman I greeted walking through Tissana replied with a dejected 'I'm hungry! There's no fish!' Sometimes, I spent hours trailing Buema on the beach, going to meet one boat after another, as she flirted and pleaded and bullied until, finally, one of her friends or relatives, tired from a long day at sea, agreed to give us something. So strong is the expectation that friendly relationships ought to be made – and made material – through exchanges of this kind that Buema could hardly contain her frustration that my own apparent popularity never *quite* manifested itself into a flood of fish:

Everywhere we go, they all greet you – 'Jennifer! Jennifer!' But they don't give you *anything*! Oh, it makes me so angry for you! If they were to say, 'Jennifer, Jennifer, look, take this fish!' – Now, *that* would be fine!

Buema's experience illustrates that, while gifts of fish tend to trace existing webs of friendship and affection, it nonetheless requires a considerable level of social skill and labour to make claims of relatedness in order to access this vital resource. The following section explores the other side of this dynamic, by revealing how bonds of affect may be built gradually over time, in part through the ongoing exchange of fish.

Gifting fish

One morning, when I joined the cluster of breakfast customers on the low benches of Fatmata's makeshift 'cookery' (restaurant), I found them – over the usual plastic bowls of fish soup and cassava – listening attentively to a fashionably dressed young stranger, Victor, a school student visiting his uncle for the holidays. By the time I arrived, he had already been holding forth for some time on the charms and conveniences of his home town, a fishing town close to the capital. Then, abruptly, his tone changed, for even Victor was prepared to admit that there was one aspect of life in Tissana that easily surpassed his home town:

Our own roads in Lungi[5] are all tarred, not like this sand you have here ... When I come here – oh! – I really feel that I am in the village. If you could see Lungi, you would not believe it. You'd think, 'This is heaven!' When I go back there, I'm going to boast to all my friends; I'll tell them that I've been eating loads and loads of fish!

In one respect, his comment was not unfamiliar. If ever I asked people what they appreciated most about life in Tissana, their answers tended to stick closely to a simple, predictable script: 'Here' – I could almost guarantee they would reply – 'we eat fine fish!' And yet it did surprise me that this particular stranger should have been so impressed by the coastal diet. Wasn't Lungi a fishing town too? As he explained:

Yes, but if I want to eat fish in Lungi I have to pay for it. At home, I can't just go to the wharf and expect someone to give me fish, free, like they do for me here. No way! Except, maybe, if you are lucky to have a brother with a boat, maybe then he will give you something ... but my brothers don't have boats – so, me, I have to buy.

As a young, unknown man, with little money and almost no connections in town, it is not immediately evident why local fishermen would choose to instigate a gift relationship with someone such as Victor. Certainly, there was little possibility – and apparently little expectation – that he would be able to return the gift. As we have seen, the Yawri Bay's population is so fluid that it is a commonplace for people to arrive in Tissana with no existing social network at all. My suggestion in this section is that the massive traffic in gifts of fish, which circulate each day across Tissana's wharf, provides one of the important material routes through which newcomers are able to become integrated into the town's sprawling network of 'potato rope' kinship.

Victor's words both mirror – and, in important ways, differ from – those of a more long-term settler in the town. Having spent his childhood and young adult life in Bo, David had also grown up accustomed to a level of urban convenience truly luxurious by Tissana's standards. Sitting outside his thatched house, he admitted that he sometimes misses the electricity, the smooth roads, and the once taken-for-granted peace of mind that

---

[5] Lungi, which is on Sierra Leone's northern Bullom coast, may once have had rather a lot in common with Tissana. However, as home to the national airport and only a short ferry ride from Freetown, the town has been targeted for some fairly extensive infrastructure development over the past decades.

had come from living within easy reach of decent medical care. And yet, he told me, he feels more prosperous in Tissana than he ever did in the city:

The first thing is that, here, we eat fish! Without buying! Even if my own boat did not catch any fish, I will go to my brothers when they 'slam' [return to land]; they will give me something to support my family...

Although both men emphasise the connection between gifts of fish and bonds of 'brotherhood', the Tissana fisherman is describing a quite different flow of causality between the two. Victor had stressed that, in his home town, not being lucky enough to have a brother with a boat, he would never be given fish; David, however – who in fact has no biological kin in Tissana – refers to all those men who gift him fish as his 'brothers'.

David is by now well established in Tissana. He is married to one of the town's best-known *banda* women and has a boat of his own. Yet, when he first arrived a decade earlier, he had neither the fishing knowledge, the financial capital, nor the social network that one might think would be necessary to set himself up in the town. He goes on to explain how, in his first few months in Tissana, more established fishermen had allowed him to subsist by scavenging the shrimps from their fishing nets:

When I first came here, I didn't know how to fish. I didn't even understand water. But when the others went to sea, to draw *sim*-boat on the sandbar, I would follow them there. I'd pick-pick the shrimps... But then, I began to think: 'Going to beg to my companions like this every day, it's such a strain!' So then, after watching them, I began fishing for myself, with a hook and line first of all.

According to David's own narrative, it was this initial willingness of the town's fishermen to give him fish – a complete newcomer – that not only allowed him to subsist through those first difficult months on the coast, but also began the gradual process of his integration into the social fabric of Tissana. These small, initial gifts were the tangible beginnings of the relationships with men he now considers to be his 'brothers'. Now himself an active member of Tissana's fishing economy, perhaps it is hardly surprising that he was eager to stress that he extends a similar generosity to the strangers on the wharf who might one day become his kin:

They say that in, like, Lungi, Goderich, Mama Beach, Funkea [all fishing towns further north along Sierra Leone's coast] they will only give you fish if you are a friend or family, or if you are loving with him... It wouldn't happen there, like it does here, that somebody would give you fish without any good relationship... If you come here as a stranger, someone will come to you, give you fish, saying, 'This is a stranger!' We so like strangers!

Given that they often lead such mobile lives – and so routinely find themselves cast in the role of 'stranger' in another *alehn* – perhaps it is hardly surprising that Tissana's fishermen tend to place such particular ideological emphasis on their willingness to give to outsiders. Here, Foday emphasises the strong sense of camaraderie that young crewmen like himself tend to experience on their arrival in an unfamiliar fishing town:

Fishermen, we all move around so much; anywhere we go, we are like one big family. We are all brothers . . . Any wharf town you go to, fishermen will welcome you, find you a place to stay, food to eat, even clothes to wear! Yes! They will even take their own trousers and give them to you. They know that, if they came on *alehn* to you, you would do the same for them.

The parallels with the ways in which David amalgamates the expectation of material generosity with a sense of assumed 'kinship' are striking. Foday's faith that he can consider any fisherman his 'brother' is predicated on a trust in the intricate gossamer web of material reciprocity that ultimately links every migratory fisherman to every other, constructing them all – even two strangers viewing one another for the first time in their lives – as though each were already established with regard to the other as both 'donor' and 'benefactor'.

We saw in David's own account of his arrival in Tissana that these small, seemingly spontaneous acts of material kindness might, over time, sediment into something altogether more substantial. Out of the loose suspension of gift-giving, his network of 'potato rope' kinship eventually settled.[6] However, if the impression I have given so far is that it is easy to build and maintain social networks, I ought to stress that only a tiny fraction of these gift relationships are likely to formalise into anything resembling a stable kinship bond. In Tissana, 'becoming' kin requires consistent material investment, and relationships that are not nurtured in this way can rapidly atrophy and fail. To illustrate this point, I turn now to look at some of the patterns according to which fish flowed into, and rice was shared within, my own complex, adoptive household.

Collapsing 'potato rope' kinship

The once-grand compound in which I lived was home to an ever-shifting population of around 30 people, too fluid and fissured to be thought of as a single 'domestic unit' in any straightforward sense. Some people considered it their permanent home: Pa Bimbola, Mama Koni, and Jacob, for example, had all lived there for most of the past three decades. Around this small core of long-term residents, other people – relatives, friends, fostered youngsters, and strangers – would come, lodge for a while, and move off again as their circumstances changed. There were

---

[6] There are clear parallels between this pattern and the ways in which Charles Piot (1999: 52–75) describes the gradual formation of Kabre 'friendships'.

usually at least a few teenage boys and young men sleeping on the parlour floor, while Buema, Si Mary, and Mama Koni all routinely rearranged their bedrooms to accommodate a couple of extra residents for a period of weeks or months.

This particular compound was larger, and therefore more complex, than most in Tissana, but the general pattern was far from unique. In a town of peripatetic fishermen and traders, it was rare for domestic arrangements to bear much resemblance to the 'English term household . . . [which] implies a special intimacy, a fusing of physiological functions and a real distinction from other types of social relations' (Harris 1981: 52). For the duration of the time that they lived there, most of the compound's residents attached themselves, with a greater or lesser degree of clarity, to one of the loose units that formed around the different cooking pots in the kitchen. Each of the adults who ate from that pot was expected to contribute to it, whether with cash, fish, or garden produce. Although these units had some of the characteristics of what we might call a family, they were not always – and certainly not only – defined by genealogical patterns of relatedness. Here, as Catrien Notermans observed in urban Cameroon, 'kinship evolves in homes through sharing food' (2008: 355). Over any one period, there were usually two to four cooking pots active within the household – although, in the churning social dynamics of the compound, these social units were in a perpetual state of emerging, dissolving, and reforming again in different constellations. At the core of this fluid social world, one pot was larger, generally better provisioned, and more stable than the rest. Throughout my stay, the rice in this pot was bought largely by myself or Jacob, and the fish was usually provided by Buema and shared by a loose collection of people whom I came to think of as my foster family. What interests me here, more than the physical migrations of people in and out of the building itself, is that, even within this single large compound, patterns of social networks were in a constant state of flux – often in direct response to people's success, or failure, to attract a flow of *plassas* fish (fish for household consumption).

Living in such cramped conditions, tempers very often ran high. In amongst all the laughter, the gossip, the intimate sharing of one another's small joys and problems, there were also frequent bursts of frustration and acrimony. The ways in which cooked rice was shared and exchanged between the different pots tended to be a fairly accurate map of the patterns of goodwill between residents. The micro-politics of sharing and withholding food were the largest single source of tension, resentment, and, sometimes, hunger.

While there is a rich literature examining how people create kinship bonds through marriage, fostering, and reciprocity, ethnographers have historically paid rather less attention to the ways in which people may sever certain relationships, or allow others to atrophy. It was Caroline Bledsoe's fieldwork in Sierra Leone that led her to make this important observation:

Arguments that groups are shaped socially must acknowledge equally the opposite potential: eliminating some ties and rendering others marginal. Divorce and infanticide are examples. However, radical efforts to sever ties are measures of last resort. Dissatisfaction between spouses, for example, is usually expressed more subtly, by neglecting sexual or domestic duties. It may also be expressed by marginalising individuals. (Bledsoe 1995: 130)

As part of her broader project to explore the micro-level politics of Mende family life, Bledsoe sought to understand how intersecting axes of stratification resulted in the 'selective neglect of children within the same household' (ibid.: 134).[7]

In Tissana, many people are living under such extreme material pressure that they are routinely forced to make extraordinarily tough choices: about which of their most intimate personal relations they can materially afford to nurture; and which they can morally and emotionally afford to neglect. Gifts of fish or rice can instigate and nurture relationships, but my field notes are also filled with examples of relationships beginning to unravel and collapse because there were no fish to bind them together. Without gifts of fish, for example, girlfriends lose interest in their lovers, and people are ashamed to visit their relatives inland. I saw with one of the families in my own compound that, without the consistent presence of a cooking pot full of fish to hold them together, even domestic units begin to dissolve, and family members scatter in search of other, more materially viable living arrangements.

Aminata had arrived at Site with five of her children, having recently fallen out with her mother in a nearby compound. With a newborn baby to care for, and a petty trading business to run, Aminata was struggling: only rarely did she find time to go down to the wharf and beg for fish. So strong is the stigma involved in feeding one's family 'dry rice' (without fish) that, on the days when Aminata had not received any gifts of fish, she simply would not cook – even if she had money. Instead, she (like many other people in Tissana) relied on the hope that one of her neighbours would share their food with her. I often heard Aminata complaining bitterly that none of her wider family or neighbours had any

---

[7] Perhaps most controversially, she suggested that women who had remarried often neglected their own children from previous marriages, in order to demonstrate loyalty to their current spouse:

Children can come, well after the biological event of birth, to have different values to their mother – values deriving from the ebb and flow of her conjugal relations and strategies of polyandrous motherhood. It should not be surprising, then, that children from former unions may have quite different health and welfare prospects than those from intact unions. (Bledsoe 1995: 139)

interest in helping her. Speaking behind her back, Buema agreed that her friend would find it difficult to persuade anyone to share her material responsibilities. 'This is what makes men afraid of Aminata. When they see how many children she has, they're afraid to marry her. They don't want to take all those children and have to feed them all.'[8]

For the many young people who describe being given insufficient food by the adults in their life, their hunger is far more than just a 'metaphor' (Notermans 2008: 370) for their sense of precariousness and exclusion; it is also the real, and potentially even dangerous, material outcome of a fragile kinship network that has failed. For days on end, Aminata's cooking pot could sit cold and empty. And, although they continued to sleep under the same roof, over the course of my fieldwork I watched as all three of her teenage children sought ways to distance themselves from a family unit that appeared to be collapsing. Thirteen-year-old Ibrahim took to selling kerosene in order to pay for his own food. Ima and Marie, on the other hand, worked increasingly hard to attach themselves to alternative cooking pots, spending their days in the compounds of aunts and grandparents, offering to do chores, and thus be fed by these other relatives. Fostering is an extremely common practice in Tissana. Sometimes, as we saw with Abu in Chapter 3, young people are sent by their parents in a distant part of the country to live with relatives on the coast. It is just as common for children to move between households much more organically, because their current guardians are simply no longer able to provide for them.

It is likely that Ima and Marie will eventually be absorbed into another household, enmeshed in new, if fragile, webs of 'potato rope' kinship: although, as we will see, absorption into new households is always a risk.

The dangers of 'becoming' kin

Elsewhere in the Mandé world, ethnographers have described infants continuing to develop biological bonds of relatedness after birth, absorbing the material substance of kinship through their mother's milk – milk that is stimulated and fortified by the man's semen through continued sexual intercourse (Fortier 2001; Cros 1990). In Tissana, by contrast, the women I knew were careful to abstain from sex while breastfeeding. Yet, in quite different ways, it was possible for the substance of relatedness to pass between a child and the people closest to their mother: not through bodily substances shared in sex, but in food. As this excerpt

---

[8] Such a statement stands in sharp contrast to earlier accounts of Sierra Leonean kinship, in which (as we saw in Chapter 1) it was taken for granted that relatively wealthier people would strive to accumulate as many wives, foster children, and tenants as possible.

from my field notes demonstrates, people often commented on the striking physical resemblances between a child and the person who had given food to his or her mother while she was pregnant.

Ever since he arrived in town, everyone has been very keen for me to meet Ba Yannie [Jacob's grandson]. 'Have you seen him yet? He looks like your own kind.' When the little boy was finally brought to visit me, his friend pointed to his nose. 'You see? White people went to his village when his mother was pregnant and gave her rice.' This morning, Buema repeated the same thing, pointing to Ba Yannie's hair: 'His hair – even if they let it grow, it's just like yours. It's smooth. It's soft, do you see it? Those white men went to Mofante with [food] supplies for the *kumbras* [breastfeeding mothers]. That's why he looks like one of you.'

There are echoes here of Janet Carsten's well-known description of relatedness in a Malaysian fishing community, where individuals come to embody their kinship identity only gradually, over the course of their lifetime, through the continuous process of giving, receiving, and consuming food together. In Tissana, much as she described, 'it is clear that not only is "social" identity...unfixed, but "physical" identity, a person's substance, is also continuously acquired and alterable' (Carsten 1995: 225). However, if this language of 'giving', 'sharing', and 'becoming kin' appears to imply selfless munificence, it is worth remembering that kinship itself 'often carries ambivalent or negative qualities, which anthropologists tend to dwell on rather less' (Carsten 2013: 245; cf. Peletz 2000).

As Peter Geschiere observed, 'both inside and outside anthropology, the general idea that intimacy breeds trust remains very influential: trust in the inner circle as a prepolitical, even ontological given' (2013: 28). This idea is not without basis. In the chaos and uncertainty of Sierra Leone's war, 'created' family networks provided the language through which it became possible for displaced, traumatised people to begin to develop new relationships of trust (Gale 2006). However, strategies to embed oneself in networks of social relationships often come with their own risks. Far from offering a special refuge of harmony and mutual altruism, the domestic sphere is often perceived as fraught with heightened danger and latent violence (Geschiere and Fisiy 1994: 325; Ajala and Ediomo-Ugong 2010).

This interweaving of intimacy and vulnerability is particularly evident in the experiences of Tissana's many foster children. The fostering of children is widespread across much of West Africa, where conceptions of 'parenthood' have historically been far more malleable than those of nuclear families.[9] Early analyses of child fostering (Goody 1982;

---

[9] Classic studies of fosterage in Sierra Leone suggest that, in the 1980s, 30 to 45 per cent of children were living in homes with adults other than their biological parents (Bledsoe 1990a; Bledsoe and Isingo-Abanike 1989).

Lallemand 1994)[10] tended to echo the publicly stated cultural ideal, in which the movement of children between households was presented as an opportunity to deepen ties within kinship networks, while also giving children a home in which they are treated with care, 'receiving equal love, attention, food, clothes and school materials' as the biological children of the house (Verhoff 2005: 373). The reality is often far more ambivalent, as various studies have revealed. As long ago as 1990, Caroline Bledsoe challenged the positive narrative with research indicating that, in Sierra Leone, fostered children often received more severe beatings and suffered higher rates of malnutrition, ill health, and mortality than children living with their birth parents (1990b; 1995).

Nicolas Argenti's work in the Cameroonian Grassfields teases out the complex historical relationship between child fostering and the older forms of pawnship and slavery 'from which fosterage was often difficult to distinguish' (2010: 229). Aside from the long precolonial history in which violent slave raiding had been endemic, this region also bears a far more intimate and disquieting history of enslavement. Throughout the precolonial period, elders – sometimes even parents – were known to sell their own young relatives into slavery (ibid.: 242–3; cf. Warnier 1995). Much more recently – indeed, within the living memory of my older informants in Tissana – it had remained an acceptable coping mechanism for struggling Sherbro parents to sell one of their children as a *wono* (domestic slave) to a wealthier household.

By the time of my fieldwork, everyone I knew in Tissana would have been horrified by the suggestion that they might buy or sell a child. The category of *wono* had become absolutely taboo. And yet, even as explicit 'slavery' has been gradually stigmatised out of public discourse, 'fostering' appears to have proliferated into a much more varied and ambivalent set of practices. Despite being publicly represented as a benign institution of love and care, the risk is that, for the most vulnerable young people, fostering 'operates as a euphemism for various forms of child labor' (Argenti 2010: 245). There is a whole tapestry of reasons why some fostered children might be very well cared for, while others 'experience fosterage as a harrowing trial' (ibid.: 229; cf. Alber, Häberlein, and Martin 2010; Notermans 2008).[11] Many of Tissana's foster parents were conscientious, loving carers to the children in their custody, and seem to have approached fostering with a genuine sense of social duty and self-sacrifice. However, it was taken for granted that foster

---

[10] See Alber (2013) for a discussion of this classic literature.

[11] In the Mende context, for example, Bledsoe argued that fostering was 'inextricably linked to wider networks of political patronage' (1990a: 75). While a child fostered from a high-status family may receive similar treatment as their guardian's biological children, those with low-status parents often find themselves filling a role more similar to that of a domestic servant.

children – especially those who had been absorbed into the household as a result of their poverty – were often expected to work the hardest, for the least reward, in order to earn their right to eat from the household cooking pot. To illustrate this tension, here is Buema's aunt, Sento, describing the sacrifices she made over her long career as a foster mother:

Right now, I've got 11 [foster children] here... all on the back of this fish that I sell! Even just now, a Ndema fisherman just came and left his son with me. He's not my relative! He just came here on *alehn*, and when he left, he asked to leave his boy here with me. To foster is not easy-oh! Strain! I manage, though; I endure. Before school, they eat. When they come out of school, they eat! It's not easy. I don't have money-oh! I don't have anything, but I do have patience.

To see the two women together today, joking on the wharf, you would have no reason to question Sento's portrayal of herself as a beneficent matriarch. However, this is how Buema recalls her young adulthood spent working under her aunt's 'parental care':

I strained for that woman! Ah! I suffered for her. I was just working non-stop, in the *banda*. You've seen that big-big *banda* she has? I didn't have time for anything else, I worked so hard! As my head hit the ground, no more, I was getting up again! At that time, my body was not fine, like it is now. I was thin-thin-thin! I didn't rest.

The increased value placed on Western-style education has created new axes of inequality within households, forcing adults to decide which of the young people in their care should be allowed to study, and which must be made to fill labour roles (cf. Alber, Häberlein, and Martin 2010). Here, Finda is contemplating the fine line between familial care and labour exploitation she observed in the home of one of her neighbours, a large-scale fish processor who, even by Tissanan standards, fostered an unusually high number of her relatives' children:

Do you see all the children she has there? Some go to school, some don't go to school... Her own children are all at boarding school. But her sister's children now: some are just there to work – to pull water from the well, to dry fish, nothing more!... If it was England, they'd say it was against 'human rights', wouldn't they? But in a place like Tissana, there are no 'human rights'.

The adult women who shared my compound would sometimes swap stories of the abuse and neglect they remember having endured as children, living under the 'care' of foster parents who had appeared more interested in exploiting their labour than protecting their well-being. For all of these women, some of their most emotive and painful childhood memories concerned being given rotten leftovers to eat. Across much of West Africa, 'eating' is a central metaphor of power (Bayart 1993

[1989]); and, in a context where 'a large stomach [is] the privilege and sign of the "big man"' (Last 2000: 374), it is often considered appropriate for children to experience a certain level of hunger (Utas 2003: 129). However, this kind of treatment is far more likely to be meted out on the most marginal members of a household. Viewed from this perspective, the intimacy expressed in the offer of food to a hungry neighbour can easily slide towards a visceral expression of control.

Jacob was constantly urging me to be more careful when consuming food cooked in other people's kitchens: 'If they offer you rice when you go down [to the other end of town], don't eat it! Do you hear?' The reason for his caution was the common belief that *ifohn wei* (bad medicine) is in wide circulation in Tissana. 'They might have put something in it,' he would warn me, sagely, '*to influence you.*' Sensing the resilience of his guest's naivety, he would never tire of trying to impress the urgency of this lesson upon me, a lesson that most of Tissana's residents had learned from early childhood. 'We are all Africans. We know each other! We know our ways. We are tricky people.' For his part, Jacob insisted that there were fewer than a handful of close family members whose cooking he would be prepared to eat; any other gifts were politely accepted and discreetly disposed of.

Harrell-Bond encountered a similar pattern among educated Freetonians in the 1970s. While giving and receiving gifts of cooked food was one of the most common ways of nurturing relationships, people were also 'highly concerned about the possibility of being poisoned' (Harrell-Bond 1978: 238). As we saw in Chapter 4, it was partly because *alehning* fishermen knew that they would have no choice but to accept food cooked by strangers that they claimed to feel so exposed to manipulation and entrapment whenever they spent the night in a foreign wharf town. In this sense, hungry children such as Ima and Marie are among the most vulnerable people in Tissana – not only because they were often undernourished, but also because their poverty placed them at the mercy of anyone who was prepared to feed them.

Conclusions

This chapter has explored the 'human economy' (Graeber 2012) of Tissana, tracing the ongoing material and emotional labour that my neighbours invested each day in attempting to negotiate webs of friendship and intimacy by giving, receiving, and 'begging' for fish on the wharf. Over the past decade, fisherfolk in Tissana, as elsewhere in West Africa, have watched with trepidation as their catches become ever smaller and less predictable. Nowadays, both men and women are more conscious than ever that their best hope of material security is to be enmeshed in strong webs of social ties that will support them when their catches fail.

There are multiple threads in the work people invest in building and managing their 'potato rope' kinship, but my focus in this chapter has been on the most materially obvious. From my own vantage point on the wharf, watching as they slid along various convoluted channels of love and obligation, fish sometimes appeared to me to be the substance from which Tissana's social fabric was created. Maurice Bloch has argued that 'sharing food is, and is always seen to be, in some way or another, the sharing of that which will cause, or at least maintain, a common substance among those who commune together' (1999: 133). Perhaps there is some truth in Bloch's suggestion that, in 'every' social context, eating together is a powerful expression of personal intimacy and 'common substance'. However, it seems obvious that the micro-politics of sharing food takes on a completely different tenor in a world – such as Tissana's – where households routinely spend their entire income on food; where many people go from one day to the next unsure about where their next meal is coming from. In a context in which most people have had the experience of going to bed without managing to eat at all, the sharing of food takes on an emotional and practical urgency that most people in wealthy countries would find difficult to imagine. To be well fed is to experience not only material security, but also the emotional and ontological security that stem from a stable sense of acceptance and social belonging. This is not a condition that all people in Tissana – and especially not all children – can take for granted. The heightened social and material fluidity of life on the Yawri Bay imposes a need for constant, exhausting social navigation. In this sense, the experience of Tissana's fisherfolk mirrors poignant accounts from ethnographers in more urban contexts across contemporary Africa, where residents are repeatedly described as struggling to manage social lives in conditions of 'routinized crisis' (Johnson-Hanks 2005: 367), precariousness, and uncertainty (Vigh 2009).

In a series of influential essays, AbdouMaliq Simone (2003; 2005; 2006) has described how, for people living in poverty in African cities, survival increasingly depends upon the agility to move between new, ever-shifting patterns of 'social assemblage' (2006), with informal social institutions constantly coalescing and reforming in new, unpredictable forms. Simone argues that, as existing social relationships are experienced as increasingly fragile and unreliable, people often respond not by narrowing their social world to a manageable scale but rather by working to build more diverse and fluid social networks (2005). While such social creativity can be celebrated on some levels (Cooper and Pratten 2015: 4), Simone's own analysis emphasises the anxiety people experience following the loss of 'predictability and support that [come] from stable social ties' (2006: 359). When the very fabric of social life is in flux, people share a sense of insecurity about 'with whom they can live and work, with whom they can talk and what kind of collective future they can anticipate' (ibid.: 360). This stark view is echoed by Achille Mbembe, who points to the 'radicalisation . . . of temporariness' as a defining – and brutal – feature of life in neoliberal Africa (quoted in Shipley 2010: 659).

In contexts such as these, where volatility permeates almost all aspects of social life, any attempt to create a meaningful, secure life can be read as an ongoing struggle against the 'corrosion of the present, both by change and by uncertainty', as Appadurai notes (2003: 47). Viewed in this light, the resources and the daily energy that Tissana's residents invest in building 'potato rope' families should not only be celebrated as a creative response to uncertainty, or even as an alternative to more rigid kinship systems that are fixed and 'rooted' in the land (Malkki 1992). This constant work of building relationships through material exchange also needs to be recognised as an unavoidable, all-consuming daily struggle to construct some sense of ontological security. As we have seen, it is not a struggle in which everyone succeeds. In a context in which relationships must be materially made and remade, rather than simply assumed, 'potato rope' families are sometimes liable to collapse as easily as they were formed.

> I sat with Hawa on the wharf one morning as she pointed out the different boats in the distance, calling each of the sailors by name as they slid towards the horizon. To her trained eye, each of those retreating boats was as instantly recognisable as the fisherman's face would have been, due to the distinctive pattern of its colourful patchwork sail. 'Like, my man's sail, for example, it's red and orange. So, when I come to the beach, I can see him straight away.'

There was a time – only a few decades ago – when it had been common for Tissana's boats to spend their entire day fishing in the shallow waters within sight of the shore. It does still happen, occasionally, that shoals of *bonga* congregate in the waters immediately around the Shenge Peninsula. On these days, if you stand on the beach and look out to sea, the water seems to be teeming with slow-motion activity. During lulls in more interesting gossip, women on the wharf would often look up and idly point out to one another which fishing grounds appeared to be popular that day, and where the different individual fishermen (entirely indistinguishable to my eye) were coming from or were going to land.

However, as we saw in Chapter 4, these shallow inshore waters have been decimated in recent decades by the profusion of unsustainable drag-net techniques. This decline in the fertility of Tissana's most local waters has combined with improved seafaring technology, which has fostered the emergence of a quite different kind of fishing culture – one in which men routinely travel far greater distances each day in search of fish. Nowadays, boat captains begin their days by listening to the rumours circulating among their fellow fishermen about which of the Yawri Bay's many fishing grounds have recently seen fish 'dying' in the greatest numbers. Even in the absence of any specific piece of intelligence, they know that their best chance of landing a decent catch is to make their way directly into deeper waters – and beyond the view of those of us on land.

Insofar as the sea has figured in my previous chapters, my focus has been on the ways in which it sustains, connects, and divides the different wharf towns along its coastline. In this chapter, I emphasise that the ocean itself is a highly complex, densely populated social world, and that the women and boat owners on the shore are palpably aware that their knowledge of this world is extremely limited. But the ocean is not the only important social space that is hidden beyond the visible horizons of Tissana's landscape. Here, as elsewhere in Sierra Leone, it is taken for granted that certain individuals – among them twins, witches, and diviners – possess an extra set of eyes, and that this privileged vision gives them access to a hidden social space, mapped onto the surface of the visible landscape.

Along the Upper Guinea Coast, ethnographers have consistently found that, even in the smallest villages – places where one might imagine that it would be almost impossible to keep anything hidden from one's neighbours for long – people invest considerable energy in infusing their words and actions with multiple layers of ambiguity (Bellman 1984; Ferme 2001; Gable 1997; Piot 1993). However, although anthropologists have explored in exhaustive detail the extent to which people work to create around themselves the charisma that comes from possessing hidden knowledge, they have paid less attention to an inevitable corollary of all this assumed secrecy: the pervasive, anxiety-inducing sense that other people know important things that they do not (Mair, High, and Kelly 2012). If you ask any Sherbro speaker how they are, they are likely to respond, with a shrug: '*La lɔ, kɛ la honɔn mu!*' ('Whatever is there, it hasn't revealed itself yet!'). This half-joking statement is repeated many hundreds of times a day in Tissana, as acquaintances exchange casual greetings. The familiar words both reflect and simultaneously work to reinforce the pervasive sense of felt ignorance and half-trust that characterises many aspects of social life on this coast.

My goal in this chapter is to explore how this episteme of secrecy and ignorance explodes beyond the seemingly 'ritual' world, to shape people's experience of their everyday economic order. In the vibrant rumours that animate everyday conversation in the fishing town, there is one anxiety that everybody shares. Boat owners, fishermen, and *banda* women alike, all were attempting to navigate their tight livelihoods through a world in which much of what affected them directly was unknowable, hidden from their view.

While beliefs in an invisible spiritual world are nothing new in Africa, anthropologists working in various parts of the continent have suggested that, in recent decades, people have begun to express a heightened sense of foreboding, that this unknowable realm has become more proximate and powerful; that it threatens to 'inhabit and overgrow' the manifest world (De Boeck quoted in Fabian et al. 2008: 143). Building on his own research in Kinshasa, De Boeck sees this deepening unease arising out of a particular moment in postcolonial African history, as growing numbers of people find themselves struggling to navigate in worlds that are – economically, politically, and socially – 'incomprehensible' (ibid.).[1] In Soweto, Adam Ashforth has made a similar suggestion: that fears about witchcraft are one expression of a broader 'spiritual insecurity' (2005: xiv; 1998), intimately entangled with the political and economic uncertainty of life in a South African township. Multiple layers of everyday anxiety and risk – arising from political oppression, poverty, rampant violent crime, and illness – feed people's conviction that their lives are shaped by 'invisible evil forces' (Ashforth 2005: 1).

From the 1990s onwards, anthropologists based in Africa have begun to recognise that discourses and practices once considered relics of a 'traditional' precolonial past have thrived and actively proliferated under conditions of 'modernity' (Geschiere 1997; Ciekawy and Geschiere 1998). In the intervening decades, a large amount of literature has emerged, tracing how local anxieties – about everything from zombie labour and vampires to witchcraft and medicine murder – have multiplied and adapted to reflect the new injustices of the postcolonial economy (Comaroff and Comaroff 2000; Meyer 1995). In many of these analyses, people's fears about the violence of the occult are understood as a vivid metaphor for the structural violence of the postcolonial world order.[2] Rosalind Shaw has painted an evocative picture, for example, of the hypermodern dystopia described by Temne informants, in which 'skyscrapers adjoin houses of gold and diamonds... street vendors roast "beefsticks" (kebabs) of human meat... and witch airports dispatch planes... to destinations around the globe' (2002: 202). She has argued, convincingly, that such images of violent extraction are founded on real historical experiences of global predation, stretching from the Atlantic slave trade to contemporary patterns of economic injustice.

Returning to Freetown in the aftermath of the civil war, Shaw encountered an even more heightened level of anxiety, about the proximity and strength of a global 'underworld', teeming with evil. For her young Pentecostal Christian informants, many of whom were struggling to recover from deeply traumatic wartime experiences, 'insistent fears, bad dreams, and memories of violence that replay again and again are interpreted as deriving from an external, demonic force' (Shaw 2007: 87). They

---

[1] De Boeck notes that:

> Something seems to have changed in the slippage between visible and invisible, in the folds of local life, between the diurnal and the nocturnal... Within the local experiential frame, the double that lurks underneath the surface of the visible world somehow seems to have taken the upper hand... making the physical world more incomprehensible every day, not only for anthropologists but also for many who inhabit these worlds on a daily basis. (quoted in Fabian et al. 2008: 143)

[2] In recent years, some commentators have begun to question whether this kind of analysis risks obscuring the specificity of our informants' anxieties, by acting as a vehicle for ethnographers to express their own concerns about the neoliberal economy (Sanders 2003; 2008; Sumich 2010).

described the horrors of war as having erupted from a *global* landscape of spiritual corruption: a hidden and highly interconnected world in which anyone from politicians, to village healers, to international statesmen could be suspected of participating in the unseen violence of witchcraft and human sacrifice. When, in 2014, many Sierra Leoneans interpreted the Ebola epidemic as arising from an international occult conspiracy, several anthropologists argued that such anxieties were based on a centuries-long experience of political violence, neglect, and exploitation (Leach 2015; Shepler 2014).

Given the extent to which people's livelihoods in the Yawri Bay are being destroyed by unaccountable fishing fleets, serving unseen markets in wealthier, more powerful parts of the world, one might expect Tissana to be fertile territory for anxieties about witches who participate in global economies of extraction. And yet, perhaps surprisingly, the witches described by Tissana's residents have far more local ambitions. Nor, as I discuss below, were Tissana's witches always described as frightening or violent – or even as being very different from their neighbours. In most conversations, the 'witch world' was represented in far more ambivalent terms, as an unseen space inhabited by a broad cast of local 'witch-eyed' actors, only some of whom use their powers for truly evil purposes. Rather than participating in a demonic international underworld, their unseen activities are usually limited to various forms of covert participation in the local economy.

This chapter unfolds across three ethnographic sections to trace the 'underneath' of Tissana's sea- and landscape, and the moral ambivalence about hidden topographies imbued with secrecy as they surface in everyday interactions. Beginning with a discussion of the 'witch-eyed' fishermen who are able to hear fish moving beneath the water's surface, I seek to emphasise that people in Tissana do not always assume 'witches' to be 'evil' by nature. What I explore in the second section of this chapter, however, is how the multiple layers of hiddenness that riddle this coastal topography work to reinforce people's conviction that their neighbours are implementing all manner of covert and nefarious strategies just beyond their frame of vision. In the final section, I reflect on how these experiences of uncertainty and half-trust are refracted through a broader 'hermeneutic of suspicion' (Ferme 2001: 7), in which Sierra Leoneans are taught from a young age both to value and to anticipate from their neighbours a certain level of creative deception.

The underside of the Yawri Bay seascape

While social scientists increasingly refer to economies defined by 'fluid' movements of peoples and ideas, our dominant image of seascapes themselves is of a curiously flat, socially characterless space, albeit one that we now expect to connect people and places, rather than separate them (Wigen 2006: 720). Tim Ingold epitomises this attitude rather neatly in his statement that 'we humans stake out our differences on the land; the sea, however, is a great dissolver – of time, of history, of cultural distinction' (1994: x). For the many thousands of fishermen who make their living from the Yawri Bay, this small, intensively utilised seascape is anything but a 'great dissolver'. When Tissana's fishermen go to sea each day, they may leave behind the relationships that characterise their social lives on the land, but they enter an equally complex social world, every bit as riven by rivalries, conflicts, and secret alliances.

I had been living in Tissana for almost a year before, one morning, a visiting boat owner from Plantain Island took a long stick and sketched a map of the Yawri Bay in sandy ground outside Pa Sila's 'cookery'. Apart from the coastline, which I recognised easily enough, Tomi's map revealed a topography altogether unfamiliar to me. He did not bother to mark any of the villages, roads, or rivers, which I tended to think of as the region's most prominent landmarks. Rather, he carefully parcelled out an intricate mosaic of distinct watery spaces, the defining characteristics of which – the depths of their seabed and the strengths of their currents – were all utterly invisible to me. On the far side of Plantain Island, for example, Tomi marked a series of small fishing grounds running away from the coast towards the Atlantic Ocean. He pointed to them in turn – 'Konah, Kaisa, Pokeh, Katatabul' – and explained how each differed from its neighbouring fishing ground in some important aspect of its invisible, underwater terrain. Beyond that, where the continental shelf slides into the deep Atlantic:

We call that 'Open' – that's the big, deep sea there, where those trawlers pass. It can be rough there. Then here, all along here, between Bompeh and Konah grounds, there is a deep channel of water. We call that 'Gutta [gutter] Ground'.

It was Tomi's map that first revealed to me just what a clear sense experienced fishermen have of the hidden, three-dimensional topography they traverse each day in their boats. But he also emphasised what a thoroughly populated and highly socialised space these fishing grounds around Plantain had become. 'First time,' he told me, 'when you went to sea, you were on your own.' Captains had relied purely on their experience to intuit where the fish might be concentrated in the ocean. Depending on the tide, the season, and weather conditions, a knowledgeable man could look at the water and make an informed guess as to where he might find fish. But really, he readily admitted, fish are not that predictable: 'Where they go – it is only God who decides that.'

The density of boats working in the Yawri Bay's waters has increased dramatically in recent decades. This, combined with the introduction of mobile phones five years earlier, had radically changed the social character of the sea: transforming it into a space in which fishing boats are far less isolated than they once were:

There are over 150 boats now, on Plantain.[3] When we go to sea, we all scatter. But now, it's not like before. We can communicate. If I've got a friend in another boat he might call me, and say, 'Are the fish dying where you are? Because here at Poke Ground, there are loads!'

The image Tomi painted, of fishermen generously collaborating to help one another at sea, is only one part of the picture. Most of the men I asked agreed that it is fairly rare to encounter fish in such massive numbers that it warrants actively inviting another boat to come and share them. In fact, in an environment where all men are essentially competing to catch the same shoals of fish, the dynamic between different fishing boats is more often one of intense, sport-like rivalry.

Travelling aboard one of the large passenger canoes (*pampas*) that commute twice weekly from Tombo to Shenge, the journey gave me and the other women on board a tantalising glimpse of a male world from which we were usually excluded (see Figure 6.1). In the course of a three-hour *pampa* journey, we might pass close enough to shout greetings to the men aboard a dozen or more of the large, so-called 'Ghana' or 'channel' boats as they stood under the glaring sun, patiently scanning the horizon about them, scrutinising the water for evidence of hidden fish shoaling just beneath the surface.

'Yes, when you see them all like that, near-near to one another, it means that the fish are there. In all those boats, they are all watching, watching, watching the water. (Yusef, crewman)

Seeing these multiple boatloads of fishermen scanning the same waters for the same shoals of fish, it would be easy to forget the possibility that each crew had set sail from a different wharf town that morning.

From my vantage point on the *pampa*, I occasionally saw one of these large boats just at the moment when its crew had broken their vigil. Their engine would be running at full speed, churning the water behind them, as the boat swerved to intercept a shoal of fish they had spotted. All the men on board were in motion, working rapidly as a team, to cast their net before any of the boats nearby were able to move to catch the same fish. On another occasion, my *pampa* passed a crew just as they were hauling their net from the water. From our cramped perches along the edge of the passenger canoe, we all turned and craned to see what kind of catch they had landed:

[3] As recently as the 1960s, Plantain had been home to a single family.

Figure 6.1 The passenger canoe (*pampa*) to Tombo

'Do you see those men there? They're pulling their net! Ah! That's hard work, there!'

'Look at all those fish! They are happy today! Look, the other crews are all watching them.'

And it was true. The sea was so congested that day that three or four other similarly sized boats were close enough in the water to have an easy view of the successful fishermen. The others had not cast their nets yet and were standing watching as their rivals dragged their heavy, glittering catch from the sea. As our *pampa* slid through the water between them, the tension was palpable. I recalled Pa Brima's comment, only a few days previously in Tissana, that: 'In the town, you see us, we fishermen all have one heart. But when I'm at sea, I don't want any man to get more than me!' Here, Mohammed paints a vivid image of the kinds of strategic games played out between rival crews as they compete against one another in the sea:

When you're all there in an open place. That boat is standing there; that one is standing there; that one is standing there: they're all watching, watching, they are all watching to see. Perhaps I might be standing here, but I can see there are fish over there [behind you]. I don't hurry-oh! I paddle small-small, I come. I paddle small-small, I come. I paddle small-small, I come... If I see fish in the water near your boat, I wouldn't call to tell you they were there-oh! No! I'd wait... wait... wait... for the right moment... then, *bam!* – I'd heave my net. Whoever casts their net first, it's done! Even if you were right there, closer to the fish than me, you don't have the right to cast your net now.

Parallel attempts to capitalise on knowledge differentials are an essential characteristic of many economic environments – from the stock market to the bazaar (Geertz 1978; Walsh 2004; Berry 2007). Yet there can be little doubt that fisheries have certain particular material characteristics that work to infuse this competition with a heightened sense of urgency. In a context in which everyone in the sea is vying to catch the same evasive resource, very often the only thing separating a triumphant boat from the many others who return home empty-handed is the fact that one crew learned, fractionally faster than its rivals, where exactly the fish were to be found. Indeed, it is a recurring characteristic of oceanic life, in otherwise disparate fishing cultures around the world, that intense competition is often paired with 'clear signs of secrecy, misinformation, and deceit' (Palmer 1990: 157; cf. Andersen 1980).

As Mark Busse reminds us: 'The materiality of property matters. The kinds of property claims that can be made depend upon the materiality of the things being claimed' (2012: 120). Or, as Pa Brima put it, rather more pithily: 'Fish get problem-oh!' If there can be any doubt as to the intensity of the competition felt between rival crews, fishermen often told me that it was common for tensions to erupt into violence:

It's a war! It's a war! It's like this: you see fish – the distance is there, far over there. I see them, too. I want to go and catch them – you also want to catch them. So, you'll paddle; I'll paddle fast to try and go and catch them. Fishermen can fight at sea-oh! Eeeee, bone to bone! Physical! Boats, they can come near to each other, like this – *fight!* They know how to fight at sea. (Alusine, crewman)

We are beginning to get a sense, then, of the complex layers of partially obscured vision that permeate Tissana's seascape. On the one hand – and I return to this important point in more detail shortly – non-seafaring fisherfolk, left behind on the shore, are always conscious of this disquieting fact: however crucial the sea is to their own fragile livelihoods, they can never know with any certainty what is taking place in that maritime world across the horizon. Yet, even if we remain, for now, with the seagoing fishermen themselves, it is clear that what knowledge they possess about their work environment is, by definition, slippery. Regardless of how experienced a boat's captain might be, there is more to mastering that endlessly fluid environment than accumulating a static corpus of knowledge. As well as steering across a topography, the physical contours of which are hidden from view beneath the water, fishermen are also working to navigate an equally complex field of socially produced knowledge, in which their friends and colleagues in other boats are as likely to be working to distort or conceal important information as they are to share it.

The intersection of the fishing economy and the esoteric episteme

As we have already seen, this pattern of daily gamesmanship in the competition to access, manipulate, and conceal knowledge from one's neighbours has as much to do with the inherent material limitations and opportunities of fishing environments as it does with any underlying 'cultural' disposition. However, when rival boats vie for the most up-to-date information in this particular region of West Africa, they do so within a very particular epistemological context in which:

Many see power in all its forms – spiritual, social, political and economic – as related to the possession of secrets... one of the certainties in a world characterised by considerable uncertainty, is that there are many secrets. Moreover, in this way of thinking, it is an incontrovertible fact that people have differential access to such secrets. (Soares 2005: 130)

To outside observers, this dynamic of concealment seems to find its most potent expression in the gendered 'secret societies' that play such an important role in customary political life. However, a person's access to powerful knowledge is not only determined by their structural position within society. In a context in which 'it is taken for granted that all people are hungry for knowledge' (d'Azevedo 1962b: 14), this 'esoteric *episteme*' (Brenner 2000) also allows for the possibility that potent secrets are concealed within the everyday material world, available to be acquired and exploited by anyone with sufficient interpretive skills.[4]

---

[4] Discussing the Mende region in which she carried out her fieldwork in the 1980s, Mariane Ferme describes a topography in which '[t]he perceptual domain is destabilised

Throughout the Mandé world, of which Sherbroland is on the periphery, it is forest hunters who are most often credited with the heightened ability to read subtle clues in the landscape, and so to access the potentially powerful forces concealed just beneath the surface of the visible world. In inland parts of Kagboro Chiefdom, where people rely heavily on bush meat as one of their main sources of animal protein, hunters are important figures in their community, and not only because they provide their neighbours with access to a much coveted food resource. Here, as elsewhere in rural Sierra Leone, hunters' skills – to see what others cannot – qualify them as individuals with an uncommon depth of wisdom and insight, 'great knowers' (Ferme 2001: 27) in a much broader sense. Here, Pa Albert is telling me about his friend and neighbour, who originally came from the same upriver region as he did:

They are not ordinary people, hunters. Like Pa Suarez: his father was a hunter and now he, too, is a hunter... When they watch an animal – maybe it is just something in the light, or the way that they move – but a hunter can know that it is a witch, turned himself into an animal. You know, very often, hunters know things that we don't know. They see things, when they are in the bush at night. But they do not easily talk about them.

Yet the very skills that Pa Albert so admired in his friend also imbue forest hunters with unpredictable – and dangerous – potential. Because they are able to enter spaces others fear, and to perceive forces that remain invisible to their neighbours, hunters are sometimes suspected of shape-shifting to animal or spirit form when they enter the bush by night (Wlodarczyk 2006). 'A hunter is not,' as Melissa Leach puts it, 'necessarily the sort of person one would want one's daughter to marry' (2000: 582). The powerfully *ambiguous* potentialities embodied by hunters are very similar to the qualities Tissana's residents attribute to the people they call 'witches'.

As other ethnographers have demonstrated, the skills of the hunter may be put to new uses in urban settings (Hansen and Verkaaik 2009: 5)[5] or frontier economies (De Boeck 2001). At sea, as in forested hunting grounds inland, experienced fishermen learn to read a combination of visible, but often extremely subtle, clues in the seascape. An acute

---

by forces that inhabit features of the landscape, that lie beneath the surface of solids and fluids' (2001: 5). Moving through a world so densely populated with unseen forces, her Mende informants understood that even 'poor strangers... may become rich and powerful through the strategic, though illicit, exploitation of secret knowledge of the landscape' (ibid.: 2).

[5] Julie Archambault (2013: 90), for example, paints an evocative picture of young Mozambican urbanites, carefully deciphering their neighbours' footprints in the sand, in order to reconstruct a secret narrative of night-time comings and goings.

observer will notice a flicker of motion just beneath the water's fluid surface, or will instinctively sense that the men in another boat are moving
just a little bit too deliberately. As Hans Lucht describes in Ghana:

Fishing depends on one's practical experience and ability to gather information
through the senses. A fisherman known to have 'good eyes' can see where, for
instance, a school of fish is moving or how the weather is developing, or 'knows'
the behaviour of sea birds and how they follow the fish. A fisherman can also
have a 'hunch', 'dream' or 'feeling' that is then collectively acted on. (Lucht
2011: 198)

In keeping with Sierra Leonean images of 'hunting' more generally, the
most masterful fishermen are credited with possessing an innate *embodied*
advantage over their competitors. Some of the largest commercial fishing
boats in the Yawri Bay employ one crew member known as the 'phone-
man': so-called because he is able to hear the fish, beneath the water, in
a way that other fishermen cannot. When the boat arrives in the fishing
ground, the phone-man enters the sea:

You know how we people, we have our different-different languages? Well, so it
is with fish – if you go in the water, if you know how to listen, you can hear them
when they talk to each other. Every different fish has his own language. They
listen to where they are . . . and they follow them – small-small, small-small. And
when they get to where [the fish] are, they wave and tell the boat to come and
cast its chain . . .
   You have to be able to swim to be a phone-man.[6] I know a bit – they showed
me a bit. But I can't do it like they do. I can hear [the fish], but I can't tell the
difference between the big ones and the small ones. (Usifu, crewman)

These exceptionally skilled crewmen are paid many times more than
anyone else in their boat – and not without good reason. If there was
one thing everyone agrees on, it is that boats with a phone-man on board
consistently bring home noticeably larger catches than their rivals. There
remains some room for disagreement, however, on the ontological status
of the phone-men themselves. Whereas Usifu emphasised the high level
of practical experience required to accurately decipher the underwater
soundscape, most people explained these abilities as one expression of
an innate, *physical* state of superhuman sensory awareness – a state that
is most simply summarised in Tissana as being a 'witch' or possessing
'witch eyes'.

Phone-men . . . have those 'witch eyes'. They can 'see'. They go into the water,
they hear the fishes when they talk – they can talk to them, they call them all into
one place. (Moses, fisherman)

---

[6] Many working fishermen, and certainly those who migrate to the coast in adulthood, do
not swim.

This slide between 'listening' for the fish and directly communicating with them was one that almost all my informants referred to. Both the Krio and the Sherbro language use a single word to denote both sensory 'hearing' and linguistic 'understanding' (*yehri* and *thee*, respectively). So, although I never heard anyone talk about a phone-man literally shape-shifting into a non-human form – as both hunters and 'witches' are described as doing in forest contexts (Jackson 1989; Leach 2000) – they are certainly assumed to take on qualities that blur the boundary between fishermen and their prey:

Mammy Kaddy (an elder): When they're casting the net, their witch goes under the water. He can be under water for a long time – maybe an hour. They gather the fish together under the water, while the boat is sitting there on the water, waiting. They know how to do that.

Me: Are they not afraid that people know they're a witch?

Mammy Kaddy: It's not so secret. No! You pay the person! People boast of it, in fact! They boast of it. And you can see, when the boats come back, the ones who have a witch get more fish.

Increasingly, though, even veteran fishermen – men with a deep embodied knowledge of the sea, acquired through long years of practice – are discovering to their dismay that the ocean has become harder to read. No amount of skill or experience is sufficient to guarantee a decent catch (cf. Lucht 2011: 198).

The underside of Tissana's townscape

What is perhaps surprising is that, when people in Tissana discuss these witch-fishermen, they do not draw any direct correlation between their special abilities and their moral character. In town, too, what sets 'witches' apart from their neighbours is not their inherent 'evil', but rather the fact that they possess 'eyes' powerful enough to see, which therefore enable them to move beyond the surfaces of the manifest world and into a shadowy spirit space 'not located in real dimensions or space or time' (Lamp 2008: 50).

In principle, the 'diffuseness and ambiguity of discourses on the occult' (Ciekawy and Geschiere 1998: 1) have long been recognised. In practice, however, whenever we privilege our own analytic models – which construct occult beliefs primarily as a vehicle for the expression of 'moral panic' about the global economic order – then we tend to incline automatically towards rather caricatured images of the witches themselves, as stylised symbols of 'evil in its most extreme forms' (La Fontaine 2011: 4). When people in Tissana discuss the 'witches' who inhabit their town and the spaces around it, they describe a more morally complex set of characters than anthropology's preoccupation with the 'poetics of pre-dation' (Comaroff and Comaroff 1993: xxvi) typically allows space to acknowledge. Here, for example, Ami is describing Tissana's thriving witch town:

Ami: You see that big-big cotton tree?...It's a big-big witch shop. Yes! They have a big-big-big shop there, at that tree. A big witch shop.
Me: What do they sell there?
Ami: Everything! Like food, rice, clothes, pans; anything you could want. They even have knives; anything you want to buy. There are loads of tin-roofed houses, and they all have generators. It's a big place! A whole town! Only we don't see it...
Me: If a person wants to buy something in that witch shop, is it the same money that we use? The same leones?
Ami: Yes, but...if you don't have those witch eyes, you can't go there.

Perhaps the most striking aspect of Ami's description of the world inhab-ited by Tissana's witches is its relative mundaneness. Rather than an exotic global hub of occult forces (cf. Shaw 2002), Tissana's underworld is imagined as a disconcertingly local place: one that maps directly onto the surfaces of the manifest world. In fact, a surprisingly large subsection of Tissana's population is assumed to have access to this realm, includ-ing most infants, twins and their siblings,[7] sorcerers, and anyone else who simply happens to have been born with eyes that enable them to see beyond the surfaces of the visible world. Here, for example, Ima and Dulai are discussing their own young children:

Ima: Asana can 'see' perfectly! He's a twin. You know that? His companion died. One time, when Dulai and I had argued, I left Asana here and went to my father's people in Plantain. He turned himself into a snake!
Dulai: Yes, it is true! I was asleep in my bed...and I saw Asana. He was standing by my bed, and then he turned himself into a snake: a big one. Really! *Ah!* Asana, Asana, he's a 'witch'! He's powerful! But I love him. I want him to go to school. Or, if not that, maybe he will be a footballer.
Ima: Baby Jenny now, in Africa, we say she's a *gbeshe*...She is the third one [the child born after twins]. She is even more powerful than a twin...She is perfect. Even though she's so small – she doesn't talk it – but she sees *everything*. She knows *everything*. But we now; we don't see. Except maybe if we go to school.

Although people with ordinary sight often describe glimpsing this world in their dreams, this sphere of Tissana's social world remains, for most

[7] A much larger proportion of people fall into this category than might perhaps be imag-ined. Even if measured by purely biomedical criteria, rates of twin births are several times higher in West Africa than elsewhere in the world. Moreover, in Sierra Leone, as elsewhere in this region, births are sometimes considered 'twin' even when only one child is born (Peek 2011). In these cases, the unborn baby may be recognisable in the placenta.

people most of the time, just beyond their vision. Yet, although Dulai and Ima draw connections between a series of familiar characteristics that are often associated with 'witchcraft' – shape-shifting, intelligence, and exceptional insight – notable in its absence is any particular concern that their children are 'wicked' or will grow up to be so. Indeed, my neighbours were quick to acknowledge that the exceptional insight that came with possessing 'witch eyes' could, potentially at least, be used in any manner of productive ways. People who had studied in high school sometimes told me that the correct English translation for the Krio word 'witch' was 'scientist', and that the foreigners who created high-tech gadgets, or who knew how to find resources such as diamonds and minerals in Sierra Leone's ground, were empowered with the same innate *embodied* potential – to see far – which gave the Yawri Bay's phone-men an advantage over their competitors. 'Your own witches,' Mama Koni told me, 'use their eyes for good.'

However, as I go on to explore in the following section, this is an economy in which it is generally taken for granted that *all* people are driven by the necessity to seize whatever narrow sliver of opportunity they have, in order to make a profit – even if, as is often the case, these 'opportunities' might involve some level of trickery or deception. My fellow lodger, David, expressed a widely held truism when he told me that 'people in Tissana are not reliable . . . If you went from [one end of town to the other], it would be hard to find five reliable people.' Living and working in such an atmosphere of pervasive half-trust, the knowledge that some people are able to act in ways invisible to their neighbours can become a source of considerable anxiety. As we will see, hidden spaces – at sea, and in the 'underworld' of the Yawri Bay and Tissana's landscape – are assumed by the majority of people who are excluded from them to be the site of all manner of illicit economic strategies.

Survival and occult economies

It goes without saying that, for the many *kustoments* and *boss-men* anxiously anticipating the boats' return on the wharf, speculation about what might be happening out of sight at sea it is a matter of intense concern. This interest is not a matter of simple curiosity. In theory at least, a large proportion of the men at work in the sea each day 'owe' their catch to a specific individual on the wharf.[8] In an economy as tight as Tissana's, people's livelihoods are very often hanging in the balance as they gaze

---

[8] In many cases, the boat in which they are fishing belongs to a land-based owner and, on four or five days of the working week, their catch is supposed to go directly and in full to that boss (see Chapter 3). Just as frequently, fishermen borrow money from a fish processor with an agreement that they will pay her back piecemeal, in fish, selling to her exclusively until the debt is finally cleared (see Chapter 4).

out to sea; they depend on the crew of their boat both catching fish and honouring their promises to bring those fish home.

However, boat owners and *banda* women are painfully aware that, the moment they move out of sight at sea, it is almost impossible to know what fishermen are actually doing. By the end of my 18 months in Tissana – much of which I spent sitting on the wharf with the *banda* women, peering out to sea, awaiting the reappearance of a particular familiar patchwork sail – I had developed a fairly strong sense of the world they imagined over the horizon, and of the slippery, strategic, economic games they 'knew' the men to be playing on the open sea. I lost track of the number of times I was told tales such as these by *banda* women or boat owners:

All the time, all the time, they're all the same. That was why I just decided to leave [the fish business] in the end. You know, one boat, I invested *so* much money, so much money – new boat, new engine, new net. I never saw even 1,000 leones from that boat. Nothing. I gave the boat to someone who I thought I could trust, a cousin of mine, and he went out and found crewmen, and then they just enjoyed themselves! They are very, very untrustworthy people, fishermen. (George Thomas, politician and former boat owner)

Well, of course, for me, right now, I don't trust my fishermen. I am heartbroken. Why? Because... those boys who fish in my boat – they don't do right by me. For the whole month, if I get any fish, I am lucky!... Always [they tell me] 'No catch!'; always 'No catch!' (Timbo, boat owner)

It is assumed by those based on land that crewmen routinely exploit the invisibility of their fishing grounds at the expense of their customers and patrons on shore, often selling their fish in secret in another wharf town along the coast; sometimes even colluding with another crew to transfer their catch into a different boat at sea. Many women described this world of hidden trickery with an air of weary authority that belied the fact that – speaking in the most literal sense – the ocean is the site of a social life they can only ever really 'know' imaginatively. When my friend Kumba asked to borrow money to buy a new canoe, claiming that he would repay our household by giving Buema fish to dry and sell, Buema was vociferous in her attempts to protect me from what appeared to her a blatant attempt to 'grift' me:

Don't give him! Don't do it, Jenny... This is where my mother bore me! I know fishermen! I know Kumba! He'll ask, and ask, and ask you for money! He'll take your money, till you can't pay your transport home, but he'll take your fish and sell them somewhere else. When he lands in Tissana, he'll say: 'Look! Here's a [single] *plassas* fish for you!'

In a curious twist of etymology, the Krio word for 'lend' is *tross* – derived from the English word 'trust' – although, in practice, debt relationships in Tissana are characterised far more often by a palpable sense of suspicion. Yet, however dubious they might be that their *tross* will be repaid, the fact remains that working *banda* women have no option but to continue investing their meagre capital, building economic relationships with seagoing fishermen. We saw in Chapter 4 that, apart from marrying a fisherman, *trossing* him cash is one of the few means by which to obtain a steady supply of fish.

There are echoes here of the fragile 'confidence' that Andrew Walsh describes as shaping the economy of his Malagasy sapphire-mining field site. In a predicament that parallels that of Tissana's land-bound fisherfolk, local gem dealers have no choice but to base their livelihoods on reciprocal relationships that they know to be dangerously brittle, dealing with international trading partners who subsequently vanish into a mysterious global sapphire market, the contours of which the dealers know themselves to be ignorant of. Faced with a reality in which traders all too often take stones on credit, never to return, Walsh's informants, like mine, navigate through an economic landscape in which:

Speculation and suspicion go hand in hand – the former as the best stand-in for unavailable certainty, and the latter as a necessary buffer against assurances of certainty and transparency in an ambiguous context that appears to offer little foothold for openness, honesty, or trust. (Walsh 2004: 226)

There is, as he notes, an inherent fragility 'in all systems of moral and economic exchange in which reciprocity and confidence play key roles' (Walsh 2009: 59). This fragility is especially marked, I would add, in contexts such as Walsh's field site and my own, where one group of economic actors is far more mobile, and so by its very nature far less amenable to be held accountable, than the other.

It is in this respect that, for the majority of people who cannot access them, the ocean and the 'underworld' share a surprisingly similar dynamic. For, although I have been at pains to stress that people with 'witch eyes' are not always necessarily 'bad' by nature, people are all too conscious that witches, like seagoing fishermen, have ample opportunity to exploit their unseeing neighbours. As the following conversation with Jacob reveals, the knowledge that their social world is so heavily populated with invisible agencies only exacerbates the common experience, shared by many in Tissana, that they have frustratingly little control over their own material livelihoods:

This is another thing. A lot of people are complaining about it: this money business . . . If you have money, you see it, you can touch it and count it, but it does not come to anything. And you can think and think and think and you do not know where all that money has gone. It leaves you just like a breeze. Just like a breeze in your hands. If someone sees you counting money, they will grow envious of you, and they put witch on you; and the money, it just goes! Nothing good will ever come of it . . .

He took a break from this monologue and looked at me: 'I hope you understand what I am saying?' For a moment, I felt that I caught a glimpse of something in Jacob's face – a desperation, which I had rarely seen before. He had had two hours' sleep that night, he told me: 'Thinking, thinking, worrying, worrying.' Fighting back tears of fatigue and frustration, he continued, wearily:

And this is what I'm saying; with the money, you see? It is like a nightmare. Do you know what a nightmare is? That is how they do it. And one minute you have the money – it is there in your hand. But no matter how careful you are, it just vanishes. Like a breeze.

There is nothing exceptional about Jacob's conviction that the structural violence of his poverty must be underpinned by some more wilful, embodied violence, actively inflicted upon him by one or other of the people closest to him. Similar rumours circulate widely through everyday conversation in Tissana, where people very often make sense of their own impoverishment through the logic that one of their neighbours must have stolen from them, invisibly, 'in a witch way', covertly robbing them of their money and good fortune. The Sherbro term for this invisible theft is *tofi*. Many share Jacob's suspicion – that, when the money they worked so hard to earn 'turns to breeze' with depressing predictability, the only explanation is that they must have been robbed imperceptibly by their 'witch-eyed' neighbours:

Sometimes, it will happen, they know how to steal from you, in a way that you cannot see. So, the person has to pay you 100,000 leones, and, as they are standing there, you count the money and it is all there. But when you go home and look again, it is only 80,000! They have stolen it by *tofi*! (Pa Dulai, elder)

If you're trying to do business with someone who has 'witch eyes', you'll never see any benefit. They will always take your money. You won't know how, because you can't see them do it. But they do it – by *tofi*. (Miriam, *banda* woman)

As we have seen, this nagging suspicion that one must have been robbed, and yet having no tangible evidence of any wrongdoing having taken place, is not limited to people's experience of doing business with 'witches'. It is a frustratingly familiar quality of economic life on the Kagboro coast, where the unrelenting material insecurity puts strain on relationships between crewmen, boat owners, and *banda* women.

The predicament faced by land-based fisherfolk is that they can rarely *really* know with absolute certainty whether they have been 'grifted', as they are apt to suspect. Fishing is, after all, an innately unpredictable business – and it has become more so in recent decades, as an ever-increasing number of crews compete to catch an ever-declining population of fish. It is quite possible that, on the many occasions when Timbo's crew returned home empty-handed, they were being completely honest: they had simply failed to catch anything. This is not, however, the explanation favoured by Timbo, George, or any of the other countless boat owners and *banda* women who are now accustomed to being disappointed on the wharf.

'If you want to go and thieve in secret, that's fine!'

However, more powerful boat owners are able to take some measures to try to keep track of their crew, even after they have moved out of sight across the sea. Here, one of Plantain Island's wealthiest *boss-men* is describing the strategies he has put in place to uncover the occasions when his crew attempt to 'play games' by secretly selling their catch in another town:

Moses: You must have somebody special in that boat who gives you information. If there is a good catch and there is any game playing, then you have to know...I have somebody in the boat. He sends messages to me, of what is happening. But [his crewmates] don't know about him.

Me: Ah, I can see that's important. I've heard stories of crewmen going and selling their fish in secret?

Moses: Yes! Of course they do that! When there's a catch...they find another port. They go there, they sell, share that money, buy fuel and then they come back at night with no catch. You, the boat owner, will never see that – unless you have somebody honest who is your eye, always ready to report them – secretly! Then I will say, 'You went to this fishing village there – I have a friend there – where is the money now?' Then the others will start to say, 'I was not party to that-oh!' Then they begin to expose themselves. [Laughs] It is very entertaining.

When I asked Jacob how a spy of this kind would be viewed by his crewmates, if he were ever discovered, his answer was unequivocal:

If [his crewmates] knew who he was, they would hate him. They would hate him, and take him to be an enemy, because that person is blocking their survival. If he is not careful maybe they would even hurt him in the sea. They might even just leave him in the sea. Yes, that can happen sometimes.

The difference between the two men's tone is striking. Jacob, for his part, recognises the stark material reality of crewmen's lives, in which, for four or five days of the working week, they have no 'legitimate' claim on the fish they work so hard to catch. In a boat as large as Moses', the two remaining days' catch must be divided between as many as 20 men, each with his own family and responsibilities on land. It is hardly surprising, then, that crewmen are often prepared to risk being caught 'cheating' with their boss's boat at sea. Employed under such conditions, the work of deceiving one's *boss-man* seems less a matter of game playing than of survival.

However, what is interesting in Moses' testimony is that, even while seeking to demonstrate that he is savvy enough to outwit his crew, he actually reveals a fairly high degree of acceptance of their low-level 'thieving', which he dismisses, laughingly, as 'very entertaining'. This attitude of partial tolerance is made much more explicit in this interview with another boat owner, Kain:

Even now, right now, I have a problem with my crewmen . . . Sometimes they steal from me. When they catch [a lot of fish], they just go and sell them somewhere else . . . It hurts me, because they should not do that but it's something you just have to bear. With a paddle boat, like mine, if you lose your fishermen, it's a problem! . . . If my crew leave me, my boat will be sitting on the wharf. This is why it's important to treat your crew well. If you encourage them, they will not leave.

If Kain recognised that his crew were so poor that 'encouraging' them entailed accepting a certain amount of 'thieving', the question remains: why did he not simply pay them a little better to begin with? It is worth noting that, working in a quite different Sierra Leonean context, Melissa Leach encountered a similar pattern of everyday 'stealing'. In her field-work in the Gola Forest, she found that a certain level of 'thieving' within households was taken for granted as a normal element of domestic life, and a necessary strategy for women whose husbands rarely gave them enough money to meet their financial obligations. In this context, men claimed 'to tolerate "theft" as it is more convenient than facing wives' incessant demands for money' (Leach 1994: 199).

The relationship between legality and morality is far from self-evident, especially in parts of the world, such as Sierra Leone, where the law has too often 'been used to justify, administer, and sanction Western conquest and plunder' (Mattei and Nader 2008: 1). As E. P. Thompson noted, in his classic study of 'poaching' in eighteenth-century England, crime is a problematic category 'when we simply take over the definitions of those who own property, control the state, and pass the laws which "name" what shall be crimes' (1975: 193–4).

Janet Roitman's research in the borderlands of the Chad Basin is particularly effective in deconstructing the relationships between legality and ethics. A large part of the economy of this frontier region consists of 'criminal' activities, ranging from smuggling and counterfeiting, to armed highway robbery. While the people she interviewed recognise that these activities are against the law, they also accept them as 'licit' livelihood strategies: not only in the limited sense that they have 'become normal practice' (Roitman 2006: 249), but also because robbery and smuggling offer valued channels for the redistribution of wealth. In post-apartheid South Africa, Adam Ashforth made a similar observation. After decades of political oppression and economic marginalisation, many young men living in townships saw robbing white people as 'a form of forcible redistribution of wealth that was more like a job of work that a morally opprobrious crime' (Ashforth 2005: 244). Indeed, he argues that many people in Soweto perceived the very category of 'crime' – at least, as it was legally defined by the government – as 'virtually an ethically neutral construct because the government was an instrument of oppression' (ibid.).

Nancy Scheper-Hughes makes a different, and rather more challenging, argument about the relationship between poverty and 'crime'. Building on research in a Brazilian shanty town, she explores the extent to which trickery and cunning become essential skills of 'social navigation' for many people living in conditions of extreme precariousness (Scheper-Hughes 2008). In some contexts, this might be read as a form of political resistance. With sufficient *malandragem* (cunning), even the most marginal shanty-town dweller might occasionally be able to beat the system that is weighed against them. However, as part of her broader campaign to avoid romanticising poverty or 'trivializing its effects on the human spirit' (Scheper-Hughes 1992: 533), Scheper-Hughes emphasises that trickery and cunning are just as often deployed in more intimate contexts. In romance, friendship, and family life, she claims, 'resilience in the context of shantytown life involves a certain amount of manipulation verging on sociopathy' (Scheper-Hughes 2008: 47).

'Cat and mouse games' similar to those I observed between boat owners and their crewmen in Tissana have been described by ethnographers working in fishing communities elsewhere (Beuving 2010: 240). This suggests that illicit strategies (and the fields of suspicion that mirror and possibly magnify them) have as much to do with the unique patterns of movement and concealment facilitated by the seascape as they do with any specific 'cultural' disposition. Nonetheless, I follow Rebecca Prentice here in suggesting that the moral salience of economic behaviours can only really be understood when viewed within the 'wider cultural contours of... daily life' (Prentice 2009: 137), and that this is especially true in cases, such as in the Yawri Bay, where people's livelihoods depend on strategies that challenge our – and sometimes also our informants' – sense of where the boundary lies between licit and illicit behaviour.[9] As I explore in the following section, it is impossible to have a meaningful discussion of the ways in which Tissana's fisherfolk evaluate the morality of trust and deception without pausing to contemplate the wider cultural context in which people work to infuse every level of social discourse with an atmosphere of secrecy (see Chapter 1).

---

[9] Working in a garment factory in Trinidad, Prentice found that certain specific forms of 'thieving' were viewed by her informants as morally legitimate. Although the same women would have condemned 'stealing' under almost any other circumstance, 'thieving a chance' on the factory floor could be celebrated as an expression of 'self-reliance, autonomy, and cunning individualism' (2009: 124).

Livelihoods, strategic deceit, and the morality of trust

Until their role was gradually encroached upon by Western styles of
schooling, the two parallel 'secret' societies – the men's Poro and the
women's Bundu – had been the main educational institutions in the
region.[10] Although it is true that the Poro society's direct political power
has atrophied fairly dramatically in recent decades on the Kagboro coast,
this has done nothing to erase the centuries-long heritage in which initiation societies played a central role in shaping the character of social
life in this region; not least by training successive generations of young
men and women in what it meant to be a responsible adult member of
Sherbro society. As part of this process, young people were inducted into
the lowest echelons of the sodality's esoteric knowledge, but they also
received training in a whole range of skills that we might recognise as
more self-evidently 'pragmatic'. Here, Pa Albert, a Sherbro elder, lists
some of the skills he was taught during his own initiation as a young man
in the 1950s:

Formerly, you used to be inside the bush for three years. In those three years, the
so'eh [the Poro elder] would teach you – how to marry, how to farm, what kind of
person to be when you grow up. In those days, they'd teach you to be responsible.
In that bush, they'd teach you how to be a hunter, how to be a fisherman. You
will be taught how to spy.

It speaks vividly to Ferme's description of Sierra Leonean social life as
shaped by a 'hermeneutic of suspicion' (2001: 7) that, when Pa Albert
listed the basic livelihood skills required by a Sherbro boy contemplating
his transition to manhood, he should include 'spying' so intuitively on
the list. Here he goes on to describe the day-to-day life of a Poro initiate
in the 1950s:

You have to learn hardship! So, your family do not bring food for you. [The
initiates] go all around the area in search of food, at night. But you have to be
very, very careful, so that no one sees you. You go in the night in search of your
food.

Like young men in the past, young female initiates continue to be actively
encouraged by their *so'ehs* (Bundu elders) to learn self-sufficiency by
thieving from their neighbours' farms under cover of night. Here, Buema
reminisces about her own time as an initiate, some 15 years ago:

Buema: We wanted to cook, but we didn't have any *plassas*, so the *so'ehs* showed
us how to thieve, and told us to go out into the bush at night. Ah! We took
a lot of food! When people came to their farms in the morning, they cried!
[Laughing]
Me: Couldn't they do anything?

[10] See Chapter 1.

Buema: *Ah!* No! Those are the rules! We were in the bush for three months – we thieved from every farm, all around here! Even just now, when you were in London, those Bundu girls came into Jacob's garden at night. They thieved his cassava, his potatoes, his pepper – everything! I laughed so much! Jacob was so angry! But then he laughed, too. There's nothing to do except laugh.

Later that day I asked Jacob for his account of the same event:

Jacob: Yes, the Bundu women stole from my garden!
Me: How did you know it was them?
Jacob: They said it! Everyone knew it was them. The women themselves told me, too.
Me: Were you angry?
Jacob: Well, I mean, yes. I was angry. But only inside myself, only inside this compound. I would never lodge a complaint to the women, because it's their right. They are a society. Those are the rules.

Although they must leave the seclusion of the Bundu bush in order to raid the gardens of their neighbours around Tissana, the young women remain protected from male eyes by the powerful – and, for non-initiates, dangerous – medicines that cover their skin.

Even if we went into the farms in the afternoon, no man can see us. We sing, so they can hear us coming. Then the men run and hide! Those who don't run, they get sick. (Aminata, petty trader)

In this sense, Poro and Bundu initiations fit very neatly within classic anthropological models of 'rites of passage', in which the 'relatively fixed and stable states' (Turner 1967: 83) of childhood and adulthood are separated by a liminal period during which young people are suspended in ambiguous limbo outside the ordinary stream of social life. However, what is striking in both Buema and Pa Albert's accounts is that learning to perform clever acts of trickery is not so much presented as evidence of the moral order turned upside down, but rather as an important training in the resourcefulness young people will need if they are to succeed in their adult lives. As Pa Albert put it: 'When you come out of the bush [after initiation], nothing will be difficult for you. You will not be lazy again.'

It is in keeping with this broader pattern, in which a certain level of strategic deceit is accepted as a necessary livelihood skill, that there is an extremely strong moral discourse against 'loose talk'. Writing of a related language group in neighbouring Liberia, Bellman (1984) described how averse her Kpelle neighbours were to open discussions of village social life. Even in cases where everybody present knew the full 'facts' of the case, they would invariably discuss them only obliquely, through the careful allusions and metaphors of 'deep talk'. The result – varying, ambiguous, and often conflicting interpretations of the world – is also apparent in Mariane Ferme's account of the Mende village where she conducted fieldwork in the 1980s: 'a person who communicates directly what she or he desires or thinks...is considered an idiot or no better than a child' (Ferme 2001: 6).

Imagine the possibilities, then, in a town such as Tissana, where – quite aside from the cacophony of dialects spoken by traders and immigrants from other parts of the country – no fewer than five languages are commonly spoken: Krio, Temne, Sherbro, Mende, and Fula. Having deliberately shifted into a 'deep' Sherbro, well beyond my comprehension, my friends would occasionally tease me: 'We're hiding from you!' ('*Hi kong ha math*!'). Yet it is not only ethnographers who are sometimes unable to understand the conversations taking place around them. Since it would be unusual for an individual to speak more than two or three languages with any degree of fluency, the result is a patchy, multilayered, polyglot fabric; one that speakers learn to manoeuvre with considerable strategy and skill – controlling which of their conversations are heard, and which remain private.

I witnessed this daily on the busy veranda of my own home. As the topic of conversation meandered, the language would switch fluidly from Krio to Temne to Sherbro to Mende and back again. Sometimes, these switches were absent-minded; but just as often, there was a strategic element of deliberate 'hiding' taking place. With each readjustment, new boundaries were being drawn between those people present who were invited to join in, and those who were being explicitly excluded from the conversation:

Although sometimes, if you have not been around with someone for a long time, you will have to be careful; because some people will pretend that they do not hear the language, but they do hear. Especially with this intermarriage. This is why it is harder now to hide. (Mama Yebu, elder)

Perhaps the most commonly expressed complaint I heard people making against the moral character of their neighbours was not that they were apt to act in secretive ways but rather that they were dangerously inclined to reveal other people's secrets. The Krio word *kongosar* can be translated into English as 'gossip' or 'snitch', and it is similarly loaded with connotations of selfishness, slipperiness, and betrayal. Here, three of my most trusted informants employ a powerful set of similes to illustrate the destructive potential of unveiling other people's hidden actions:

To be nice to a person's face, then wait until they go over there to talk badly of them – we say it is the same thing as if, when your friend dies, you wait three days, then come and chop up their body and eat them...But it is a very, very big problem here. It is just too common. (Kumba, fisherman)

The violence of the language Kumba chooses here to describe a simple act of speech is arresting. Throughout West Africa, analogies relating to cannibalism are typically reserved to describe only the most extreme forms of wilfully antisocial behaviour (Bayart 1993 [1989]; Pratten 2007). However, both Buema and Pa Albert go further: emphasising the real-world danger that is unleashed whenever a person speaks something that ought to have remained silent:

A *kongosar* is worse than a thief... *Kongosar* heaves confusion. It scatters families... It ends marriages. *Kongosar* kills people. (Buema, petty trader)

You know about the witchcraft we have here, and you know what it can do. It is very, very bad. But when you look at it, *kongosar* is heavier than witchcraft... It can even lead to murder. (Pa Albert, elder)

What initially surprised me about the passion with which my informants denounced *kongosars* was that they did not reserve their criticism for instances when they suspected the gossip to be false. On the contrary, as Jacob explains to me here, *kongosars* are to be feared the most when they reveal a genuine hidden truth:

Jacob: *Kongosars* are telling the truth about the person, but that person did something hidden and you go and tell the person who they stole from, or whatever. It is a very bad thing!
Me: But isn't it the person who stole who is bad?
Jacob: Well, yes... Yes, to steal is bad. But the person who is stolen from does not know who did it! He might grow annoyed, annoyed, annoyed, but, in the end, he will just leave his case to God. But if you go and tell him who did it, he might just explode with anger! And whose fault is that? It is the *kongosar*'s fault, isn't it? Because the person [the thief] went and did his business in secret, but you who knows and tells the [victim], you are the bad person now.

So, on the one hand, unseen behaviour itself carries clear implications of criminality and is often assumed to relate to illicitly obtained wealth. Yet, as much as people worry that their neighbours and business partners are covertly defrauding them, the fact that *kongosars* are relentlessly undermining the secrecy that others work so hard to construct and maintain is the cause of almost as much anxiety.

This apparently contradictory moral stance was rendered particularly stark for me when I heard the following speech, delivered at a political rally in Tissana. The speaker, who was representing Sierra Leone's governing party, is the same former boat owner whom we heard, a few pages ago, despairing that the fishermen he once employed had been 'very, very untrustworthy people'. Faced with a crowd of fisherfolk he needed to impress, his tone was altogether different:

The government has made a promise to ban some [environmentally unsustainable] fishing methods, like channel fishing. And we will stick by that promise! But what you do, if you want to go and thieve in secret, that is fine! What you do when you are out at sea is left to you. But it is those *kongosar*people [snitches] who are the problem here! It is them that you have to be careful of. (George Thomas, politician)

Conclusions

Writing almost 30 years ago, Suzette Heald raised the point that, although many African societies have historically bracketed thieving together with witchcraft as similar kinds of behaviours deserving of similar kinds of punishment, this correlation is almost never acknowledged in the literature. According to Western conceptions of the material world, the former is a 'real' economic crime while the latter belongs in the sphere of 'mystical ... or arcane beliefs and practices' (Heald 1986: 86; cf. Niehaus 2012). However, if lack of 'hard evidence' is reason enough to assume that occult economies belong in the realm of 'ideas, not behaviours' (La Fontaine 2011: 14), we would have to extend a similar logic to dismiss much else that people in Tissana know about their material and economic world.

Part of the difficulty in any comparative discussion of 'witchcraft' is that there is a limit to how far we can meaningfully collapse specific local ideas into a universal ethnographic category. The English word 'witch' comes encrusted with a thick patina of associations – originally drawn from European history, but long since overlaid with decades of ethnographic discussion. In Tissana, the single most fundamental characteristic of a 'witch' is their ability to see, and so move, into a shadow world that runs alongside the everyday visible landscape. While it might be tempting to presume a deep ontological divide between the mundane world and this unseen space, there is, as Peter Geschiere observed in Cameroon, 'at the most a distinction of access ... the two domains are intricately intertwined in everyday life' (quoted in Fabian et al. 2008: 139).

Such descriptions of the everyday landscape present a challenge to Western epistemology, which usually relies on an authoritative, objectifying gaze as the root of knowledge. Michael Jackson has gone further than most anthropologists in attempting to move beyond this ethnographic impulse to produce an authoritative account of the world. Instead, his writing emphasises 'the sense of living in a place, of experiencing it from all sides, moving and participating in it instead of remaining on the margins like a voyeur' (Jackson 1989: 8). This 'cubist' approach comes to life particularly vividly in his discussion of witchcraft, in which he reveals 'the essential provisionality of beliefs, how they are manipulated, called upon, suspended, invested with different emotional values ... in different situations by different individuals' (Jackson 1978: 34). If interrogated directly about witches, his informants tended to paint a generic image of malicious, devious, violent individuals (Jackson 1989: 90). And yet, what is most interesting about Jackson's work is his willingness to embrace the ambiguity and 'polysemy' of specific stories about witchcraft, as they emerge in the lives and relationships of actual people.

In short, *suwa'ye* [witchcraft] . . . denotes an indeterminate power or faculty. And though this power of *suwa'ye* is in essence 'wild' or extrasocial, whether it becomes good or bad depends entirely on how it is harnessed or used. (Jackson 1989: 93)

More recently, Harry West's (2008) acclaimed book *Ethnographic Sorcery* similarly emphasises the complexities and contradictions of witchcraft – not so much a clearly defined set of evil practices as a diffuse field of thought and action that encompasses many shades of morality and aspects of life. It is, West argues, this amorphous quality that makes witchcraft discourse such a powerful medium for reflecting on the hidden operations of power that shape everyday life.

I was initially rather surprised that the stories people told about witches did not reflect the global economies of violence and extraction that have so explicitly shaped this coastline's history. My neighbours were very well aware that Plantain Island had once been the site of one of the busiest slave forts on the Upper Guinea Coast, and are equally conscious of the role played by international trawlers in undermining their coastal ecosystem and personal livelihood chances. And yet, as Cooper and Pratten note, 'recognizing the power of distant forces on present life does not necessarily help people to resolve the immediate uncertainties and insecurities that they experience' (2015: 7). In everyday life, Tissana's fisherfolk tend to focus their anxieties much closer to home (cf. Booth, Leach, and Tierney 1999: 23; Schoepf and Schoepf 1988).

The 'witch-eyed' people who inhabit the hidden spaces around the town's landscape are remarkable not for their inherently 'evil' character, but rather for their ability to see, and thus to move and act, in spaces their neighbours cannot see. In this respect, the ocean and the underworld share a surprisingly similar dynamic for the majority of people who are excluded from them. Both spaces are fundamentally integrated within Tissana's everyday material economy yet are located just beyond the edges of the publicly visible townscape. There are resonances here with Simmel's classic attempt to generalise the experience of inhabiting a world permeated with secrecy. 'The secret offers, so to speak, the possibility of a second world alongside the manifest world; and the latter is decisively influenced by the former' (Simmel 1964 [1950]: 330). In Tissana, as Simmel had predicted, individuals' knowledge that their neighbours have access to hidden spaces fosters a sense of their material environment as 'enlarged', stretching far beyond the limits of their own sensory experience. In an economy as fragile and unpredictable as Tissana's, most people experience their ignorance of these hidden spaces as a source of palpable anxiety.

The instability of economic life is compounded by the legacy of a civil war in which many became accustomed to regarding social life with an all-embracing and deep-rooted sense of unease. In Tissana, much as Lotte Meinert has described in post-war Uganda:

Trust – in personal relations, institutions, truths, and places is less familiar here, and something people may achieve in specific relations and institutions over time... Trust is a tricky social achievement that people may encourage themselves and each other to work toward, even while reminding themselves that there is great instability and unpredictability in who and what can actually be trusted. (Meinert 2015: 199)

Theorists have debated whether trust is a fundamental characteristic of human nature (Løgstrup 1997 [1956]) or whether trust relationships should more meaningfully be understood as a site of permanent struggle,[11] one entailing a contested and ambivalent 'leap of faith' (Simmel 1964 [1950]). The philosopher Esther Pederson (2015) recently tried to move beyond these ontological arguments by developing a framework for understanding trust and distrust as attitudes that are highly sensitive to an individual's social environment. According to Pederson, whether a person is inclined to be trusting of others depends to a large extent on their own life history and their own experiences of past social interactions. But these personal stories always play out within a broader topography of cultural norms, and a shared public discussion about the nature of social life. Pederson coins the term 'prima facie trust/distrust' to refer to the instinctive way in which people tend to respond to social situations, based on this taken-for-granted knowledge of the world (ibid.: 106). It is, she argues, at the intersection between public discourse and personal experience that we 'learn to expect that people will be either reliable or unreliable' (ibid.: 107). In its positive form, 'prima facie trust' is similar to what Niklas Luhmann calls 'confidence'. Writing for a readership in wealthy, liberal democracies, Luhmann describes confidence as the 'normal' response to most situations:

You are confident that your expectations will not be disappointed: that politicians will try to avoid war, that cars will not break down or suddenly leave the street and hit you on your Sunday afternoon walk. You... have to neglect, more or less, the possibility of disappointment. You neglect this because it is a very rare possibility, but also because you do not know what else to do. The alternative is to live in a state of permanent uncertainty. (Luhmann 1988: 97)

---

[11] See Geschiere (2013) for an excellent discussion of trust in anthropology.

For many people struggling to balance fragile livelihoods in precarious and unpredictable economic conditions, the kind of unquestioning confidence described by Luhmann would appear to be an almost unimaginable luxury. Johnson-Hanks' (2005) ethnography describes people in southern Cameroon embracing – or at least resigning themselves to – the pervasive unpredictability that permeates all aspects of social, personal, and economic relations. She describes her interlocutors navigating through life with a 'subjunctive' disposition: a continual openness to change and an awareness of the likelihood that, whatever plans one makes, they are likely to collapse. One outcome of this stance, she argues, is that people feel little pressure to behave in ways that are transparent, trustworthy, or predictable:

After all, if corruption and witchcraft are inevitable and 'everyone' engages in them, why resist? As a result of the common view that Cameroon is in crisis, the values assigned to specific social actions are remarkably fluid, with sometimes devastating consequences. (Johnson-Hanks 2005: 366)

Ethnographers elsewhere in sub-Saharan Africa have suggested that this sense of insecurity encompasses, but is not confined to, people's interactions in the material world. As Adam Ashforth has described in Soweto, 'the prevalence of misfortune stimulates an enormous profusion of interpretive endeavors' (1998: 65). People may find themselves submerged in epistemic anxiety, knowing that unseen agencies are acting in their lives – but not knowing what these are, or how to safely engage with them (Ashforth 2005: 485). Faced with such conflicting images of the invisible world, people feel overwhelmed with doubt about the fundamental forces shaping their existence.

And yet, even in this ambience of 'prima facie *distrust*' (Pederson 2015: 109), individuals' social and economic survival continues to depend on the ability to forge relationships founded on patterns of reciprocity. Anthropological discussions of gift exchange have been so overshadowed by classic theories about the 'spirit' of reciprocity (Mauss 1990 [1925]) that we have tended to downplay the importance – and the frightening fragility – of *trust* as the real centre of gift relationships. As Andrew Walsh has revealed, in a wonderful article on failed reciprocity in a Malagasy sapphire-mining economy:

The gift and the grift aren't so far apart as some might assume. Where the rhythm of the gift is ideally regular and continuous – give, receive, reciprocate; give, receive, reciprocate; give, receive, reciprocate – the rhythm of the grift differs only by one beat – give, receive, reciprocate; give, receive, reciprocate; give, receive . . . nothing. (Walsh 2009: 65)

In common with Walsh's informants, people in Tissana understood all too well that reciprocal relations are inherently fragile. In situations such as these – where 'the most needed relationships are the ones that have the most potential to do the most harm' (ibid.: 59) – trust is never a 'natural' response to social interactions, but rather the result of a deliberate, anxiety-provoking process of deliberation and the weighing up of risk. However, it would be simplistic to read individuals' justified *anxiety* – at having to negotiate their livelihoods through so slippery a social sphere – as evidence that they are condemning their neighbours' *morality* in any straightforward way. People in Tissana find themselves navigating through an economic landscape in which they know that they have the best chance of scraping together a reasonable living if they risk tricking their rivals at sea and their *boss-man* and business partners on land – and they know that this is as true of their neighbours as it is of themselves. Faced with a reality in which, as Jacob once put it to me, 'whenever a person is poor, you know he is tricky', people make sense of these relationships in part through a long-standing aesthetic, which values concealment as an art as much as it fears it as an act of deception.

7   Material words

In this final ethnographic chapter, I return to the problem introduced at the beginning of the book, as we watched Tito give away half a million leones' worth of fish in return for the spoken blessings of 'the mammies, the girlfriends, the brothers, to *all those people who just came and begged, no more*' (my emphasis). On days when they are successful at sea, it is common for fishermen to distribute a large proportion of their precious catch among the crowds of people who gather to meet them on the shore. As we have seen, men give gifts of fish to their lovers, relatives, customers, and friends – but also to strangers with whom they have no existing relationship at all. One thread that has run throughout this book has been an exploration of the various ways in which people use material gifts as a means of strategically forging and strengthening useful social bonds. However, in fishermen's own accounts, they invariably emphasised that their reason for *wapping* (gifting fish) was *not* to nurture social ties with the specific individual they gave to, nor even to promote a positive reputation for themselves within the community as a whole. Rather, they would insist that the most powerful motivation beyond almost any material gift is to accumulate 'blessings'.

In this chapter I will argue that blessings are – as fishermen claim – a powerful mobilising force in Tissana's political economy. Notwithstanding its etymological root in Christian English, the term 'blessing' has been adopted in the Sierra Leonean context to signify a concept for which there is no direct analogue in Anglo-American English. While they appeal for their ultimate effectiveness to God or Allah, blessings actually emerge in Tissana's social fabric at a far more grounded level, in the concrete everyday interactions between two individuals. For there is only one way to accumulate them, and that is to be actively 'given' them by another person uttering aloud the words 'May God bless'. The people I knew in Tissana were consistent and absolutely explicit that these simple spoken words carry a weight far beyond mere expressions of gratitude or goodwill. As Pa Albert once put it: 'You can give that person any other thing, but the best thing you can give them is a blessing. That blessing is like a ray behind them through their life.'

As this quote begins to suggest, people discuss blessings, and circulate them, as a latently material element of the economy. Blessings generally – indeed, in my experience in Tissana, *only*– offered in response to material gifts of fish or money, and the benefit of receiving a blessing is described in equally narrow, and equally material, terms. I only ever heard blessings referred to as being desirable for their ability to bring material success, or success in this world; they are never described as bringing spiritual salvation or any similarly intangible measure of well-being. More effusive beneficiaries of fish on the wharf make this very explicit in the wording of their blessings to fishermen: 'May Allah give you twice that which you have given me', 'May the Lord give you plenty-plenty money', and so on.

As we will see below, there are some broad continuities between the ways in which my informants imbued spoken blessings with material power, and the ways in which people elsewhere in Sierra Leone and West Africa also do so. However, I want to begin by emphasising what is *peculiar*, and therefore intriguing, about Tissana's wharf-side bless-ing economy. In her fieldwork in southern Sierra Leone in the 1980s, Caroline Bledsoe (1992) was also struck by the considerable energy her informants invested in seeking to accumulate blessings. In common with my neighbours in Tissana, Bledsoe's informants expressed a strong faith in the concrete material force of these words, to 'make [a person] prosper...the major support or lever that will lift someone to better himself' (ibid.: 182). Her neighbours explained, just as mine did, that there is no way to accumulate this vital resource *except* through interper-sonal relationships: they were gifted from one individual to another, and always in return for offerings of a more tangible kind. Here, however, the ethnographic continuities end. For, in the rural economy described by Bledsoe, blessings were only ever transferred along certain, narrowly defined chains of hierarchical relations: from ancestors to high-ranking living patrons to their dependants, as a reward for long periods of loyal subordination.

The rapid, opportunistic circulation of fish and blessings across Tis-sana's wharf seems almost anarchic by comparison. As blessings do not function to naturalise existing patterns of social authority, we might won-der why it continues to make sense to people in Tissana that these spoken words are valuable as things in themselves. Where does this value come from? And what are its consequences for individuals' everyday economic survival?

This discussion fits within a long tradition in West African regional ethnography in which researchers have often recognised that their infor-mants draw no sharp categorical distinction between material and imma-terial elements of their environment (e.g. Jędrej 1976; Tonkin 2000). My contribution here is that I interrogate *how* these seemingly esoteric ques-tions of '(im)materiality' obtain relevancy in people's lives through their everyday livelihood practices, through the work they invest in economic exchange. In this respect, my project could be read as the mirror of Ferme's. Her analysis of the 'underneath of things' is concerned with 'the *material bearers of meaning* inscribed onto the rural Sierra Leonean landscape' (Ferme 2001: 14, emphasis added):

> Despite the fact that anthropologists have begun to pay attention again to questions of secrecy, their focus is still primarily on discursive domains, on historical memory, and generally at the level of consciousness. Instead, my focus here moves beyond the paradigm of consciousness toward an analysis of the material bearers of collective memory and an examination of those contested meanings. (Ferme 2001: 9)

By contrast, my own interest lies in exploring the practical consequences that arise from the fact that spoken words are often imbued with a weight and a value that have little to do with 'meaning'.

This chapter explores the genealogy and function of words as 'things' across three sections. I begin by describing the unusual characteristics of orality in Tissana, where, despite basic levels of literacy, spoken words are credited with carrying as much weight as their written form. In a town in which almost every person is tied into a complex network of small and large debts, spoken pledges circulate through Tissana's economy in such large volumes that they could meaningfully be described as the town's second currency. The second part of the chapter is concerned specifically with the exchange of spoken blessings. Following a general discussion of 'prayer economies' (Last 1988) elsewhere in the ethnographic literature, I trace the genealogy of Tissana's unusually fluid, unstructured trade in blessings. Changes in coastal society over recent decades mean that contemporary fisherfolk have little interest in working to maintain relationships with the ancestral spirits, who, elsewhere in Sierra Leone, are credited with 'underwriting' the value of blessings passed between a patron and their dependant (Bledsoe 1992).

In the final section of the chapter, I seek to understand how – despite such radical shifts in the social context within which they are offered and received – the words themselves continue to be credited with carrying substantial value. Here, I discuss how speech is woven through the very fabric of material culture in Sierra Leone. With a particular focus on 'swear medicines', the section reveals that spoken language is often credited with a material force of its own, in ways that might have little to do with communicating a message. This quality of materiality enables spoken blessings to retain a sense of weight and value, even through periods of dramatic socio-economic change. This has powerful consequences for the livelihood decisions of fishermen in the Yawri Bay and for the survival of those people who gather to meet them each day on the wharf.

An oral economy

To develop this argument, I begin by looking at the most routine ways in which people in Tissana strategically circulate spoken words in their everyday lives. As we have already begun to see in previous chapters (especially Chapter 4), in such a cash-strapped environment it is all but impossible to function as an economically active person without becoming enmeshed in a complex, constantly fluctuating web of petty loans and debts. Yet, despite the fact that most people in Tissana are able to read and write, none of this elaborate web of credit and debt is ever recorded in written form.

Such a complete disinterest in creating written contracts indicates a faith in the binding force of spoken language that academics once assumed was characteristic only of preliterate societies. Writing over 30 years ago, Malian anthropologist Hampâté Bâ (1981) set out to capture the essence of an African 'oral tradition' that was, as he saw it, on the brink of being eclipsed by invasive colonial forms of literate knowledge. In this regard, his argument was echoed by proponents of the 'literacy thesis': scholars such as Walter Ong (1991), Eric Havelock (1982) and Jack Goody (1977), all of whom agreed that writing, 'more than any other single invention' (Ong 1991: 78), transforms human consciousness and patterns of thought.

However, whereas Ong and his colleagues had viewed this transformation through the triumphalist framework of modernist intellectual progress – one that culminated, for the literate, in a 'realisation of fuller, interior, human potentials' (Ong 1991: 82; cf. Collins 1995) – Bâ's attention was focused in exactly the opposite direction. It is with the nostalgic tone of one who imagines his cherished subject vanishing rapidly from view that Bâ paints a rather idealised image of an African 'oral society' that literacy had yet to infiltrate.

Bâ's argument is partly materialist in nature. In the absence of any technology to capture words and ossify them as text – where the only words are words spoken – then, he argued, people must, by definition, have a fundamentally different relationship to speech. Without written signatures or documents, there is no frame of reference by which spoken words are made to appear transient or insubstantial in comparison. Speech is enabled to carry a far greater social burden than we now tend to allow it in fully literate societies: 'Man is bound by the word he utters. He is committed by it. He is his word and his word bears witness to what he is. The very cohesion of society depends on the value of and respect for the spoken word' (Bâ 1981: 185). Despite their ideological differences, all these scholars were united on one thing: wherever the technology of writing is introduced, it inexorably usurps the important functions that, in more 'traditional' societies, human voices were once allowed to perform. 'The deep sacred bond that used to unite man and word disappears' (ibid.: 167). Yet, such neatly predetermined teleologies have long since fallen out of fashion in anthropology, and rightly so.

Lying on the coast, Sherbros were the first of Sierra Leone's 'native' peoples[1] to come into sustained contact with Euro-Americans, and Shenge's residents are proud that their town was home to the first Western-style school outside Freetown. Finda, a visiting fish trader from Kono, was echoing a widely held stereotype when she told me: 'Well, one thing those Sherbros do have, is intelligence. They're clever-oh! They had books before any of the rest of us did.' Education still continues to be highly valorised in Tissana, and parents or foster parents often make considerable sacrifices in order to enable the young people in their households to attend school for as many years as possible.

Yet, the fact is, outside the classroom, writing has almost no visible place in everyday material culture. It is a three-hour journey to the nearest place where one might, conceivably, buy a newspaper. There is no postal service. Pens and notebooks, although widely available, belong within a clearly delimited realm of material culture, and are associated exclusively with the activities of schoolchildren. Nobody I knew even used the text message function on their mobile phone. Whatever prestige may be attached to literacy, it does not seem to alter the fact that, in virtually every practical sense, Tissana remains an oral society.

As one might imagine, this persistent orality has important repercussions for the way in which the local economy functions. For example, I once spent a day shadowing an experienced fish trader, Esta, as she collected her load of dry fish, ready to return to her market in Koidu. Upon her arrival, over a month previously, she had visited 17 of her regular customers and had decided how to *tross* (loan) her cash between them. Over the long intervening weeks, I had grown used to seeing Esta gracefully killing time on one or other of her friends' verandas while her *banda* women *kustoments* 'worked' her money, often re-*tross*ing it to their own fishermen *kustoments* as a means of securing fish on the wharf, or sometimes using the cash for other purposes, in the hope of earning it back before Esta came to collect her debts. Now, though, their time had run out.

As Esta marched cheerfully from one *banda* to the next, I was struck by the level of personal charm and mental dexterity required to do her job well. Even as my eyes adjusted to the half-light of another unfamiliar smokehouse, she would already be crouched on the earth floor beside her customer, scanning the baskets of dried fish piled around her, assessing how much each was worth, and judging whether they fitted the description of the orders she had made. Her affable demeanour belied the

---

[1] As opposed to the mixed, freed-slave/migrant population of Freetown.

seriousness of these conversations, for there was a significant amount of money at stake. In total, she had brought over six million leones (around £1,100) with her to the coast, much of which had been entrusted to her by her fellow market traders in Koidu, to procure fish on their behalf. Neither Esta nor any of her customers had made any written record of their transactions. Yet, despite the amount of time that had passed, no chink showed in her confidence in the accuracy of her memory: she knew precisely what was owed to her, and by whom.

It was the tail end of the rainy season and fishing had been slow. Not all her customers had managed to gather enough fish to fulfil the promises made all those weeks earlier. What was striking, though – when one considers how much time had passed and how desperately close to the edge of subsistence many of these *banda* women live – was that not one of Esta's customers made any attempt to fudge or deny the size of her debt. In each case, they simply negotiated a price for what fish they did have, and begged Esta to carry the shortfall over until her next visit. The example is a mundane one, but it is multiplied myriad times across Tissana's economy. As we have seen, almost everyone – whether a boat owner, trader, crewman, or *banda* woman – is similarly embedded in a personal network of customers and clients. Yet, despite the fact that most people in Tissana are able to read and write, none of this elaborate interlocking tangle of verbal contracts is ever committed to paper.

A similar pattern is replicated on much smaller scales and within shorter cycles of time. Shenge-Tissana pulses with a constant circulation of petty traders. Traders hawking everything from doughnuts to pharmaceutical drugs to second-hand fashion relentlessly circle around Tissana's houses and *bandas*. The following excerpt from my field notes describes a familiar scene on the veranda of my own home, as one of these roving traders passed through our compound:

Hoisting her heavy rubber *baff*-pan to the ground, she rattled out her weary sales pitch: 'Pepper! I've got pepper-oh! One cup. One grand.[2] One week! Four cups. Three grand. One week!' I had never met this woman before, and nobody else in our compound greeted her with any familiarity either. Yet she proceeded, without hesitation, to measure out the different quantities of chilli requested by each of the various women on the veranda. And, without asking for payment, or making any written record of the debt, she continued on her route.

The 'one week' so integral to this trader's pricing plan referred to the amount of time she would allow her customers before returning to collect their debts. By the time she had managed to distribute her entire load of chilli peppers, in various-sized lots in households up and down the wharf, she would have (what seemed to me) an extraordinary amount of information to remember. Yet the vast majority of hawkers operate in

---

[2] One thousand leones.

this way. Many thousands of similar spoken pledges are made in Tissana each week – from 1,000 leones (£0.20) for a cup of chilli peppers up to 500,000 (£100) for a load of fish. And, regardless of whether these promises are exchanged between long-established *kustoments* or mere acquaintances, not one is underscored by written records.

This is certainly not to say that business always runs as smoothly as in Esta's case above. On the contrary, disputes are extremely common. My housemate Buema made and hawked soap for a living, so I witnessed up close the frustrations inherent in a livelihood based on petty debt collection. More often than not, she returned home from yet another evening spent touring town attempting to locate the many small payments owed her, announcing:

If you say 'one week' [then for] two weeks, three weeks, they hold your money! If they don't pay me my soap money, I'll make a sober-sober palaver! I'll cuss them in the street, bitter-bitter one! And you know I know how to make a palaver!

Yet, simply because verbal contracts are not always easily fulfilled, this does nothing to detract from Bâ's broader point: that where people do not rely on the technology of writing, 'the very cohesion of society depends on the value of and respect for the spoken word' (Bâ 1981: 167). The enormous volume of verbal pledges that circulate each day through Tissana's economy is a fundamental element of livelihoods in a town in which, as my friend Ami once put it, 'If you don't have a market, you don't eat!'

Academics once took for granted that wherever the technology for writing exists, spoken words will necessarily come to be perceived as ephemeral in comparison (cf. Goody 1977; Ong 1991). Yet people in Tissana could quite easily make written records of their contracts, if they wanted to. Despite operating in an economic atmosphere of widespread half-trust, they choose not to. This persistence of people's faith in oral agreements seems to speak to an intuitive respect for the power of spoken words that the availability of writing has done little to diminish.

Given the value of orality in Tissana, it perhaps makes sense that some words have more 'substance' to them as they have come to be used, shared, and exchanged in the well-worn 'trade routes' that link people and things together. In the following section, I outline a brief genealogy of blessing exchange in Tissana, tracing how these valuable words have come to be traded in quite different ways in the commercial fishing economy than would have been the case in subsistence farming villages.

Blessing economies

The exchange of spiritual blessings for tangible forms of material wealth is, in fact, a fairly well-documented phenomenon, and one that appears in religious traditions well beyond West Africa, across the broader Christian and Islamic worlds. A common thread linking analyses of blessing economies in all these various contexts is that they are presented as explicitly hierarchical systems: blessings are distributed in patterns that both mirror and reinforce broader structures of socio-political power. From West Africa (Last 1988; Soares 2005) to South Asia (Ewing 1983; Werbner 1998), ethnographers working in explicitly religious contexts have repeatedly described a pattern by which Islamic blessings are distributed 'downward' through networks of religious patronage. In each of these examples, high-ranking individuals considered to have privileged access to God are uniquely empowered to bestow blessings, and do so only in exchange for offerings of material tribute from their disciples.

In rural Pakistan in the 1980s, for example, Katherine Ewing describes people adhering to a cosmological order in which God's blessing is assumed essential for physical health, material well-being, and spiritual salvation. Yet God himself is imagined as such a remote, all-powerful leader that he is wholly inaccessible to ordinary men and women. Only a tiny minority of privileged individuals, living saints who trace their ancestry to Mohammed, are capable of receiving or communicating God's blessing:

[The saints'] authority is symbolised by spiritual blessing, which has flowed from God to his Prophet Muhammed and then eastward with the saints. Others can come into contact with this blessing and benefit from it, but they cannot transmit it, because blessing cannot flow through their impure or undeveloped souls. (Ewing 1983: 256)

Ordinary people must therefore maintain a face-to-face relationship with their saint, who gives them blessings in return for material offerings of tribute. The blessings themselves may be communicated in a whole range of material or immaterial forms, from recited Qur'anic verses to complex written amulets. In all cases, however, what is most strongly emphasised is that only the saint's unique expertise and spiritual charisma render these blessings effective (Ewing 1984).

Benjamin Soares' study of religious leaders in Mali reveals how a similarly hierarchical economy of blessings was adapted to meet the new social and political conditions of the postcolonial state. Just as in rural Pakistan, it had long been the case that Malian individuals sought access to spiritual development, as well as the rewards of 'wealth, power, social prestige, progeny and good health' in this world (Soares 1996: 744), by cultivating personal relationships with living saints. The exchange of gifts for prayers had long been one of the most salient features of the saint–follower relationship. However, Soares explores how, in the 1980s and 1990s, 'visits to the religious leaders [had] increasingly come to resemble a market-place, in that contact with them [had] come to be

mediated on an unprecedented scale by both commodities and money'
(Soares 2005: 170). The most famous Malian saints had accumulated
extravagant material riches through this increasingly commodified form
of blessing exchange by learning to reserve their most 'powerful' forms
of prayer for their most lavishly generous supplicants, 'so that the elites
might obtain what they desire' (ibid.: 173–4).

Despite the obvious differences between them, one of the most salient
characteristics linking these two examples is that blessings always move
in the same direction: from elevated individuals who are considered
somehow closer to God than ordinary people, towards their followers
who give material gifts of tribute in return, 'as a mark of respect or
in gratitude for a blessing bestowed' (Werbner 1998: 104). The same,
intuitively logical, 'downward' flow of blessings also underpins Murray
Last's (1988) account of Nigeria's 'prayer economy', and enables Maurice Bloch (1986) to understand spiritual blessing as a powerful political
force in Madagascar.

The most detailed existing descriptions of blessing exchange in Sierra
Leone can be found in Caroline Bledsoe's (1992) account of her fieldwork in Mende-speaking parts of the country in the 1980s. Her account
suggests that blessing exchange in this region has historically been characterised by a similar pattern of self-evident hierarchy. While she never
suggests that it would be possible to accumulate lavish material wealth in
exchange for blessings, blessing exchange does appear to have been one
means by which those in positions of relative power were able to further
entrench their claims to gerontocratic authority. In Bledsoe's account,
she consistently describes blessings as 'ancestral blessings', and (rather
as Ewing describes in rural Pakistan) maintains that the effectiveness of
these prayers depends upon a message being communicated up through
a string of relationships between visible and invisible sentient beings:

Because God does not want to face a barrage of individual supplicants of
unproven merit, he requires requests to come through the proper authority
channels. Standing between God and a living supplicant, therefore, is a long,
hierarchical chain of mediating ancestors – living as well as dead – through whom
God confers blessings on families and the young. (Bledsoe 1992: 191)

Carol MacCormack made a similar claim with reference to the Sherbro
coastal region, that 'ancestors are the ultimate source of blessings' (1986:
117). According to this vision of the social and cosmological order, spoken blessings carry meaningful power only when they are communicated
within certain kinds of social relationship. 'For both Muslim and Christian Mende,' Bledsoe tells us, 'elders bless younger kin, parents bless
children, uncles bless nephews, masters bless apprentices, teachers bless
students, etc.' (1992: 191). Such patterns of blessing exchange map
neatly onto a broader political economy of wealth in people, in which

securing the loyalty of a large pool of dependants is the most important measure of a person's wealth and power (d'Azevedo 1962a; Guyer 1995). In order to earn the blessings that will determine their chances of future success, 'subordinates' took care to 'display gratitude to their benefactors through labour, remittances, and unquestioning loyalty' (Bledsoe 1992: 191–2).

In my own fieldwork, I occasionally heard accounts of blessings being mobilised in this way, particularly as the means by which traditional teachers were able to demand long-term loyalty from their apprentices. For example, Jacob's stepson, Sheku, who was born in a farming village near Tissana, had been apprenticed to a Qur'anic teacher for approaching a decade. Throughout this ten-year training, Sheku had lived with his teacher and worked on the older man's farm. Now that Sheku had completed his Arabic studies, Jacob was worried that his teacher might choose to hold his young apprentice hostage, with the simple threat of withholding blessing:

Jacob: That teacher has ten or 15 students. And those boys are working hard for him! They clear his farmland, they lay his farm . . . Now Sheku has finished his studies, but we will have to pay a lot of money to release him . . . To release him, we have to pay two bags of rice, one goat, one sheep . . . Ah, it is a lot of money! You see that? He's a rich man, that teacher . . .

Me: What will happen if you don't pay?

Jacob: Sheku will just have to stay there and work [on his teacher's farm]. Unless he just leaves. He could just leave. But if he does that [without paying], his teacher will never bless him. And without that blessing he will never prosper.

So, just inland from Tissana, a patron–client economy of blessings continues to operate very similarly to the one described by Bledsoe and MacCormack in the 1980s, and continues to be mobilised in ways that directly reinforce more visible ties of dependency and subordination. For most people on the coast, this economy of patronage and dependence is extremely familiar: if they did not migrate to the coast themselves in adulthood, the vast majority of Tissana's fisherfolk are the children or grandchildren of people who grew up in farming communities similar to the one where Sheku lives. One thing that is evident in Jacob's description of his stepson's predicament is that he fully understands and respects the coercive power of spoken blessings, when used in this way, to police 'traditional' expectations of filial loyalty from a young dependant to his patron.

Within Tissana itself, however, blessings circulate through the economy in an entirely different way. It remains the case in the commercial fishing economy, as in more 'traditional' economic settings, that blessings are held to be extremely powerful: a person's relative ability to accumulate them is assumed to account for much of the difference between a successful and an unsuccessful life. Yet, in all my observations of spoken blessings being exchanged in Tissana – and they were, as already mentioned, spoken as a common daily occurrence on the wharf – these encounters barely ever took place between a patron and his or her dependant. Nor did I ever hear anyone refer, in any way whatever, to the mediating role of ancestors in rendering these spoken words meaningful and powerful. Indeed, while neighbours, and perhaps even kin, might bless one another on occasion, these exchanges were understood to be most important – *and most potent* – when they took place between two individuals who had no prior relationship at all.

If asked to describe the ideal model of blessing exchange, fisherfolk would describe showing material generosity to a stranger and receiving a blessing in return. In the following monologue, a visiting town chief was mediating a disagreement between two of the residents in my compound: Aminata and her teenage daughter, Ima. Notice how he mobilises the promise of future blessing in order to convince the teenager that she ought to be more obedient to her mother:

'Look,' he said, pointing to me. 'We have our stranger sitting here. I, too, am a stranger . . . If you're not used to warming water for your mother, how will you know to do it for a stranger? If you're not used to sweeping for your mother, how will you know to do it for a stranger? There are some children: the moment a stranger arrives in the house, they will know to ask, "Do you want hot water or cold [to wash with]?" It doesn't matter if you're as beautiful as heaven, if you don't have blessings you'll never go anywhere in life.'

Pa Stevens' advice to Ima reveals an important transformation in the way in which people understand the value and the power of blessings. Bledsoe described 'ancestral blessing' as a gift that, by its very nature, is handed down from the ancestral realm, via living elders, to their children in exchange for filial loyalty. Yet, in the coastal economy, local models of blessing have evolved in such a way that Pa Stevens had to draft in another character – 'the visiting stranger' – in order to convince Ima that she had a hope of accumulating blessings through good behaviour at home.

The fact that Tissana's residents should have stopped considering ancestral spirits to be 'the ultimate source of blessings' (MacCormack 1986: 117) raises two interconnected questions. Firstly, what has changed in the social fabric of coastal economies to undermine people's faith in the power of their ancestors? Secondly, and rather more problematically, why do people continue to value spoken blessings, and to seek to accumulate them, when the ancestors who previously underwrote their value have essentially faded from the social landscape? I address these two questions in turn in the final two sections of this chapter.

Where have all the ancestors gone?

In 1971, few would have questioned Igor Kopytoff's assertion that 'ancestor cults and ancestor worship loom large in the anthropological image of sub-Saharan Africa' (1971: 129). Yet, 30 years on, Cole and Middleton were noting the 'strange absence' of ancestor-related practices in discussions of religion and ritual on the continent (2001: 1). There have been various attempts to theorise this apparently widespread shift in the centre of gravity of spiritual life. Fields (1985), for example, argued that people lost trust in their ancestors when they failed to protect them against the violence of colonialism; and that the institution was further devalued by elders' willingness to collude with colonial regimes. In Ghana, Meyer (1999) suggested that, in the wake of the profound socio-economic changes brought about by colonialism, ancestors simply lost their cultural relevance. The pattern is not consistent, however. In at least some parts of the continent, people continue to inhabit 'a landscape densely populated by ancestral presence' (Cole and Middleton 2001: 1), leading some to suggest that it is *anthropologists*, rather than the people they study, who have lost interest in ancestors (McCall 1995).

In Chapter 6, I discussed the immediacy of the 'underworld' in people's everyday experience: unseen, yet powerfully felt just beyond the visible surfaces of landscape and seascape around Tissana. In everyday conversation, my neighbours were interested in this hidden space primarily because it was inhabited by morally ambivalent and potentially dangerous spirits (*min* in Sherbro or 'devils' in Krio) and the 'witches' whose defining characteristic was the ability to transmogrify between human, animal, and spirit form.[3]

Far more rarely, some of my oldest informants would tell me that the town's ancestors dwelled similarly close at hand, moving through a terrain only slightly removed from the farms and homes of their living relatives. This compression of genealogical history into the contemporary landscape is a familiar theme in the ethnographic literature on this region. Some of the most interesting ethnography in recent decades has explored the ways in which people inhabit a landscape still seething with material and immaterial traces of the past (Ferme 2001; Shaw 2002; Argenti 2007).

In agrarian villages across the Upper Guinea region, genealogical history is usually traced back to a single putative ancestor figure: the person credited with founding that community and first laying claim to its land. In this context, knowledge of local genealogical history may have powerful political consequences. The more convincingly an individual is able

---

[3] The terms *min* and devil describe a far more varied cast of spiritual beings: from harmless masked dancers to the invisible but terrifying Poro devil (see Jędrej 1974).

to claim direct descent from the town's founder, the more likely they are to be recognised as a holder of the land, and to achieve the status of a wealthy patron (Sarró 2010; d'Azevedo 1962b). This expectation – that the only history worth attending to is the kind embedded in the immediate landscape – is illustrated vividly here in Mariane Ferme's description of a Mende forest landscape in the 1980s:

> A casual walk through forest paths can take one by several [grave] sites, and if someone in the company has specific knowledge of them, the conversation often turns to the ruin's history... As the Mende proverb puts it, 'A stranger recognises a new grave, but does not know who lies in it.' The crucial knowledge of the underneath of things is not limited to the surface recognition of a grave site but, rather, reaches down into the deeper history of those who are under the surface and into how they got there. (Ferme 2001: 26)

In Ferme's description of this agrarian topography, the presence of human remains in the ground seems to stand as a testament to the indivisibility of land and history, and to the fact that certain people, with privileged knowledge, have the right to lay claim to both.

In many classic ethnographic accounts, ancestors are described as having been integral to a lineage system in which kin groups comprised dead as well as living members. Writing in 1986, Carol MacCormack described how, at that time, the people who inhabited the area around the Sherbro Coast based their social organisation on descent from named ancestors and ancestresses. 'Ancestors, the living, and those not yet born constitute a great chain of being': a 'continuum of existence' that was punctuated, but not severed, by birth and death (MacCormack 1986: 117). According to this image of the cosmological order, it was important to engage directly with ancestors, and to respect them as active participants in everyday material life. Ancestors who in life had been important lineage elders retained real power and authority over surviving kin, who attempted to win their benevolence through gifts – usually of food and alcohol. Some of the people whom I knew in Tissana continued to take these obligations seriously. For example, Pa Albert (who was over 80 years old) always kept a pan of rice aside:

> For the person who may come in the night, looking for a place to sleep... They won't talk to you. You won't even see them... any day, any day, the dead may pass. If they come, and they see that there is nothing there to eat, they will just leave in disgust.

Kopytoff suggested redefining 'ancestors' as 'dead elders' in order to highlight the extent to which these seemingly otherworldly figures were in fact embedded within, and integral to, the familiar micro-politics of extended family life:

It is striking that African 'ancestors' are more mundane and less mystical than the dead who are objects of 'worship' should be in Western eyes. African elders, on the other hand, look more mystical to us than we are willing to allow the living to be. Similarly, Africans treat their living elders more 'worshipfully' than the English term 'respect' conveys, and they treat the ancestors with less 'respect' and more contentiousness than the term 'worship' should allow. (Kopytoff 1971: 140)

This suggests that, if we are to understand the diminishing relevance of ancestors in social life, we need to consider how broader patterns of kinship are shifting and evolving. In some contexts, ancestor-related practices are a fertile space in which different members of a community may compete to establish alternative visions of history, kinship, and the spirit world, and their continued importance in everyday material life. Inconsistencies and tensions within these practices can shed light on 'how connections between the living and the dead, the present and the past, and youths and elders are not only forged but also disputed' (Rasmussen 2000: 16). In Sherbro farming villages, there are certain key points in the agricultural calendar when the relationship is made especially explicit between the contemporary population and the community's ancestors, who continue, in some senses, to reside alongside them. Village ancestors must be begged permission, for example, whenever a fresh farm is cleared, or a new crop planted. This annual cycle of rituals serves to reinforce a powerful expectation that belonging in a place – and being able to prosper there – depends upon being able to claim historical 'roots' in the land (Sarró 2010; d'Azevedo 1962b; Knörr and Filho 2010).

However, as we have seen in Chapters 3 and 5, old patterns of land-based dependency between 'landlords and strangers' (Dorjahn and Fyfe 1962) have been replaced in the maritime context with newly fluid means of claiming social belonging – and social power. Elderly residents, who had lived in Tissana since the town was a subsistence village, could remember a time when the whole community used to come together to publicly honour their ancestors. However, such events are, as Mi Yoki describes here, increasingly rare:

First time, when I was young, we used to leave food in this deep forest here, for the ancestors, pour libation . . . We'd make gladdy-gladdy [celebrate], we'd dance until dawn. But now, they don't do it anymore . . . They say they are Muslim, they refuse to do it. Things are changing now, for many, many reasons.

At a national level, there is some evidence that broader changes in the religious landscape may be acting to exacerbate lines of tension between Christianity, Islam, and indigenous religious practices. A central feature of the rapid expansion of Pentecostal Christianity across Africa, for example, has been a move to vilify 'traditional' forms of spirituality, redefining local spirits as demonic forces, and undermining trust in traditional healers by labelling them 'witch doctors'. In an era of deepening social and economic insecurity, the Pentecostal 'gospel of prosperity' has won adherents with its seductive promise of a spiritual route to material well-being (Meyer 2004; Pfeiffer, Gimbel-Sherr, and Augusto 2007; Shaw 2007); part of the appeal of the movement is that it promises access to globalising modernity, through a theology that rejects 'traditions' as not just 'backward' but dangerous (Meyer 1995).[4] While Pentecostal Christianity is far from being a dominant religious force in Tissana, my informants were certainly aware of the emergence of new, more hardline Christian voices. One of my most trusted informants, Pa Yanker, a respected elder within both the Methodist church and the Poro society, often expressed his unease and regret at these changes, which were perceived as filtering into Kagboro from Freetown: 'The churches are so many now. And they preach against everything! Preach against societies, preach against everything!'

In a parallel development, the increased presence of externally educated Muslim clerics in urban areas has contributed to the gradual emergence of more purist tendencies within Sierra Leonean Islam (O'Brien and Rashid 2013: 176). This forms part of a broader regional trend, in which many parts of West Africa are going through a period of Islamic renewal, when 'what was a once self-evident Muslim identity must now be continually redefined in terms of "correct" practices set in opposition to "improper" ones' (Masquelier 2008: 42).[5]

For the time being, most people in Tissana remain fairly sanguine about their religious 'identity', and that of their neighbours. However, as stricter interpretations of both Christianity and Islam filter into everyday discourse in places such as Tissana, many people are feeling increasingly uneasy about their own syncretic religious practices.

Like Pa Brima there: he was head of his [Poro] society in Ndema, you know? And what do you see him doing now? Just praying, praying, praying all the time; asking his god for forgiveness. A lot of these men now, when the Poro devil passes, they don't even go outside. But the Bundu women are not so prepared to change their ways. (Jacob, Sherbro elder)

---

[4] As Meyer has noted, this 'demonization by no means implies that the former gods and spirits will disappear out of people's lives. As servants of Satan they are still regarded as real powers that have to be dealt with in a concrete way' (Meyer 1999). This observation has led her to suggest a direct connection between the growing popularity of Pentecostalism and the widely described spike in anxieties about witchcraft and the occult.

[5] In Niger, for example, Adeline Masquelier (2008) described the anxiety her informants felt in response to reported sightings of a 'veiled she-devil'. At a moment when Nigerien Islam is becoming increasingly exclusive to other forms of religious belief, the veiled spirit seemed to prompt such particular unease because she forced people to acknowledge the 'porousness of categorical boundaries' (ibid.: 43).

Although Islam and Christianity have both been practised in Sierra Leone for centuries, I often heard people claim that in recent years religious practice has become less tolerant of syncretism with so-called 'native ways' – including paying respect to the ancestors. There are also powerful socio-economic reasons why Tissana's contemporary residents have allowed the town's ancestors to fade from view as powerful actors in the local social scene.

In contrast to farming economies inland, there is no longer any particular stigma attached to being a 'stranger'. It is not that anyone questions the fact that the oldest 'aristocratic' lineages are the sole rightful holders of the land around Shenge,[6] but, in an increasingly ocean-facing economy, these ancestral claims bring very little in the way of actual socio-economic privilege. Here, the best hope of achieving material security and prosperity has depended, for several generations now, not on land rights but rather on boat ownership. We have seen throughout this book that the Sierra Leonean stereotype of modern fisherfolk is that they are always half-ready to up-anchor and set sail for a new wharf town. As a town of migrants, almost everyone's ancestors lived and died somewhere else. As if in recognition of the new disconnect between ancestral history, identity, and place, the largest single grave site on the Kagboro coastline is filled not with the bodies of important ancestors but with those of unknown, unnamed strangers. Here, Buema recalls the aftermath of one particularly horrifying boat disaster some 15 years ago:

There were so many bodies. The people who went out in their boats to get them, they just heaved them out of the water, like sharks – whomp, whomp, whomp. They're all buried at the wharf in Shenge. When you die at sea, the wharf is your grave... They put them two by two in the graves. When you stand on Shenge Wharf, from the jetty all the way until you meet those rocks, it's all one grave. They came from all over – Bo, Kenema, Kono, Plantain: all over. They came here to work. They were traders. When they pulled their bodies from the water, it was only their clothes you would recognise them by.

If, as Tuan has argued, '[r]ootedness in the soil and the growth of pious feeling toward it seem natural to sedentary agricultural peoples' (1977: 156), then in Tissana what we appear to be observing is the 'naturalness' of this relationship unravelling. While it is no doubt true that, as he put it, 'places become special... whenever the people believe it to be not only their home, but also the home of their guarding spirits and gods' (ibid.: 150), one could just as well state the relationship the other way around: that places become home to guarding spirits when people believe them to

[6] Indeed, I was told of one dispute, several years before my arrival, when an elderly Mende man had attempted to claim ownership of the land his family had been farming for decades. Always the story was repeated with the same incredulous punchline: 'But he was a Mende! Came, his people came to this place! How could he own the land?'

be special. Nowadays, Tissana's population is so unashamedly fluid, and its economy so squarely oriented to the ocean, that ancestral rootedness in the land has a diminishing relevance in people's lives.

Yet, as Buema's story about the boat disaster reminds us, there are very real dangers associated with adopting an itinerant livelihood in a country where the transport system and emergency services are as impoverished as Sierra Leone's. The events Buema described are tragically unexceptional. Within recent living memory, there have been several similarly catastrophic boat disasters in the waters around Shenge. The mass grave beneath the town's wharf is unmarked and rarely mentioned, but there is no one in Shenge who does not know, as they walk across the beach to travel aboard a *pampa* (passenger canoe), that beneath their feet lie the bodies of hundreds of unnamed travellers who lost their lives on similar journeys. The reasons fisherfolk cite for needing to accumulate blessings reflect the new anxieties of their highly unsettled lives. Quite aside from the dangers associated with sea travel itself, itinerant fisherfolk are justifiably nervous of falling into any kind of difficulty while in an unfamiliar town, far beyond the reach of their friends and kin. As one trader recounted to me:

When I first started coming to buy fish here in Kagboro [Chiefdom], I couldn't sleep at night I was so afraid . . . Because, you know, if a trader disappears, nobody would even notice! They'd say, 'Maybe she's gone to Shenge', 'Maybe she's gone to Plantain.' They wouldn't know I'd disappeared. Because they don't know me. They don't know my people. (Esta, trader)

For people whose lifestyle routinely takes them beyond what is familiar and safe, beyond the reassuring presence of a strong network of kin and long-term neighbours, the protective, generative potential of blessings takes on an added salience.

People in Tissana are not averse to reminding their neighbours of the importance of accumulating blessings as a means of encouraging others to be generous with their material resources. To draw an example from my own experience, it was generally assumed among my neighbours in Tissana that, as a white person, I must be lavishly wealthy. I had difficulty figuring out how to morally navigate the onslaught of requests that were made of me each week, so Buema, as my closest friend in the town, often took it upon herself to try to protect me from these demands. It was not a role that won her many admirers. On one occasion, Aminata came to my room to offer some furtive advice: 'Don't listen to Buema, if she tells you not to [be generous to] people. Do you hear?' She glanced around to make sure that Buema was not within earshot, before leaning a little closer to warn me in an urgent stage whisper: 'You have come far! You are here, far away from your home and your family. Let you get home safe and with well body. Every time you give to a person, they must say, "Thank you, Jenny. May God bless.'"

Of course, I was far from being the only person in town who was 'far away from my home and my family'. Many of the men I saw each day, landing fish on Tissana's wharf, were relative strangers in town and surrounded by people they barely knew. In the restlessly fluid maritime economy, many others knew that they would shortly move on again, leaving behind the hard-won networks of 'potato rope' kin that offered their only real source of material security. In this quote, for example, David makes it very clear that his key motivation for trading fish for blessings on the wharf is his knowledge that, as an *alehning* (migrating) fisherman, he will soon be a stranger himself, and in particular need of the good fortune and protection that blessings are known to bring:

The reason I give people fish is that . . . there are some goodnesses that you do – as long as you're here, in your own home town, you'll never receive any payment. But when you go out [far away from home] – at that time, just when you don't expect it at all, somebody will give you something, and say: 'Take this. You use it.' It's a blessing. Like, if I were to give you fish now, you'd say, 'Ah, may God bless; may the Lord make your business prosper!' Allah will take your voice faster!

As we have seen, the busy, multidirectional circulation of spiritual blessings through Tissana's wharf-side economy stands in contrast to the model of the 'prayer economy' more familiar in the ethnographic record, whereby blessings pass along a certain kind of narrowly defined route, from a spiritually elevated patron to his or her subordinate. The fact that Tissana's fisherfolk have moved so decisively away from this model reflects a broader set of transformations in the coastal economy, as social hierarchies based on ancestry and land ownership have been replaced by increasingly complex, fragile, shifting webs of 'potato rope' kinship.

However, these changes also raise an analytical problem: how is it possible that spoken blessings continue to hold value in Tissana's economy in the absence of the ancestor spirits and clear social hierarchies that, until recently, provided the formal explanation for their power? There are intriguing parallels here with the history of money in the global economy. There were many who feared that the removal of the dollar from the gold standard would cause the implosion of the American economy. And yet, despite such a radical shift in the context within which they were being offered and received, people continued to take it for granted that banknotes were capable of conveying economic value:

Whether we look to the emergence of modern stock markets in northwestern Europe in the seventeenth century, or to postbellum greenbacks, or to the closing of the gold window in 1971 and the breakdown of the Bretton Woods agreements that lent an aura of stability to money through the middle of the twentieth century, we find similar debates about the relationship between 'real' economic value and 'insubstantial' fictions of fiat currencies and finance and a concern about the effects of the transition from 'true' money to the promissory kind on the fabric of society itself. (Maurer 2006: 29)

Even if the value of money is, as Bill Maurer puts it, 'a fantastical endeavor' (2006: 16), this does nothing to detract from the powerful – indeed, *world-shaping* – reality of that material value.

As I discuss in the following section, with a particular focus on 'medicines', spoken words are woven through the very fabric of material culture in Sierra Leone, and often in ways that have little to do with communicating a message. By contemplating the substance of words within material culture more broadly, my argument is that spoken blessings can be understood as valuable *things* in their own right, rather than only as a message or a promise conveyed between ancestral spirits and living persons. This echoes other ethnography from the Upper Guinea region (Jędrej 1976), and suggests a limit to the argument made by Stanley Tambiah that, in contexts where people appear to behave as though certain spoken words carry an inherent 'magical' force, such language is nonetheless better understood as deriving power by virtue of its 'capacity to communicate with [sentient spiritual beings] and thereby influence their actions' (Tambiah 1968: 178).[7] It is this very materiality without recourse to ancestral force that has made it possible for blessings to retain their exchange value as they circulate from one economic context to another.

Words and the substance of medicine

'Medicines' play a conspicuous role in the socio-political lives of all Sierra Leone's major language groups (Jędrej 1976). Referred to in Sherbro as *ifohn*, and in Tissanan Krio as 'fetish medicines', this category encompasses an array of objects and substances that is hugely heterogeneous in material form and practical function. Some medicines appear as bulky objects, wrapped in bundles of cloth or string; others are worn as amulets, consumed as liquids or powders, or rubbed as a lotion on skin. As their Krio name suggests, some *ifohn* may be used to cure illnesses,[8] but they are also deployed to influence people's bodies in a whole range of more

---

[7] Describing the seemingly nonsensical 'demon language' used in Sinhalese exorcism rituals, for example, Tambiah argued that, although the words spoken were 'largely unintelligible' to the exorcist and his audience alike, they were 'nevertheless based on a theory of language the demons can understand … the spells have power by virtue of secrecy and their capacity to communicate with demons and thereby influence their actions' (Tambiah 1968: 178).

[8] Pharmaceutical drugs are described as *ifohn*, along with more esoteric and carefully guarded forms of medicinal substance.

covert and potentially ambivalent ways: to poison, seduce, or otherwise disempower their subject. We have already seen throughout this book that fishermen and *banda* women routinely deploy 'fetish' technologies as part of their mundane economic strategies: to protect their property against thieves; to increase their chances of catching fish; and, in particular, to attempt to influence their relationships with the people with whom they do business.

The one characteristic linking this seemingly eclectic array of substances is that all are 'impregnated with supernatural force' (Little 1967 [1951]: 227). What interests me in the context of this chapter's discussion is that in many cases this 'supernatural force' becomes animated only when spoken words are uttered into the material substance of the *ifohn*. A focus on medicines therefore reveals how often spoken words are mobilised in Tissana as 'illocutionary acts': that is, speech acts that are unconcerned with communicating 'meaning', but rather that are intended to bring about a direct material effect in the world (cf. Lambek 1990). Similar technologies for empowering inanimate objects by infusing them with spoken recitations recur in many parts of the Islamic world (Ewing 1983; Skinner 1978), as well as elsewhere in tropical Africa (MacGaffey 1988), and provide a neat microcosm for imagining how words and objects might shade into one another, in a context in which 'matter' is obliged to be neither passive nor silent. This is not an entirely radical insight.

Ethnographers have often pointed to *ifohn* as evidence that, in the Upper Guinea region, no clear distinction can be drawn between discursive forms of knowledge and the concrete world of things (e.g. Bellman 1975; Tonkin 2000). However, existing discussions of immaterial forces tend to focus on a rather narrowly defined range of overtly 'ritual' behaviours, and such forces tend to be explored within a broader frame of interest in the political power of secrecy. As Murphy puts it, *ifohn* 'designate the most fearful secret forces in the [Sierra Leonean] cosmology of power' (1998: 567). It is an *ifohn*, for example, that sits at the heart of every initiation sodality and which, ultimately, is said to complete the conversion of children into gendered adults (Jędrej 1976); ethnographers have been interested in understanding how the aura of secrecy surrounding these substances works to legitimise the considerable power wielded by society elders (Bledsoe 1984; Murphy 1980). Anthropologists have also been intrigued by the popular discourses that describe powerful 'big persons' deriving their charisma from the secret use of 'bad medicines' (*ifohn wei*): substances acquired by violent means at the ruthless expense of more vulnerable people (Shaw 1996; Richards 1996).

This emphasis on the relatively high-level (and/or sinister) political uses of *ifohn* tends to detract attention from fact that medicines exist in myriad forms, most of which are rather banal. Mariane Ferme's (2001) ethnography marked an important step towards considering the presence of unseen forces behind the visible surfaces of 'everyday' material things, but her focus on the high levels of specialist skill required to decipher clues scatted through the material landscape also reinforced the impression that a practical knowledge of immaterial forces is the preserve of a small minority of people. By considering the material exchange value of spoken blessings, our attention is drawn to the fact that *all* fisherfolk seek to harness and capitalise upon immaterial forces as part of the routine work of managing their fragile livelihoods. In keeping with this broader goal, I turn now to consider one particularly common form of *ifohn*: swear medicines. In the following section, I discuss how words addressed to these medicines have real material consequences for the workings of economic life in Tissana.

Swear medicines

In Tissana, strategies for preventing theft are a common matter of concern. As we have seen in Chapter 6, levels of economic mistrust are high here, and not without good reason. The physical contours of the coastal landscape are such that lovers, neighbours, and business partners are constantly moving in and out of view. So, in an unpredictable, threadbare economy, people are highly conscious of their constant vulnerability to theft and fraud. If a person has been cheated or stolen from, there are two accepted courses of action available. If he or she believes that they know who was responsible for the crime, they may summon that suspect directly to court. However, those people who have weathered the chieftaincy court system typically warn that it is a time-consuming, expensive, and ultimately frustrating process. A far more common strategy is to threaten to 'swear' upon an *ifohn ranka* ('swear medicine') that will 'catch' and usually kill the culprit if they fail to confess in time.

As with all *ifohn*, swear medicines are privately owned and will only be effective if used with the formally expressed permission of the medicine's owner, permission that is generally paid for in cash (Jędrej 1976). In extreme cases (a very major theft, for example), swearing can become an involved and highly public process. If the victim of a crime can afford the time and considerable expense, he or she might choose to apply to the Chieftaincy Office in Shenge and obtain an official 'swear licence', giving authorisation to employ the services of a recognised medicine owner. In a handful of famous cases, individuals from Tissana have even been known to travel to the other end of Sierra Leone to seek out a particular ritual specialist, known for possessing a powerful medicine on which they swear.

Ifohn ranka come in a variety of forms. How, exactly, the swearing itself is enacted – and how its repercussions are felt – vary dramatically from one case to another. In 'official' cases, when authority has been sought from the elders of Kagboro Chiefdom, swearing becomes a very high-profile public performance. In the days leading up to the moment when the curse is finally spoken, the town crier walks the streets, raising an 'alarm' and giving the thief one final opportunity to confess and escape the full weight of their punishment.

Or, at least, this is what I was told. For, in fact, such official cases are extremely rare and none took place during the time I was in Tissana. A far more affordable option is to pay a local medicine owner for the use of their *ifohn* and then carry out one's own swearing in a private, pared-down fashion. It is in this more common use of swear medicines, stripped of the extra legitimisation of bureaucracy, that we see that the fundamental weight of the medicine lies in the spoken words themselves:

Here, it is enough just to talk it: to say, 'This person stole from me,' or whatever. Sometimes, people will even go outside at night, naked, and talk it; say it aloud. If it is true, if it is a straight case, you will see, very quickly, something will happen to [the thief] . . . Very often, when someone's children are dying it is because they have a swear on them. But, as soon as they confess, you will see their children will start to live again. (Pa Albert, elder)

This act of speech has powerful consequences and is not to be treated lightly. Indeed, the power of swear medicines is so widely accepted that, in any case of serious misfortune, there will almost always be speculation that it must be the result of an old curse. I saw this discourse being played out under tragic circumstances when my young neighbour Sina lost her third and last remaining child:

You see Sina now? You hear – even her mother said it – it is an old swear that has caught her. It was Mary Sese. At that time we were all in this house together. Sina stole something from Mary – I can't remember what it was. At that time, she wasn't married yet, she hadn't borne children yet. When you hear people say, 'Swears don't catch', well, no, they don't catch *now* . . . When you have married, when your children all die, that is when you see the swear. It is only now we're seeing that swear catch Sina. And they say Mary is in . . . Funkea! You see? Who is going to go all the way there to find her [to cancel the swear]? (Fatti, petty trader)

The memory was still fresh in my friends' minds of the time, a couple of years before my arrival, when a trader visiting the neighbouring town of Bendu had had all his money stolen. Having done all he could to investigate the theft in person, he eventually returned to his home near Waterloo, where – it was widely agreed – he must have sworn on a medicine known as '*ifohn lamp'eh*':

What else could he do? It was his father's money . . . So, he went back home and he put a swear on that money. They say three people have died from that swear so far! For a whole year, Bendu was burning. They'd put out one fire – look! Another fire had started in the next *banda*. That was a powerful swear. (Kumba, fisherman)

Ifohn lamp'eh catches its subjects 'by fire'. But, according to common interpretation, the unusual virility of that particular medicine was a result of the words the young man must have used when he addressed the *ifohn*. The curse was worded to target not only the person directly responsible for the theft, but also anyone who sheltered him; those people, once infected by the curse, became similarly contagious themselves and could inadvertently pass it on to anyone who helped them:

So it was just spreading, like that. It happened: one person went to Plantain Island and, after two or three days, there was a fire there, too! So people became afraid, even to shelter someone. It gave people who came from this area a bad reputation – even as far as Tombo! Even as far as Waterloo! That lasted for some months! People would forget, forget, and then it would catch again! Until the person finally confessed [to the theft]. And then it stopped. (Pa Sufyan, elder)

So, while swearing on *ifohn ranka* is recognised as a legitimate form of justice, the young man's particular choice of wording was criticised as a reckless mishandling of the medicine's power.

Although such curses were the subject of daily animated discussion, and would inevitably be threatened at the climax of all the most heated arguments, my own experience was that people threatened to use swear medicines with far more enthusiasm than they actually enacted them. One day, for example, Buema was enraged to discover that 10,000 leones had been stolen from her purse. The culprit must have been someone in our house – of that she was certain. With a stamina that never failed to astound me, she stood on our veranda for two hours straight, 'talking fire' at a volume that would have been audible several compounds away. Finally, she announced that she was going to swear on that stolen money. If there could be any doubt about how serious such a move would be, she repeated again and again, in her majestic full-lunged bellow: 'Let them eat my money with their life! If they return it, even if they throw it under my door, no problem! But if they eat my money . . . they will never steal again, except in the grave!'

The next morning, the money had not been returned. Buema went to meet a local medicine owner and paid her 4,000 leones to prepare a swear medicine. She then set about gathering the various material ingredients that were needed to activate this particular medicine: fish, a pawpaw, and a miniature cooking pot borrowed from one of her neighbours. At each point, she conspicuously announced the progress she was making. Yet, when I asked Jacob about it, he replied wearily:

She's not going to swear. I won't let her. She's just trying to scare the person so that they return the money. This is what happened with Alimatu last year. Someone stole her money and, when she said she was going to swear, she found the money on top of her bag... But, even if they don't repay Buema, I won't let her do it. Swearing is dangerous! Sometimes it catches the person who you don't expect. Or maybe the person who took that money cooked food and gave it to you – you don't know. And then you say you want to catch 'the person who ate my money'. Sometimes it catches the person who you don't expect.

Buema's money never was returned, but nor did she ever employ that swear medicine. As this example demonstrates, people are so wary of the volatile powers unleashed by the words of a curse that most are reticent about actually using them. Yet this does nothing to diminish their concrete relevance to people's economic lives. In a chiefdom with only four under-resourced police officers, and a highly fluid population of over 30,000 residents, people's shared respect for the efficacy of spoken curses is one of the most important disciplinary forces regulating economic behaviour.

Conclusions

I began this chapter by asking how something as light and impalpable as a spoken blessing is able to carry a material exchange value, just as fish do. Perhaps we ought to pause here to question why this valuation would even appear surprising. In the post-industrial North, the vast majority of the money upon which people depend for almost every aspect of their daily lives never exists in any material form. One important conceptual difference between these impalpable conveyers of wealth and the ones that circulate through Tissana's economy is that the former exist as digits – on pay slips, receipts, and computer screens; they are rarely written manually these days, but they are nonetheless a literary expression of value. By contrast, I have sought to illustrate that, although most people in Kagboro are quite capable of reading and writing, Tissana remains an oral economy in almost every practical sense. So many thousands of spoken pledges of debt are exchanged in Tissana each day that these speech acts could meaningfully be described as the town's second market currency. With this in mind, I have sought to understand how certain spoken words come to be endowed with a weight of material value in Tissana's economy.

The 'meaning' of the words 'May God bless' might appear fairly self-evident. However, as Webb Keane (2008) warns us, we should be very wary of assuming that religious words or rituals are transparent windows to religious 'beliefs'. The fact that individuals enact the same ritual behaviours – exchanging similarly worded blessings, for example – is no guarantee that they share the same knowledge about the 'meaning' of those words, nor the source of their power. And if this is true everywhere, it is nowhere more vividly demonstrated than in locations such as rural Sierra Leone, where explicitly esoteric practices result in knowledge about the material order being extremely unevenly distributed.

When we begin from the assumption that ritual words cannot be reduced to evidence of thoughts, then, analytically speaking, the tangible, enduring qualities that enable them to be exchanged and to move into different social contexts – their materiality, in this sense – suddenly begin to appear as their *least* problematic characteristic (Keane 2008). This slide of words, from language to artefact, is far from being unique to West Africa; nor even, indeed, to 'religious' contexts. In a radically different environment – in the bureaucracy of international diplomatic negotiation – Annelise Riles (1998) has explored the ways in which policy documents come to be valued as objects of prestige exchange: ritually presented, collected, and conspicuously displayed by conference delegates who, in fact, are highly unlikely ever to read their contents. In both cases, complex, painstakingly constructed textual artefacts are used and circulated as autonomous semiotic forms, the 'meaning' of which has become quite independent of the words embedded within them (cf. Coleman 1996).

Nonetheless, it is important to emphasise, as I have done in this chapter, that when people in Sierra Leone exchange valuable words, they do so within a very specific epistemological context. In his classic study of Mende swear medicines, Jędrej argued that 'whereas ancestors must be begged or cajoled for help with offerings of food... [i]n *hale* [medicines] men have a power over which they have complete control' (1974: 44–5). My experience in Tissana was that people were actually rather wary of the unexpected chains of causality they might unleash in their use of swear medicines. However, Jędrej's broader point holds true: by deploying a swear medicine, people are not appealing to spirits, or ancestors, or even God to intervene in their lives. Rather, the words contained within or addressed to an *ifohn* seek to activate the transformative powers inherent within the substance of the material world itself. My argument is that people in Tissana extend a similar intuitive understanding to spoken blessings, valuing these words for a capacity that is independent of their 'meaning': the ability to bring about direct, albeit unstable, consequences in the material world.

It is because people seek to accumulate and manipulate spoken blessings as powerful *things* that these spoken words have retained their material value, even as the social context in which they are exchanged has been transformed beyond recognition. As Webb Keane puts it:

> as objects that endure across time, [religious language] can, in principle, acquire features unrelated to the intentions of previous users or the inferences to which they have given rise in the past. This is in part because as material things they are prone to enter into new contexts ... Their very materiality gives them a historical character. (Keane 2008: S124)

His argument could be read alongside Appadurai's important observation that material objects are capable of leading complex, sometimes unpredictable, 'social lives', and may come to be valued in quite different ways by different people, as they cycle from one economic context to another. As he argues, 'we have to follow the things themselves, for their meanings are inscribed in their forms, their uses, and their trajectories' (Appadurai 1986: 4–5).

In the case of the spoken blessings that I witnessed being exchanged on Tissana's wharf, we can see the historical trajectory of these material forms stretching in two directions. In Tissana, as in many parts of West Africa, people often make the link between European wealth and their supposed possession of powerful 'secrets' (Bledsoe and Robey 1986). In d'Azevedo's description of early encounters between European missionaries and Gola speakers in neighbouring Liberia, we can begin to imagine how Christian language might have become incorporated within existing 'regimes of value' (Appadurai 1986: 4), and, in the process, become imbued with a weight of material value quite different from anything Europeans themselves had previously imagined possible (cf. Pietz 1985):

> [T]hose who came from lands across the sea [kwi] in great ships with wealth of strange new goods and knowledge were courted and admired for the djike dje – the 'new ideas' – which they possessed. Kwi had wealth and weapons to buy and enforce authority over the land ... Furthermore, they came with their own teachers who also had a 'book', which contained the laws of their god ... The Gola looked upon the early Western missionary in much the same way as he had always looked upon the itinerant Muslim trader and scholar. It was considered advantageous to encourage them in order to learn their ways and the secrets of their power. (d'Azevedo 1962b: 30)

In the present historical moment, Sierra Leonean fisherfolk are once more living through a period of social upheaval. Leading newly mobile, cosmopolitan lives, most have lost interest in maintaining social relationships with the ancestral spirits who, until recently, were formally credited as providing the power behind spoken blessings (Bledsoe 1992). And yet, rather than fading from the economic topography, what we see is that spoken blessings are now valued in new ways, as they are circulated through novel kinds of economic relationship. In a stretched, unpredictable economy, the material value imbued in blessings has powerful consequences in people's lives. It enables those with nothing to survive, because fishermen – eager to take every available precaution to mitigate the insecurity of their own precarious livelihoods – are prepared to invest considerable resources in earning the blessings of neighbours and strangers on the wharf.

8 Conclusion

This book has offered an ethnographic glimpse into a dynamic, but previously largely unstudied maritime world: a precarious, fluid, frontier economy, quite different from the agrarian villages that have historically shaped our knowledge of the Upper Guinea region. The past 50 years have been a period of profound social and economic transformation across the Yawri Bay, as settlements such as Tissana have mushroomed from tiny fisher-farmer hamlets to multi-ethnic hubs of commercial fishing, fish processing, and trade. Perhaps the best-known contribution made by ethnographers of Sierra Leone over the years has been a rich literature focusing on the ways in which 'the powerful presence of the past' (Knörr and Filho 2010) is woven through the social and material fabric of everyday life (Ferme 2001; Shaw 2002; Basu 2007). Some of the most influential work of the post-civil war period has sought to trace the genealogy of contemporary social tensions within rural communities back through a centuries-long history of Atlantic and domestic slavery (Richards 2005; Peters 2010). However, when we see how rapidly the Yawri Bay's emergent fishing towns have acquired new, more fluid, structures of power and kinship, it reminds us of the dangers of overly reifying the past. In a recent conversation about the particular challenges of 'theorising from Africa', Achille Mbembe argued that in many parts of the continent people are experiencing a period of such dramatic social and economic transformation that:

> The ways in which societies compose and invent themselves in the present – what we could call the creativity of practice – is always ahead of the knowledge we can ever produce about them . . . 'the social' is less a matter of order and contract than a matter of composition and experiment. (quoted in Shipley 2010: 654–5)

Certainly this resonates well with my own experience in Tissana. Like many youthful 'frontier' towns or other sites of proto-urbanisation (e.g. Mitchell 1956; Walsh 2003; Beuving 2010), arrivals in Tissana often experience it as a space of new freedoms and possibilities. But the Yawri Bay is also a space of considerable social, moral, and ontological uncertainty. Even as the town's neophyte fisherfolk learn to adapt to this fickle,

fluid maritime world, they are already having to improvise *new* livelihood strategies to cope with the rapid depletion of their coastal ecology.
In the five empirical chapters, I have traced some of the moral fissures
and material tensions that surface throughout the town's social fabric, as
emergent patterns of gendered mobility and shifting modes of economic
relationships have led people to reconsider previously taken-for-granted
knowledge about what constitutes kinship, intimacy, social power, and
responsibility.

The book makes two broad contributions to the anthropology of West
Africa. Firstly, my ethnography adds another layer of nuance to the existing literature exploring the relationship between economies and moralities, both in the Upper Guinea region and more widely. The study sits
within a recent wave of research aiming to shed light on the stark realities
of lives lived in poverty. In a global economic climate in which 'precarity has inserted itself into the heart of anthropology itself' (Muehlebach
2013: 238), some of the most compelling ethnography to emerge over
the past few years has been concerned with exploring the opportunities,
anxieties, and constricted forms of agency available to people navigating
conditions of extreme economic uncertainty (Archambault 2013; Mills
2013; Han 2012; Simone 2005). Much of my empirical discussion has
been concerned with exploring various corollaries of a single basic underlying tension: for many of those who choose to migrate to the Yawri Bay,
the greatest appeal of maritime life is that it appears to offer a kind
of moral simplicity and personal independence that would be unthinkable within the patron–client strictures of a farming village. However,
the reality is that, in a material environment as stretched as Tissana's,
it is difficult to survive without becoming re-enmeshed in new forms of
potentially extractive relationship.

The second contribution has been to explore how such ongoing material insecurity intersects with and is productive of Sierra Leone's famous
'hermeneutic of concealment' (Ferme 2001: 6), as well as its particular construction of the material order. Running as a thread throughout
the ethnographic chapters, we have seen repeated examples of the ways
in which unambiguously pragmatic livelihood strategies are interwoven
with material strategies that might appear to belong to the sphere of
'ritual' or 'esoteric' practice. Anthropologists working in Sierra Leone
have often pointed to the ways in which spiritual agencies are seen to
inhabit material substances, in a context in which hidden, sequestered
realms of knowledge and action play a central role in political life. What
I have worked to reveal through my ethnographic discussion is how these
particular constructions of (im)materiality are both revealed and produced through the mundane practices of artisanal fishing, gift exchange,
and relatedness. My approach has been to treat the material value of fetish
medicines, curses, and blessings not so much as a matter of 'belief', but

rather as a simple economic *fact* with direct consequences for the ways in which people seek to balance their tight livelihoods.

Contested freedoms

A common tension running through many aspects of everyday relations in Tissana is that, while people aspire to 'freedom', networks of intimate social relations provide the strongest available source of material security. Over the years, ethnographers have often returned to the argument, made by both Marx (2000 [1946]) and Simmel (1978 [1900]), that market-based systems of reckoning value and mobilising labour have the effect of eroding social bonds, replacing them instead with a system of fleeting and impersonal transactions. The classic ethnographic literature on 'modernisation' is rich with examples of people responding to these transformations with a profound sense of unease (Bohannan 1959; Taussig 1980). However, the people I knew rarely expressed regret for the lost morality of 'traditional' village life. Quite the contrary: the rural hinterland is most often caricatured as a space of inhumane patrimonial extraction.

Chapter 3 introduced Tissana through the personal narratives of migrants who, at different points over the past 50 years, chose to risk everything to flee conditions in their home villages, which they described as exploitative or dangerous, and begin a new life on the sea. For some readers, these stories will have a familiar ring: there are striking resonances between the accounts of the village émigrés I knew in Tissana and the grievances expressed by ex-combatants when asked to explain what prompted them to join one of the factions in Sierra Leone's civil war (Peters and Richards 1998). We saw some of the ways in which neophyte fishermen attempt to safeguard their newfound independence: choosing to live recklessly 'in the moment' rather than become trammelled by the obligations and responsibilities associated with close social bonds. However, the chapter ended by acknowledging that such stated aspirations to 'freedom' are rarely more than fleetingly realised. Vulnerable crewmen navigate a narrow line between dependency and destitution, always at risk of falling into patterns of indentured labour that people in Tissana likened to 'slavery' (wono).

Chapter 4 developed a similar line of argument, although this time through the lens of gendered economic relations. In an apparent inversion of more familiar narratives of economic nostalgia, the people I knew in Tissana looked back longingly to their town's fleeting economic 'boom', during which the sale of fish on the wharf seemed to come close to a simple, *impersonal* market. As catches have become smaller and less predictable in recent decades, women's livelihoods have come under even greater pressure than those of the fishermen with whom they do business, and many *banda* women reflect on their creeping material impoverishment through a discourse that emphasises the growing necessity of nurturing intimate social relationships with the men whose fish they want to buy. However, in contrast to the existing literature on 'fish for sex' in East African fisheries (Béné 2007), the focus of the chapter was not on female victimhood. Rather, I sought to reveal the creativity of women's material strategies, as they work to initiate and cement trading partnerships with men: sometimes through public loans of cash, gifts of rice, and good advice; sometimes by more covert means, including sexual seduction or the strategic deployment of fetish medicines (*ifohn*).

Chapter 4 was also the first ethnographic chapter to discuss the powerful sense in which space is gendered in the maritime topography, with profound repercussions for the ways in which members of both genders are able to manage their social and economic lives. While Tissana's women lead largely sedentary lives, seagoing fishermen are, by contrast, extremely mobile. Men routinely opt to land their boats, and sell their catch, on the wharf of a town other than their home. When they do, the transactions that take place on those foreign wharfs are often charged with a heightened sense of urgency, opportunity – and risk. There are fascinating echoes of much longer-standing regional constructions of gender, in which young people are considered to become fully male or fully female only after periods spent in ritual segregation in their respective societies' 'bush'. And, as in those more ritualised contexts of segregation, the borderland spaces where men and women come back into contact are 'highly charged and potentially dangerous' (Bledsoe 1984: 465). According to their playful moral narratives, fishermen claim to fear becoming entrapped on these foreign shores: first seduced, and later bound to their new *kustoment* by bonds of monetary indebtedness.

These tales of economically predatory seductresses are one example of a much more diffuse set of tensions that recur in various guises throughout the book, but which are explored most explicitly in Chapter 5. However much fishermen might self-romanticise the 'free mobility' and rugged masculinity of their unpredictable lives, this very unpredictability results in enormous day-to-day anxiety – for themselves and, perhaps especially, for the people with whom their lives are entangled. For cosmopolitan elites, confident of their long-term material security, constant movement and social change may be empowering. However, speaking here about the urban poor in Mumbai, Arjun Appadurai captures the unrelenting sense of insecurity experienced by people for whom life is both socially fluid and materially precarious:

Many things in life have a temporary quality – not only physical resources, spatial resources, and housing but also social, political, and moral relations . . . A huge amount of their social energy and personal creativity is devoted to producing, if not the illusion, then the sense of permanence in the face of the temporary. The phenomenology of the temporary must be carefully distinguished by group location in the political economy...The temporariness of things if you are a high-level speculator in the derivatives market of Bombay is very deeply different than if you are living in a viaduct in Bombay. (Appadurai 2003: 47)

Surviving in this unpredictable economy without a strong network of social relations would be a risky strategy indeed. In Chapter 5, we saw how the massive daily traffic in gifts of fish and dishes of rice that move between fishing boats, kitchens, and homes across the townscape can be read as an ever-shifting map of each person's 'potato rope' kin. There is a very real sense in which these gifts are the substance out of which Tissana's social fabric is woven. However, beneath the initial impression of munificence and mutual generosity, there are two respects in which this traffic in gifts points towards more ambivalent dynamics in Tissana's social life. Firstly, the sheer volume of this gift economy is evidence of the unrelenting material work people are required to invest simply to construct some semblance of social security, in a context where one's *subabu* is liable to leave town at any moment. As we saw, this is not a struggle at which everyone succeeds. Because 'potato rope' bonds must be *made* and then materially *remade* rather than simply assumed, the poorest families are liable to collapse and unravel as rapidly as they were formed.

Secondly, set against a broader historical context in which the most intimate relationships have often been the site of greatest exploitation, the material relationships that people work so hard to create and nurture are also often regarded with a deep sense of moral ambivalence. Where many people are only just managing to balance their fragile livelihoods, the pragmatics and morality of exchange are rooted in the fundamental material needs of *survival*. Few substances are more strongly coveted, more emotive, or more immediately powerful than food. But complex expressions of social power may also be smuggled alongside the most innocuous-looking gift of rice; with 'fetish' medicines widely in circulation, a gift of rice is at once the substance of survival and, potentially, a potent expression of control.

As this final point reveals, and as I move on to discuss in more detail in the following section, careful attention to the materiality of everyday economic transactions can provide a window into people's shared knowledge of the fabric of the material order, and the kinds of agency people are able to exert through material substances.

Economies and materialities

The complexity of the relationship between cosmologies and economies has been a recurrent preoccupation in European social science since at

least the nineteenth century. Max Weber (2001 [1930]) is often credited as the first important theorist to acknowledge that religious beliefs
not only reflect but also help produce people's economic behaviours. In
his best-known study, he explored how the Protestant Reformation set
in motion a series of profound changes in the character of economic
life across northern Europe. His argument can be read, at least in part,
as a move to counterbalance Marx's (2000 [1946]) claim that religious
belief systems are all ultimately shaped by human activity to reproduce
the economic order and naturalise its inequalities. Over the subsequent
years, ethnographers and historians have repeatedly arrived, by various
routes, at the same discovery: 'While it may not matter much which
came first, economies or culture, it is important to keep the intercon-
nection in mind, for changing one often changes the other' (Blim 2012:
345). Comaroff and Comaroff (1985) illustrated, for example, that the
'conversion' that Protestant missionaries were attempting to precipitate
in colonial South Africa reached far beyond conveying the theological
teachings of the Bible. The missionaries' efforts to disseminate their
'Protestant world view' led them to intervene in every material aspect
of Tswana life, attempting to radically reconfigure Tswana attitudes on
everything from labour to time, space, and the self.

There is a long history of interest among ethnographers of the Upper
Guinea Coast in attempts to unravel the complex ways in which the
material world is inhabited and animated by unseen agencies (Ferme
2001; Bledsoe and Robey 1986; Jędrej 1974; 1976; Tonkin 1979; 2000;
Bellman 1975). An insight that these ethnographers seem to share is
that Sierra Leone's particular constructions of (im)materiality can be
understood as one facet of a broader politics of secrecy. According to this
view, 'true' knowledge of the material order can be possessed by only
a small minority of especially skilful or powerful persons. In Chapter 6,
my own ethnography added to this literature, by exploring how Sierra
Leone's long-standing cultural aesthetic of concealment intersects with
the physical contours of a maritime topography. As we saw, the Yawri
Bay seascape provides ample opportunity for people to move in and
out of view, across the watery horizon, or into the hidden spaces of
the 'witch world'. From my own limited vantage point on the wharf, I
witnessed the considerable fields of suspicion and anxiety that circulate
around these hidden spaces, as people assume that their neighbours are
covertly defrauding them just beyond their frame of view. To this extent,
my ethnography supports the widespread image of this region as one in
which practical strategies of secrecy and concealment are an important
element of many aspects of social, political, and economic life.

And yet, in other respects, my goal has been to erode this aura of
esotericism that infuses so many ethnographic accounts of the Upper
Guinea Coast. With its seemingly mysterious secret societies, elaborate

practices of esoteric knowledge, and dark history of slavery and violence, rural Sierra Leone has proven particularly fertile ground for ethnographers with a poetic preference for the other-worldly. Almost a century has passed since Edwin Walter wrote of Sherbroland that 'such a country evidently deserves to be called a land of mystery' (1917: 160); to a greater or lesser degree, a similar tone has continued to permeate much of the writing about this region ever since (Ellis 1999; Wlodarczyk 2006). In the wake of a civil war that was characterised in the global media as both appallingly barbarous and inscrutably exotic, those of us working to describe everyday life in Sierra Leone have an even stronger responsibility than most to be wary of any representation that smacks of exoticism. For the people who live there, there is nothing 'mysterious' about the daily, grinding struggle to survive in a place such as Tissana.

By focusing on people's everyday judgements of the material value of different substances – from life-sustaining foodstuffs, to unseen *ifohn*, and impalpable words – we gain insights into an embodied knowledge of the (im)material order that is not secret at all, but rather taken for granted, and shared by all people. This methodological approach was developed most explicitly in Chapter 7, where I sought to illustrate that, under certain circumstances, spoken words carry a material exchange value within Tissana's everyday economic order. Beginning at the most seemingly mundane level, I argued that, although most people in Tissana learned to write at school, they do not use written records as part of their economic relationships. In a world in which almost everyone is embedded in complex webs of credit and debt, spoken promises are valued as highly as written contracts would be in a more literary society. These oral pledges circulate through the everyday economy in such high volumes that they could meaningfully be described as the town's second currency. I then moved on to consider seemingly more 'esoteric' or 'supernatural' expressions of the material value invested in words. From the blessings that fishermen accept on the wharf in exchange for their precious catch, to the ways in which spoken words are woven into the material fabric of various power objects, people in Tissana accept that spoken language can exert a direct influence in the material world, in a way that has little to do with communicating 'meaning'. We saw that, because people seek to accumulate and manipulate spoken blessings as powerful *things*, these spoken words have retained their material value, even as the social context in which they are exchanged has transformed almost beyond recognition.

Here, my research relates to that familiar genre of ethnographic writing that interprets people's stories of 'the occult' as a series of moral commentaries directed against the injustices of the 'modern' economic order (Comaroff and Comaroff 2000; Ciekawy and Geschiere 1998; Geschiere 1997; Shaw 1997a; 1997b). Other anthropologists have criticised this trope for reproducing familiar moral binaries in ways that risk obscuring the moral complexity of real people's economic experience (Sanders 2003; 2008; Sumich 2010). What is questioned less often, however, is the underlying assumption that narratives presenting 'occult' activity as a route to material enrichment should be read as a metaphorical trope reflecting on economic life, not as a window onto the material *workings* of economic life. What Sanders shares with the anthropologists whose work he criticises is a view of popular African economic discourses that 'hover over the material world but [do not] permeate it' (Ingold 2000: 340). A broader critique might seek to emphasise that people's fears about the violent strategies available to their most ruthlessly greedy neighbours are informed by the same basic knowledge of the material world that also shapes their own mundane livelihood strategies.

So, for example, in Sherbro-speaking regions of Sierra Leone, there is a long genealogy of the knowledge that human body parts may be used to concoct extremely potent forms of 'fetish medicine' (*bor-fima*), capable of imbuing previously ordinary individuals with exceptional charisma. Throughout the first half of the twentieth century, Sherbroland was notorious for the reputed power of its Bor-fima society;[1] this was a secretive sodality described as similar in structure to the Poro or Bundu, except for the fact that members would take turns to sacrifice one of their dependants to replenish the sodality's powerful medicine (Burrows 1914; Gray 1916; Kalous 1974). Many Sierra Leoneans take it for granted that similar technology remains an important source of power for contemporary 'big' persons (Shaw 1996; Ferme 2001). Interrogating the truth of these stories falls beyond the scope of this book (but see Pratten 2007).

However, what we have repeatedly seen throughout this book is that less powerful forms of 'fetish' (*ifohn*) – often incorporating the hair, clothes, or nail clippings of the individual they are intended to influence – are in common circulation throughout Tissana's covert economy. Alongside the town's busy trade in gifts of rice and fish runs a parallel, though less tangible, traffic in *ifohn* (fetish medicines). Most people claim to disapprove of their use, yet the common circulation of 'fetish medicines' is also taken to be an integral element of everyday economic negotiations. As we saw in Chapters 4 and 5, these hidden substances are widely regarded as being among the most effective, affordable, and commonplace means of creating, strengthening, or otherwise manipulating the webs of relatedness that will make the difference between a person's relative prosperity and their destitution.

The interesting point in the context of my own discussion is that, if medicine murder is to 'make sense' as a plausible route to wealth and

---

[1] Known to English speakers as the 'Man-Leopard' or 'Alligator' society, depending on the method used to dispose of victims.

influence, it requires a particular set of assumptions – not only about *who* holds power and how they might be prepared to abuse it, but also, at a more ontological level, about what power *is*, how it functions, and how it operates through human bodies and material substances. The same basic knowledge of the material world that underpins people's fears of occult violence also informs these more banal economic encounters, by dictating how it is possible for a person to exert their agency in and through material things.

Conclusion

This book has revealed various facets of the work invested by Sierra Leone's fisherfolk as they struggle to create some semblance of personal security in a context of often desperate scarcity. As we have seen, these material anxieties are compounded by the fact that the basic rules of social life appear to be chronically unstable. Even as patterns of gendered intimacy, family belonging, and patrimonial responsibility are shifting into new, unpredictable forms, people in Tissana devote a huge amount of their energy and material resources in attempting to strategically nurture the 'right' networks of personal relationships: the social bonds that will be able to catch them when their fish catches fail.

However, if the empirical focus of this book has been on fishing, gift exchange, and relatedness, then these everyday livelihood practices have turned out to be a surprisingly fertile way of examining what Foucault once called 'the order of things' (2005 [1966]). As we have seen, people's most pragmatic livelihood strategies are often informed by a set of convictions about the material order, and about the scope of human agency within that order, that I did not share with my informants. Ethnographers working in Sierra Leone have often pointed to the intriguing relationship between material things and unseen agencies (Ferme 2001; Jędrej 1974; 1976; Tonkin 2000), although rarely through the lens of mundane economic exchange.

When we acknowledge the material value of spoken words, or the material force of mundane fetish technologies within Tissana's economic transactions, two things happen. Firstly, this expanded view of economic life allows us to glimpse the ways in which people intuitively understand the fabric of their material world, and the threads of causality that hold it together. Secondly – and arguably more importantly – we are immediately granted a much broader panorama of the material strategies people use to obtain credit, to negotiate a gift of fish, to protect themselves from witchcraft attacks: in short, *to survive* in this desperately stretched economy. It matters that people believe that spoken blessings possess a weight of material value. This is not just an issue of representation or 'belief'; it has real consequences for people's livelihoods. Like fish or rice, blessings are the stuff out of which economic – and therefore social – relations are made.

Perhaps we cannot fully understand anyone's economic behaviour without first asking: what kinds of substances are materially capable of holding value? What kinds of substances can be possessed, or traded, or used to exert a direct influence within the physical world? Given the 'fantastical' (Maurer 2006: 16) quality of money itself, there are few places in the world where these deceptively simple questions would not yield complex and fascinating answers. By considering the ways in which people practise social constructions of (im)materiality through their everyday economic behaviours, we can begin to glimpse how 'the order of things' shapes, and is simultaneously shaped by, people's practical and micro-political struggles for survival.

Bibliography

Abramowitz, S. 2014. 'How the Liberian health sector became a vector for Ebola', *Cultural Anthropology*, 7 October, www.culanth.org/fieldsights/ 598-how-the-liberian-health-sector-became-a-vector-for-ebola (accessed 8 October 2014).

Abu-Lughod, L. 1991. 'Writing against culture' in E. Lewin (ed.), *Feminist Anthropology*. Oxford: Blackwell Publishing, pp. 137–62.

Acheson, J. M. 1981. 'Anthropology of fishing', *Annual Review of Anthropology* 10: 275–316.

Ajala, A. S. and E. N. Ediomo-Ugong. 2010. '"It's my stepmother": witchcraft, social relations, and health security in Ibibio, South-South Nigeria', *Anthropos* 105 (2): 455–70.

Alber, E. 2013. 'The transfer of belonging: theories on child fostering in West Africa reviewed' in E. Alber, J. Martin, and C. Notermans (eds), *Child Fostering in West Africa: new perspectives on theory and practices*. Leiden and Boston MA: Brill, pp. 79–107.

Alber, E., T. Häberlein, and J. Martin. 2010. 'Changing webs of kinship: spotlights on West Africa', *Africa Spectrum* 45 (3): 43–67.

Aldridge, T. J. 1894. 'Wanderings in the hinterland of Sierra Leone', *Geographical Journal* 4 (2): 123–40.

Aldridge, T. J. 1910. *A Transformed Colony. Sierra Leone as it was, and as it is: its progress, peoples, native customs and undeveloped wealth*. Westport CT: Negro Universities Press.

Allison, E. H. and A. Janet. 2001. 'HIV and Aids among fisherfolk: a threat to "responsible fisheries"?', *Fish and Fisheries* 5 (3): 215–34.

Andersen, R. 1980. 'Hunt and conceal: information management in Newfoundland deep-sea trawler fishing' in R. Andersen (ed.), *In Secrecy: a cross-cultural perspective*. New York: Human Sciences Press, pp. 205–28.

Appadurai, A. 1986. 'Introduction: commodities and the politics of value' in A. Appadurai and I. Kopytoff (eds), *The Social Life of Things*. Cambridge: Cambridge University Press, pp. 3–63.

Appadurai, A. 1990. 'Disjuncture and difference in the global economy', *Public Culture* 7 (2): 295–310.

Appadurai, A. 2003. 'Illusion of permanence: interview with Arjun Appadurai', *Perspecta* 34: 44–52.

Archambault, J. S. 2013. 'Cruising through uncertainty: cell phones and the politics of display and disguise in Inhambane, Mozambique', *American Ethnologist* 40 (1): 88–101.

Bibliography

Argenti, N. 2007. *The Intestines of The State: youth, violence, and belated histories in the Cameroon Grassfields*. Chicago: University of Chicago Press.

Argenti, N. 2010. 'Things that don't come by the road: folktales, fosterage, and memories of slavery in the Cameroon Grassfields', *Comparative Studies in Society and History* 52 (2): 224–54.

Ashforth, A. 1998. 'Reflections on spiritual insecurity in a modern African city (Soweto)', *African Studies Review* 41 (3): 39–67.

Ashforth, A. 2005. *Witchcraft, Violence, and Democracy in South Africa*. Chicago: University of Chicago Press.

Astuti, R. 1999. 'At the centre of the market: a Vezo woman' in S. Day, E. Papataxiarchis, and M. Stewart (eds), *Lilies of the Field: marginal people who live for the moment*. Boulder, CO: Westview Press, pp. 83–95.

Bâ, A. H. 1981. 'The living tradition' in J. Ki-Zerbo (ed.), *General African History. Volume 1: Methodology and African prehistory*. Nairobi: East African Publishers, pp. 166–205.

Ballinger, P. 2006. 'Watery spaces, globalizing places: ownership and access in postcolonial Croatia' in J. Laible and H. J. Barley (eds), *Contemporary Studies in Economic and Financial Analysis*. Bingly: Emerald Group, pp. 153–7.

Barber, K. 1995. 'Money, self-realisation and the person in Yoruba texts' in J. Guyer (ed.), *Money Matters: instability, values and social payments in the modern history of West African communities*. London: James Currey, pp. 205–24.

Bashkow, I. 2000. '"Whitemen" are good to think with: how Orokaiva morality is reflected on Whitemen's skin', *Identities* 7 (3): 281–332.

Bashkow, I. 2006. *The Meaning of Whitemen: race and modernity in the Orokaiva cultural world*. Chicago: University of Chicago Press.

Basu, P. 2007. 'Palimpsest memoryscapes: materializing and mediating war and peace in Sierra Leone', in F. De Jong and M. Rowlands (eds), *Reclaiming Heritage: alternative imaginaries of memory in West Africa*. Walnut Creek, CA: Left Coast Press, pp. 231–59.

Bayart, J.-F. 1993 [1989]. *The State in Africa: the politics of the belly*. London: Longman.

Bellman, B. 1975. *Village of Curers and Assassins: on the production of Fala Kpelle cosmological categories*. The Hague: Mouton and Co.

Bellman, B. 1979. 'The paradox of secrecy', *Human Studies* 4 (1): 1–24.

Bellman, B. 1984. *The Language of Secrecy*. New Brunswick, NJ: Rutgers University Press.

Béné, C. 2007. 'Women and fish-for-sex: transactional sex, HIV/Aids and gender in African fisheries', *World Development* 36 (5): 875–99.

Bentor, E. 2008. 'Masquerade politics in contemporary southeastern Nigeria', *African Arts* 41 (4): 32–43.

Berlin, I. 1969 [1958], 'Two concepts of liberty' in *Four Essays on Liberty*. Oxford: Oxford University Press.

Berliner, D. 2010. 'The invention of Bulongic identity (Guinea-Conakry)' in J. Knörr and W. T. Filho (eds), *The Powerful Presence of the Past: integration and conflict along the Upper Guinea coast*. Leiden: Brill, pp. 253–71.

Berry, S. 2007. 'Marginal gains, market values, and history', *African Studies Review* 50 (2): 57–70.

Beuving, J. 2010. 'Playing pool along the shores of Lake Victoria: fishermen, careers and capital accumulation in the Ugandan Nile perch business', *Africa* 80 (2): 224–48.

Bledsoe, C. 1980. 'The manipulation of Kpelle social fatherhood', *Ethnology* 19 (1): 29–45.

Bledsoe, C. 1984. 'The political use of Sande ideology and symbolism', *American Ethnologist* 11 (3): 455–72.

Bledsoe, C. 1990a. '"No success without struggle": social mobility and hardship for foster children in Sierra Leone', *Man: New Series* 25 (1): 70–88.

Bledsoe, C. 1990b. 'School fees and the marriage process for Mende girls in Sierra Leone' in P. Reeves and R. Gallagher Goodenough (eds), *Beyond the Second Sex: new directions in the anthropology of gender*. Philadelphia: University of Pennsylvania Press, pp. 181–210.

Bledsoe, C. 1992. 'The cultural transformation of Western education in Sierra Leone', *Africa* 62 (2): 182–202.

Bledsoe, C. 1995. 'Marginal members: children of previous unions in Mende households in Sierra Leone' in S. Greenhalgh (ed.), *Situating Fertility: anthropology and demographic inquiry*. Cambridge: Cambridge University Press, pp. 130–53.

Bledsoe, C. and U. Isingo-Abanike. 1989. 'Strategies of child-fosterage among Mende grannies in Sierra Leone', in R. J. Lesthaeghe (ed.), *Reproduction and Social Organisation in Sub-Saharan Africa*. Berkeley: University of California Press, pp. 442–74.

Bledsoe, C. and K. Robey. 1986. 'Arabic literacy and secrecy among the Mende of Sierra Leone', *Man: New Series* 21 (2): 202–26.

Blim, M. 2012. 'Culture and economy' in J. Carrier (ed.), *A Handbook of Economic Anthropology*. Cheltenham: Edward Elgar, pp. 344–60.

Bloch, M. 1986. *From Blessing to Violence: history and ideology in the circumcision ritual of the Merina*. Cambridge: Cambridge University Press.

Bloch, M. 1999. 'Commensality and poisoning', *Social Research* 66 (1): 133–49.

Bloch, M. and J. Parry (eds). 1989. *Money and the Morality of Exchange*. Cambridge: Cambridge University Press, pp. 1–32.

Bohannan, P. 1959. 'The impact of money on an African subsistence economy', *Journal of Economic History* 19: 491–503.

Bolt, M. 2012. 'Conundrums of cash: wage rhythms and wealth circulations on the Zimbabwean–South African border'. Paper presented at CAS@50, Conference Centre for African Studies, Edinburgh, June.

Bolten, C. 2008. '"This place is so backward": durable morality and creative development in northern Sierra Leone'. Unpublished PhD thesis, University of Michigan.

Booth, D., M. Leach, and A. Tierney. 1999. *Experiencing Poverty in Africa: perspectives from anthropology*. London: Overseas Development Institute.

Bordanaro, L. I. 2009. 'Introduction: Guinea-Bissau today? The irrelevance of the state and the permanence of change', *African Studies Review* 52 (2): 35–45.

Boswell, D. M. 1969. 'Personal crises and the mobilization of the social network' in J. Mitchell (ed.), *Social Networks in Urban Situations: analyses of personal relationships in Central African towns*. Manchester: Manchester University Press, pp. 245–96.

Boyle, J. 2003. 'The second enclosure movement and the construction of the public domain', *Law and Contemporary Problems* 66 (1/2): 33–74.

Braidotti, R. 1994. *Nomadic Subjects: embodiment and sexual difference in contemporary feminist theory*. New York: Columbia University Press.

Braudel, F. 1995 [1966]. *The Mediterranean and the Mediterranean World in the Age of Philip II. Volume 1.* Berkeley: University of California Press.

Brenner, L. 2000. *Controlling Knowledge: religion, power and schooling in a West African Muslim society.* London: Hurst.

Browne, K. 2009. 'Economics and morality: introduction' in K. Browne and L. Milgram (eds), *Economics and Morality: anthropological approaches.* Lanham, MD: Rowan Altamira, pp. 1–40.

Bürge, M. 2011. 'Riding the narrow tracks of moral life: commercial motorbike riders in Makeni, Sierra Leone', *Africa Today* 58 (2): 59–95.

Burkhalter, B. and R. F. Murphy. 1989. 'Tappers and sappers: rubber, gold and money among the Mundurucu', *American Ethnologist* 16 (1): 100–16.

Burrows, D. 1914. 'The Human Leopard Society of Sierra Leone', *Journal of the Royal African Society* 13 (50): 143–51.

Busse, M. 2012. 'Property' in J. Carrier (ed.), A Handbook of Economic Anthropology. *Second edition.* Cheltenham: Edward Elgar, pp. 111–27.

Carrier, J. G. 1997. *Meanings of the Market: the free market in Western culture.* Oxford: Berg.

Carrithers, M. 2005. 'Anthropology as a moral science of possibilities', *Current Anthropology* 46 (3): 433–56.

Carsten, J. 1995. 'The substance of kinship and the heat of the hearth: feeding, personhood, and relatedness among Malays in Pulau Langkawi', *American Ethnologist* 22 (2): 223–41.

Carsten, J. 2013. 'What kinship does – and how', *HAU: Journal of Ethnographic Theory* 3: 245–51.

Caulker-Burnett, I. 2010. *The Caulkers of Sierra Leone: the story of a ruling family and their times.* Bloomington, IN: Xlibris.

Christiansen, C., M. Utas, and H. E. Vigh. 2006. 'Introduction: navigating youth, generating adulthood' in C. Christiansen, M. Utas, and H. E. Vigh (eds), *Navigating Youth – Generating Adulthood: social becoming in an African context.* Uppsala: Nordiska Afrikainstitutet.

Ciekawy, D. and P. Geschiere. 1998. 'Containing witchcraft: conflicting scenarios in postcolonial Africa', *African Studies Review* 41 (3): 1–14.

Cole, G. 2008. 'Religious plurality and economic sustainability: the impact of Muslim merchants on the colonial economy of nineteenth-century Freetown', *African Economic History* 36: 79–94

Cole, J. and K. Middleton. 2001. 'Rethinking ancestors and colonial power in Madagascar', *Africa* 71 (1): 1–37.

Coleman, S. 1996. 'Words as things: language, aesthetics and the objectification of Protestant evangelicalism', *Journal of Material Culture* 1 (1): 107–28.

Collier, P. 2000. *Economic Causes of Civil Conflict and their Implications for Policy.* Washington, DC: World Bank.

Collins, J. 1995. 'Literacy and literacies', *Annual Review of Anthropology* 24: 75–93.

Comaroff, J. and J. L. Comaroff. 1985. *Body of Power, Spirit of Resistance.* Chicago: University of Chicago Press.

Comaroff, J. and J. L. Comaroff. 1993. 'Introduction' in J. Comaroff and J. L. Comaroff (eds), *Modernity and its Malcontents: ritual and power in postcolonial Africa.* Chicago: University of Chicago Press, pp. xi–xxxvii.

Comaroff, J. and J. L. Comaroff. 2000. 'Millennial capitalism: first thoughts on a second coming', *Public Culture* 12 (2): 391–7.

Coole, D. and S. Frost. 2010. 'Introducing the new materialisms' in D. Coole and S. Frost (eds), *New Materialisms: ontology, agency and politics*. Durham, NC: Duke University Press, pp. 1–43

Cooper, E. and D. Pratten. 2015. 'Ethnographies of uncertainty in Africa: an introduction' in E. Cooper and D. Pratten (eds), *Ethnographies of Uncertainty in Africa*. New York: Palgrave Macmillan, pp. 1–16.

Cornwall, A. 2002. 'Spending power: love, money, and the reconfiguration of gender relations in Ado-Odo, southwestern Nigeria', *American Ethnologist* 29 (4): 963–80.

Cornwall, A. 2003. Whose voices? Whose choices? Reflections on gender and participatory development. *World Development* 31 (8): 1325–42.

Cornwall, A. 2007. 'Myths to live by? Female solidarity and female autonomy reconsidered', *Development and Change* 38 (1): 149–68.

Cornwall, A., E. Harrison, and A. Whitehead. 2007. 'Gender myths and feminist fables: the struggle for interpretive power in gender and development', *Development and Change* 38 (1): 1–20.

Coulter, C. 2009. *Bush Wives and Girl Soldiers: women's lives through war and peace in Sierra Leone*. Ithaca, NY: Cornell University Press.

Creighton, M. and L. Norling. 1996. *Iron Men, Wooden Women: gender and seafaring in the Atlantic world*. Baltimore: Johns Hopkins University Press.

Cresswell, T. 2006. *On the Move: mobility in the modern Western world*. London: Routledge.

Cros, M. 1990. *Anthropologie du Sang en Afrique: essai d'hématologie symbolique chez les lobi du Burkina Faso et de Côte-d' Ivoire*. Paris: L'Harmattan.

Crosby, K. H. 1937. 'Polygamy in Mende country', *Africa* 10 (3): 249–64.

d'Andrade, R. 1995. 'Moral models in anthropology', *Current Anthropology* 36 (3): 399–408.

d'Azevedo, W. 1962a. 'Common principles of variant kinship structures among the Gola of western Liberia', *American Anthropologist* 63 (4): 504–20.

d'Azevedo, W. 1962b. 'Uses of the past in Gola discourse', *Journal of African History* 3 (1): 11–34.

da Col, G. 2012. 'The poisoner and the parasite: cosmoeconomics, fear, and hospitality among Dechen Tibetans', *Journal of the Royal Anthropological Institute* 18 (S1): 175–95.

Dalsgaard, S. 2013. 'The commensurability of carbon: making value and money of climate change', *HAU: Journal of Ethnographic Theory* 3 (1): 80–98.

Davis, D. L. and J. Nadel-Klein. 1992. 'Gender, culture and the sea: contemporary theoretical approaches', *Society and Natural Resources* 5 (2): 135–47.

Davis, J. 1992. 'The anthropology of suffering', *Journal of Refugee Studies* 5 (2): 149–61.

Day, S., E. Papataxiarchis, and M. Stewart. 1999. 'Consider the lilies of the field' in S. Day, E. Papataxiarchis, and M. Stewart (eds), *Lilies of the Field: marginal people who live for the moment*. Boulder, CO: Westview Press, pp. 1–24.

De Boeck, F. 2001. 'Garimpeiro worlds: digging, dying and "hunting" for diamonds in Angola', *Review of African Political Economy* 28 (90): 548–62.

De Boeck, F. 2015. '"Poverty" and the politics of syncopation: urban examples from Kinshasa (DR Congo)', *Current Anthropology* 56 (11): S146–58.

De Certeau, M. 1984. *The Practice of Everyday Life*. Berkeley: University of California Press.

Deleuze, G. and F. Guattari. 2004 [1987]. *A Thousand Plateaus: capitalism and schizophrenia*. London: Continuum.

Denov, M. and C. Gervais. 2007. 'Negotiating (in)security: agency, resistance, and resourcefulness among girls formerly associated with Sierra Leone's Revolutionary United Front', *Signs* 32 (4): 885–910.

Dolan, C. and D. Rajak. 2011. 'Introduction: ethnographies of corporate ethicizing', *Focaal* 60 (Summer): 3–8.

Dolan, C. and L. Scott. 2009. 'Lipstick evangelism: Avon trading circles and gender empowerment in South Africa', *Gender and Development* 17 (2): 203–18.

Dorjahn, V. R. and C. Fyfe. 1962. 'Landlord and stranger: change in tenancy relations in Sierra Leone', *Journal of African History* 3 (3): 391–7.

Douglas, I. 1999. 'Fighting for diamonds: private military companies in Sierra Leone' in J. Cilliers and P. Mason (eds), *Peace, Profit or Plunder? The privatization of security in war-torn states*. Johannesburg: Institute for Security Studies, pp. 184–5.

Edelman, M. 2012. 'E. P. Thompson and moral economies' in D. Fassin (ed.), *A Companion to Moral Anthropology*. Chichester: Wiley-Blackwell, pp. 49–66.

EJF. 2012. *Pirate Fishing Exposed: the fight against illegal fishing in West Africa and the EU*. London: Environmental Justice Foundation (EJF).

Ellis, S. 1999. *The Mask of Anarchy: the destruction of Liberia and the religious dimension of an African civil war*. London: Hurst.

Elyachar, J. 2005. *Markets of Dispossession: NGOs, economic development, and the state in Cairo*. Durham, NC: Duke University Press.

Ewing, K. 1983. 'The politics of Sufism: redefining the saints of Pakistan', *Journal of Asian Studies* 42 (2): 251–68.

Ewing, K. 1984 'The Sufi as saint, curer, and exorcist in modern Pakistan', *Contributions to Asian Studies* 18: 106–14.

Fabian, J., P. Geschiere, G. ter Haar, F. De Boeck, and M. L. Bastian. 2008. 'Review symposium on *Ethnographic Sorcery* by Harry West', *African Studies Review* 51 (3): 135–47.

Fanthorpe, R. 2006. 'Integrating chieftaincy conflicts in colonial Sierra Leone: elite competition, popular uprising and ritual control over sociality'. Paper presented at 'The Powerful Presence of the Past: Historical Conflict in the Upper Guinea Coast', Max Planck Institute for Social Anthropology, Halle.

Ferguson, J. 1999. *Expectations of Modernity: myths and meanings of urban life on the Copperbelt*. Berkeley: University of California Press.

Ferguson, J. 2006. *Global Shadows: Africa in the neoliberal world order*. Durham, NC: Duke University Press.

Ferme, M. 2001. *The Underneath of Things: violence, history and the everyday in Sierra Leone*. Berkeley: University of California Press.

Ferme, M. 2014. 'Hospital diaries: experiences with public health in Sierra Leone', *Cultural Anthropology*, 7 October, www.culanth.org/fieldsights/591-hospital-diaries-experiences-with-public-health-in-sierra-leone (accessed 8 October 2014).

Fields, K. 1985. *Revival and Rebellion in Colonial Central Africa*. Princeton: Princeton University Press.

Fortier, C. 2001. 'Le lait, le sperme, le dos. Et le sang?', *Cahiers d'Études Africaines* 41: 97–138.

Foster, R. 2013. 'Things to do with brands: creating and calculating value', *HAU: Journal of Ethnographic Theory* 3: 44–63.

Foucault, M. 2005 [1966]. *The Order of Things: an archaeology of the human sciences*. London: Routledge.

Friedman, M. 1962. *Capitalism and Freedom*. Chicago: University of Chicago Press.

Fumanti, M. and D. Rajak. 2013. 'Small and mid-range towns in Africa: continuity, change and new frontiers in urban ethnography'. Unpublished manuscript.

Fyfe, C. 1962. *A History of Sierra Leone*. Oxford: Oxford University Press.

Gable, E. 1997. 'A secret shared: fieldwork and the sinister in a West African village', *Cultural Anthropology* 12 (2): 213–33.

Gale, L. A. 2006. 'Sustaining relationships across borders: gendered livelihoods and mobility among Sierra Leonean refugees', *Refugee Survey Quarterly* 25 (2): 69–80.

Gale, L. A. 2007. 'Bulgur marriages and "big" women: navigating relatedness in Guinean refugee camps', *Anthropological Quarterly* 80 (2): 355–78.

Gberie, L., R. Hazleton, and I. Smillie. 2000. *The Heart of the Matter: Sierra Leone, diamonds and human security*. Ontario: Partnership Africa Canada.

Geertz, C. 1978. 'The bazaar economy: information and search in peasant marketing', *American Economic Review* 68 (2): 28–32.

Geschiere, P. 1997. *The Modernity of Witchcraft: politics and the occult in postcolonial Africa*. Charlottesville: University of Virginia Press.

Geschiere, P. 2013. *Witchcraft, Intimacy, and Trust: Africa in comparison*. Chicago: University of Chicago Press.

Geschiere, P. and C. Fisiy. 1994. 'Domesticating personal violence: witchcraft, courts, and confessions in Cameroon', *Africa* 64 (3): 323–41.

Gilroy, P. 1993. *The Black Atlantic: modernity and double consciousness*. Cambridge, MA: Harvard University Press.

Goody, E. 1982. *Parenthood and Social Reproduction: fostering and occupational roles in West Africa*. Cambridge: Cambridge University Press.

Goody, J. 1977. *The Domestication of the Savage Mind*. Cambridge: Cambridge University Press.

Graeber, D. 2012. 'On social currencies and human economies: some notes on the violence of equivalence', *Social Anthropology/Anthropologie Sociale* 20: 411–28.

Gray, A. 1916. 'The human leopards of Sierra Leone', *Journal of the Society of Comparative Legislation: New Series* 16: 195–8.

Groes-Green, C. 2013. '"To put men in a bottle": eroticism, kinship, female power, and transactional sex in Maputo, Mozambique', *American Ethnologist* 40 (1): 102–17.

Gudeman, S. 2012. 'Vital energy: the current of relations', *Social Analysis* 56 (1): 57–73.

Gupta, A. and J. Ferguson. 1997. *Anthropological Locations: boundaries and grounds of a field science*. Berkeley: University of California Press.

Guyer, J. I. 1995. 'Wealth in people, wealth in things: introduction', *Journal of African History* 36 (1): 83–90.

Guyer, J. I. 2004. *Marginal Gains: monetary transactions in Atlantic Africa*. Chicago: University of Chicago Press.

Han, C. 2012. *Life in Debt: times of care and violence in neoliberal Chile*. Berkeley: University of California Press.

Hansen, T. B. and O. Verkaaik. 2009. 'Introduction: urban charisma on everyday mythologies in the city', *Critique of Anthropology* 29 (1): 5–26.

Harrell-Bond, B. 1978. 'The fear of poisoning and the management of urban social relations among the professional group in Freetown, Sierra Leone', *Urban Anthropology* 7 (3): 229–51.

Harris, O. 1981. 'Households as natural units' in K. Young, C. Wolkowitz, and R. McCullagh (eds), *Of Marriage and the Market: women's subordination in international perspective*. London: CSE Books, pp. 48–67.

Hart, K. 2012. 'Money in twentieth-century anthropology' in J. Carrier (ed.), *A Handbook of Economic Anthropology*. Second edition. Cheltenham: Edward Elgar, pp. 166–82.

Harvey, D. 2006. *Spaces of Global Capitalism*. London: Verso.

Hasty, J. 2005. 'The pleasures of corruption: desire and discipline in Ghanaian political culture', *Cultural Anthropology* 20 (2): 271–301.

Hau'ofa, E. 1993. 'Our sea of islands' in V. Naidu, E. Waddell, and E. Hau'ofa (eds), *A New Oceania: rediscovering our sea of islands*. Suva: School of Social and Economic Development, pp. 2–16.

Havelock, E. A. 1982. *The Literate Revolution in Greece and its Cultural Consequences*. Princeton: Princeton University Press.

Hayek, F. A. 1944. *The Road to Serfdom*. Oxford: Routledge.

Heald, S. 1986. 'Witches and thieves: deviant motivations in Gisu society', *Man* 21 (1): 65–78.

Helmreich, S. 2011. 'Nature/culture/seawater', *American Anthropologist* 113 (1): 132–44.

Hoffer, C. P. 1972. 'Mende and Sherbro women in high office', *Canadian Journal of African Studies* 6 (2): 151–64.

Hoffman, D. 2007. 'The city as barracks: Freetown, Monrovia, and the organization of violence in postcolonial African cities', *Cultural Anthropology* 22 (3): 400–28.

Hoffman, D. 2011. *Thoute War Machines: young men and violence in Sierra Leone and Liberia*. Durham, NC: Duke University Press.

Højbejerg, C. K., J. Knörr, and W. P. Murphy. 2016. 'Introduction: deconstructing tropes of politics and policies in Upper Guinea coast societies' in C. K. Højbejerg, J. Knörr, and W. P. Murphy (eds), *Politics and Policies in Upper Guinea Coast Societies: change and continuity*. London: Palgrave Macmillan.

Holsoe, S. E. 1977. 'Slavery and economic response among the Vai (Liberia and Sierra Leone)' in S. Miers and I. Kopytoff (eds), *Slavery in Africa: historical and anthropological approaches*. Madison: University of Wisconsin Press, pp. 287–303.

Honwana, A. 2014. '"Waithood": youth transitions and social change. Response to Syed Mansoob Murshed' in D. Foemen, T. Dietz, L. de Han, and L. Johnson (eds), *Development and Equity: an interdisciplinary exploration by ten scholars from Africa, Asia, and Latin America*. Leiden: Brill.

House-Midamba, B. and F. K. Ekechi. 1995. 'Introduction' in B. House-Midamba and F. K. Ekechi (eds), *African Market Women and Economic Power: the role of women in African economic development*. Westport, CT: Greenwood Press, pp. xi–xix.

Howell, S. 1997. 'Introduction' in S. Howell (ed.), *The Ethnography of Moralities*. London: Routledge, pp. 1–24.

Humphreys, M. and J. M. Weinstein. 2004. *What the Fighters Say: a survey of ex-combatants in Sierra Leone, June–August 2004*. New York and Stanford: Post-Conflict Reintegration Initiative for Education and Empowerment (PRIDE), Columbia University and Stanford University.

Humphreys, M. and J. M. Weinstein. 2006. *Who Rebels? The determinants of participation in civil war*. New York and Stanford: Post-Conflict Reintegration Initiative for Education and Empowerment (PRIDE), Columbia University and Stanford University.

Hunter, M. 2010. *Love in the Time of AIDS: inequality, gender, and rights in South Africa*. Bloomington: Indiana University Press.

Hutchinson, S. 1992. 'The cattle of money and the cattle of girls among the Nuer 1930–83', *American Ethnologist* 19 (2): 294–316.

Ibrahim, A. F. and S. Shepler. 2011. 'Introduction to special issue: everyday life in postwar Sierra Leone', *Africa Today* 58 (2): v–xii.

Ingold, T. 1994. 'Foreword' in G. Palsson (ed.), *Coastal Economies, Cultural Accounts: human ecology and Icelandic discourse*. Manchester: Manchester University Press, pp. vii–x.

Ingold, T. 2000. *The Perception of the Environment: essays on livelihood, dwelling and skill*. London: Routledge.

Ingold, T. 2007. 'Materials against materiality', *Archaeological Dialogues* 14 (1): 1–16.

Jackson, M. 1978. 'Ideology and belief systems in change', *Canberra Anthropology* 1 (2): 34–41.

Jackson, M. 1989. *Paths Toward a Clearing: radical empiricism and ethnographic inquiry*. Bloomington: Indiana University Press.

Jackson, M. 2005. 'Storytelling events, violence, and the appearance of the past', *Anthropological Quarterly* 78 (2): 355–75.

Jȩdrej, M. C. 1974. 'An analytical note on the land and spirits of the Sewa Mende', *Africa* 44 (1): 38–45.

Jȩdrej, M. C. 1976. 'Medicine, fetish and secret society in a West African culture', *Africa* 46 (3): 247–357.

Johnson-Hanks, J. 2005. 'When the future decides: uncertainty and intentional action in contemporary Cameroon', *Current Anthropology* 46 (3): 363–85.

Jones, A. 1983. *From Slaves to Palm Kernels: a history of the Galinhas country (West Africa), 1730–1890*. Wiesbaden: F. Steiner.

Jorion, P. 1988. 'Going out or staying home: migration strategies among Xwla and Anlo Ewe fishermen', *MAST: Maritime Anthropological Studies* 1 (2): 129–55.

Kalous, M. 1974. *Cannibals and Tongo Players of Sierra Leone*. Auckland: Self-published.

Keane, W. 2008. 'The evidence of the senses and the materiality of religion', *Journal of the Royal Anthropological Institute* 14 (S1): S110–27.

Knörr, J. and W. T. Filho. 2010. 'Introduction' in J. Knörr and W. T. Filho (eds), *The Powerful Presence of the Past: integration and conflict along the Upper Guinea coast*. Leiden: Brill, pp. 1–26.

Kopytoff, I. 1971. 'Ancestors as elders in Africa', *Africa* 43 (2): 129–42.

Kopytoff, I. and S. Miers. 1977. 'African "slavery" as an institution of marginality' in I. Kopytoff and S. Meirs (eds), *Slavery in Africa: historical and anthropological approaches*. Madison: University of Wisconsin Press, pp. 3–85.

La Fontaine, J. 2011. 'Ritual murder?' Interventions Series 3. St Andrews: Open Anthropology Cooperative Press.

Lallemand, S. 1994. *Adoption et mariage: les Kotokoli du centre du Togo*. Paris: L'Harmattan.

Lam, V. W. Y., W. W. L. Cheung, W. Swartz, and U. R. Somaila 2012. 'Climate change impacts on fisheries in West Africa: implications for economic, food and nutritional security', *African Journal of Marine Science* 34: 103–17

Lambek, M. 1990. 'Certain knowledge, contestable authority: power and practice on the Islamic periphery', *American Ethnologist* 17 (1): 23–40.

Lamp, F. J. 1985. 'Cosmos, cosmetics, and the spirit of Bondo', *African Arts* 18 (3): 28–43.

Lamp, F. J. 2008. 'Temne twins (*tà-bàri*) should share everything. Do you mean *everything?*', *African Arts* 41 (1): 50–65.

Last, M. 1988. 'Charisma and medicine in Northern Nigeria' in D. B. C. O'Brien (ed.), *Charisma and Brotherhood in African Islam*. Oxford: Oxford University Press.

Last, M. 2000. 'Children and the experience of violence: contrasting cultures of punishment in Northern Nigeria', *Africa* 70 (3): 359–93.

Laurenti, G. 2008. *Fish and Fishery Products: world apparent consumption statistics based on food balance sheets 1961–2003*. Rome: Food and Agriculture Organization.

Leach, M. 1994. *Rainforest Relations: gender and resource use among the Mende of Gola, Sierra Leone*. Edinburgh: Edinburgh University Press.

Leach, M. 2000. 'New shapes to shift: war, parks and the hunting person in modern West Africa', *Journal of the Royal Anthropological Institute* 6 (4): 577–95.

Leach, M. 2015. 'The Ebola crisis and post-2015 development', *Journal of International Development* 27: 816–34.

Little, K. L. 1948. 'The Poro society as an arbiter of culture', *African Studies* 7 (1): 1–15.

Little, K. L. 1966. 'The political function of the Poro: part II', *Africa* 36 (1): 62–72.

Little, K. L. 1967 [1951]. *The Mende of Sierra Leone: a West African people in transition*. London: Routledge and Kegan Paul.

Løgstrup, K. E. 1997 [1956]. *The Ethical Demand*. Translated by F. R. Løgstrup. Notre Dame, IN: University of Notre Dame Press.

Lucht, H. 2011. *Darkness Before Daybreak: African migrants living on the margins in southern Italy today*. Berkeley: University of California Press

Luetchford, P. 2012. 'Economic anthropology and ethics' in J. Carrier (ed.), *A Handbook of Economic Anthropology*. Second edition. Cheltenham: Edward Elgar, pp. 390–404.

Luhmann, N. 1988. 'Familiarity, confidence, trust: problems and alternatives' in D. Gambetta (ed.), *Trust: making and breaking cooperative relations*. Oxford: Basil Blackwell, pp. 94–107.

MacCormack, C. P. 1977a. 'Biological events and cultural control', *Signs* 3 (1): 93–100.

MacCormack, C. P. 1977b. 'Wono: institutionalised dependency in Sherbro descent groups (Sierra Leone)' in S. Miers and I. Kopytoff (eds), *Slavery in Africa: historical and anthropological approaches*. Madison: University of Wisconsin Press, pp. 181–204.

MacCormack, C. P. 1980. 'Proto-social to adult: a Sherbro transformation' in C. MacCormack and M. Strathern (eds), *Nature, Culture and Gender*. Cambridge: Cambridge University Press, pp. 95–118.

MacCormack, C. P. 1982. 'Control of land, labor, and capital in rural southern Sierra Leone' in E. G. Bay (ed.), *Women and Work in Africa*. Boulder, CO: Westview Press, pp. 35–53.

MacCormack, C. P. 1986. 'Dying as transformation to ancestorhood: the Sherbro coast of Sierra Leone' in D. Sich (ed.), *Sterben und Tod Eine Kulturvergleichende Analyse*. Heidelberg: Internationalen, pp. 117–26.

MacCormack, C. P. 2000. 'Land, labor, and gender' in A. Lugo and B. Maurer (eds), *Gender Matters: rereading Michelle Z. Rosaldo*. Ann Arbor: University of Michigan Press, pp. 37–53.

MacGaffey, W. 1988. 'Astonishment and power: the visual vocabulary of Kongo *minkisi*', *Journal of Southern African Studies* 14 (2): 188–203.

Mair, J., C. High, and A. Kelly. 2012. 'Introduction: making ignorance an ethnographic object' in C. High, A. Kelly, and J. Mair (eds), *The Anthropology of Ignorance: an ethnographic approach*. New York: Palgrave, pp. 1–32.

Malkki, L. 1992. 'National geographic: the rooting of peoples and the territorialization of national identity among scholars and refugees', *Cultural Anthropology* 7 (1): 22–44.

Manson, K. and J. Knight. 2012. *Sierra Leone*. Chalfont St Peter: Bradt Travel Guides.

Marquette, C. M., K. A. Koranteng, R. Overå, and E. B.-D. Aryeetey. 2002. 'Small-scale fisheries, population dynamics, and resource use in Africa: the case of Moree, Ghana', *Ambio* 31 (4): 324–36.

Marx, K. 2000 [1946].'The German ideology' in D. McLellan (ed.), *Karl Marx: selected writings*. Oxford: Oxford University Press, pp. 175–208.

Masquelier, A. 2008. 'When spirits start veiling: the case of the veiled she-devil in a Muslim town of Niger', *Africa Today* 54 (3): 39–64.

Mattei, U. and L. Nader. 2008. *Plunder: when the rule of law is illegal*. Oxford: Blackwell.

Maurer, B. 2006. 'The anthropology of money', *Annual Review of Anthropology* 35: 15–36.

Maurer, B. 2011. 'Money nutters', *Economic Sociology* 12 (3): 5–12.

Mauss, M. 1990 [1925]. *The Gift: the form and reason for exchange in archaic societies*. New York: W. W. Norton.

McCall, J. 1995. 'Rethinking ancestors in Africa', *Africa* 65 (2): 256–70.

McGovern, M. 2012. 'Life during wartime: aspirational kinship and the management of insecurity', *Journal of the Royal Anthropological Institute* 18 (4): 735–52.

McGovern, M. 2015. 'Liberty and moral ambivalence: postsocialist transitions, refugee hosting, and bodily comportment in the Republic of Guinea', *American Ethnologist* 42 (2): 246–61.

McGregor, J. 2008. 'Patrolling Kariba's waters: state authority, fishing and the border economy', *Journal of Southern African Studies* 34 (4): 861–79.

Meinert, L. 2015. 'Tricky trust: distrust as ontology and trust as a social achievement in Uganda' in *Anthropology and Philosophy: dialogues on trust and hope*. New York and Oxford: Berghahn.

Menzel, A. 2016. 'Betterment versus complicity: struggling with patron–client logics in Sierra Leone' in C. K. Højbejerg, J. Knörr, and W. P. Murphy (eds), *Politics and Policies in Upper Guinea Coast Societies: change and continuity*. London: Palgrave Macmillan.

Meyer, B. 1995. '"Delivered from the powers of darkness": confessions of satanic riches in Christian Ghana', *Africa* 65 (2): 236–55.

Meyer, B. 1999. *Translating the Devil: religion and modernity among the Ewe in Ghana*. Edinburgh: Edinburgh University Press for the International African Institute.

Meyer, B. 2004. 'Christianity in Africa: from African independent to Pentecostal-charismatic churches', *Annual Review of Anthropology* 33: 447–74.

Miller, D. 2005. 'Introduction' in D. Miller (ed.), *Materiality*. Durham, NC: Duke University Press, pp. 1–50.

Mills, E. 2013. 'Embodied precarity: the biopolitics of AIDS biomedicine in South Africa'. Unpublished PhD thesis, Institute of Development Studies, Sussex.

Mintz, S. 1985. *Sweetness and Power: the place of sugar in modern history*. New York: Penguin.

Mitchell, J. C. 1956. *The Kalela Dance: aspects of social relationships among urban Africans in northern Rhodesia*. Manchester: Manchester University Press.

Mol, A. and J. Law. 1994. 'Regions, networks and fluids: anaemia and social topology', *Social Studies of Science* 24 (4): 641–71.

Moore, H. 1993. 'The differences within and the differences between' in T. del Valle (ed.), *Gendered Anthropology*. London: Routledge, pp. 193–204.

Muehlebach, A. 2012. *The Moral Neoliberal: welfare and citizenship in Italy*. Chicago: University of Chicago Press.

Muehlebach, A. 2013. 'On precariousness and the ethical imagination: the year 2012 in sociocultural anthropology', *American Anthropologist* 115 (2): 297–311.

Murphy, W. P. 1980. 'Secret knowledge as property and power in Kpelle society: elders versus youth', *Africa* 50 (2): 193–207.

Murphy, W. P. 1998. 'The sublime dance of Mende politics: an African aesthetic of charismatic power', *American Ethnologist* 25 (4): 563–82.

Murphy, W. P. 2010. 'Patrimonial logic of centrifugal forces in the political history of the Upper Guinea coast' in J. Knörr and W. T. Filho (eds), *The Powerful Presence of the Past: integration and conflict along the Upper Guinea coast*. Leiden: Brill, pp. 27–54.

Nakayama, S. 2008. 'City lights emblaze village fishing grounds: the re-imaginings of waterscape by Lake Malawi fishers', *Journal of Southern African Studies* 34 (4): 803–21.

Niehaus, I. 2012. 'From witch-hunts to thief-hunts: on the temporality of evil in the South African Lowveld', *African Historical Review* 44 (1): 29–52.

Nordstrom, C. 2007. *Global Outlaws: crime, money, and power in the contemporary world*. Berkeley: University of California Press.

Notermans, C. 2008. 'The emotional world of kinship: children's experiences of fosterage in East Cameroon', *Childhood* 15 (3): 355–77.

Nunley, J. 1988. 'Purity and pollution in Freetown: masked performance', *TDR* 32 (2): 102–22.

Nyamnjoh, F. B. 2005. 'Fishing in troubled waters: *disquettes* and *thiofs* in Dakar', *Africa* 75 (3): 295–324.

O'Brien, K. and I. Rashid. 2013. 'Islamist militancy in Sierra Leone', *Conflict, Security and Development*, 13 (2): 169–90.

Olivier de Sardan, J.-P. 1992. 'The exoticizing of magic from Durkheim to "postmodern" anthropology', *Critique of Anthropology* 12 (1): 5–25.

Ong, A. 1988. 'The production of possession: spirits and the multinational corporation in Malaysia', *American Ethnologist* 15 (1): 28–42.

Ong, W. J. 1991. *Orality and Literacy: the technologizing of the word*. London: Routledge.

Otto, T. and R. Willerslev. 2013. 'Introduction. Value as theory: comparison, cultural critique, and guerilla ethnographic theory', *HAU: Journal of Ethnographic Theory* 3: 1–20.

Overå, R. 2001. 'Institutions, mobility and resilience in the Fante migratory fisheries of West Africa'. CMI Working Papers 2001:2. Bergen: Chr. Michelsen Institute.

Oyewumi, O. 1997. *The Invention of Women: making an African sense of Western gender discourses*. Minneapolis: University of Minnesota Press.

Palmer, C. 1990. 'Telling the truth (up to a point): radio communication among Maine lobstermen', *Human Organisation* 49 (2): 157–63.

Pederson, E. O. 2015. 'An outline of interpersonal trust and distrust' in S. Liisberg, E. O. Pedersen, and A. L. Dalsgård (eds), *Anthropology and Philosophy: dialogues on trust and hope*. New York and Oxford: Berghahn, pp. 104–17.

Peek, P. M. 2011. 'Introduction: beginning to rethink twins' in P. Peek (ed.), *Twins in African and Diaspora Cultures: double trouble, twice blessed*. Bloomington: Indiana University Press, pp. 1–38.

Peletz, M. 2000. 'Ambivalence in kinship since the 1940s' in S. Franklin and S. McKinnon (eds), *Relative Values: reconfiguring kinship studies*. Durham, NC: Duke University Press, pp. 413–44.

Peters, K. 2010. 'Generating rebels and soldiers: on the socio-economic crisis of rural youth in Sierra Leone before the war' in J. Knörr and W. T. Filho (eds), *The Powerful Presence of the Past: integration and conflict along the Upper Guinea coast*. Leiden: Brill, pp. 323–55.

Peters, K. 2011. 'The crisis of youth in postwar Sierra Leone: problem solved?', *Africa Today* 58 (2): 129–53.

Peters, K. and P. Richards. 1998. '"Why we fight": voices of youth combatants in Sierra Leone', *Africa* 68 (2): 183–210.

Pfeiffer, J., K. Gimbel-Sherr, and O. J. Augusto. 2007. 'The Holy Spirit in the household: Pentecostalism, gender, and neoliberalism in Mozambique', *American Anthropologist* 109 (4): 688–700.

Phelan, J. 2007. 'Seascapes: tides of thought and being in Western perceptions of the sea'. *Working paper*. London: Goldsmiths University.

Pietz, W. 1985. 'The problem of the fetish', *RES: Anthropology and Aesthetics* 9: 5–17.

Pietz, W. 1987. 'The problem of the fetish II', *RES: Anthropology and Aesthetics* 13: 23–45.

Piot, C. 1993. 'Secrecy, ambiguity, and the everyday in Kabre culture', *American Anthropologist* 95 (2): 353–70.

Piot, C. 1999. *Remotely Global: village modernity in West Africa*. Chicago: University of Chicago Press.

Pratten, D. 2007. *The Man-Leopard Murders: history and society in colonial Nigeria*. Edinburgh: Edinburgh University Press.

Pratten, D. 2008. 'Masking youth: transformation and transgression in Annang performance', *African Arts* 41 (4): 44–60.

Prentice, R. 2009. '"Thieving a chance": moral meanings of theft in a Trinidadian garment factory' in K. E. Browne and B. L. Milgram (eds), *Economics and Morality: anthropological approaches*. Plymouth: Altamira Press, pp. 123–41.

Rajak, D. 2011. *In Good Company: an anatomy of corporate social responsibility*. Stanford: Stanford University Press.

Rasmussen, S. J. 2000. 'Alms, elders, and ancestors: the spirit of the gift among the Tuareg', *Ethnology*, 39 (1): 15–39.

Reader, J. 1997. *Africa, a Biography of the Continent*. New York: Vintage Books.

Reno, W. 2003. 'The underneath of things: violence, history, and the everyday in Sierra Leone by Mariane Ferme', *Journal of Modern African Studies* 41 (1): 153–62.

Richards, P. 1986. *Coping with Hunger: hazard and experiment in an African rice-farming system*. London: Allen and Unwin.

Richards, P. 1996. 'Chimpanzees, diamonds and war: the discourses of global environmental change and local violence on the Liberia–Sierra Leone border' in H. Moore (ed.), *The Future of Anthropological Knowledge*. London: Routledge, pp. 139–55.

Richards, P. 2004. 'Controversy over recent West African wars: an agrarian question?' Occasional paper. Copenhagen: Centre of African Studies, University of Copenhagen.

Richards, P. 2005. 'To fight or to farm? Agrarian dimensions of the Mano River conflicts (Liberia and Sierra Leone)', *African Affairs* 104 (417): 571–90.

Riles, A. 1998. 'Infinity within the brackets', *American Ethnologist* 25 (3): 378–98.

Robbins, J. 2004. *Becoming Sinners: Christianity and moral torment in a Papua New Guinean society*. Berkeley: University of California Press.

Rodney, W. 1966. 'African slavery and other forms of social oppression on the Upper Guinea coast in the context of the Atlantic slave-trade', *Journal of African History* 7 (3): 431–43.

Rodney, W. 1970. *A History of the Upper Guinea Coast, 1545 to 1800*. Oxford: Oxford University Press.

Roitman, J. 2005. *Fiscal Disobedience: an anthropology of economic regulation in Central Africa*. Princeton: Princeton University Press.

Roitman, J. 2006. 'The ethics of illegality in the Chad Basin' in J. Comaroff and J. L. Comaroff (eds), *Law and Disorder in the Postcolony*. Chicago: University of Chicago Press, pp. 247–72.

Roitman, J. 2007. 'The efficacy of the economy', *African Studies Review* 50 (2): 155–61.

Sanchez, A. 2012. 'Deadwood and paternalism: rationalizing casual labour in an Indian company town', *Journal of the Royal Anthropological Institute* 18 (2): 808–27.

Sanders, T. 2003. 'Reconsidering witchcraft: postcolonial Africa and analytic (un)certainties', *American Anthropologist* 105 (2): 338–52.

Sanders, T. 2008. 'Buses in Bongoland: seductive analytics and the occult', *Anthropological Theory* 8 (2): 107–32.

Sarró, R. 2002. 'Book review: *The Underneath of Things: Violence, history, and the everyday in Sierra Leone* by Mariane Ferme', *African Affairs* 101 (404): 439–41.

Sarró, R. 2010. 'Map and territory: the politics of place and autochthony among Baga Sitem (and their neighbours)' in J. Knörr and W. T. Filho (eds), *The Powerful Presence of the Past: integration and conflict along the Upper Guinea coast.* Leiden: Brill, pp. 231–52.

Scheele, J. 2012. *Smugglers and Saints of the Sahara: regional connectivity in the twentieth century.* Cambridge: Cambridge University Press.

Scheper-Hughes, N. 1992. *Death Without Weeping: the violence of everyday life in Brazil.* Berkeley: University of California Press.

Scheper-Hughes, N. 2008. 'A talent for life: reflections of human vulnerability and resilience', *Ethnos* 73: 25–56.

Schoembucher, E. 1988. 'Equality and hierarchy in maritime adaptation: the importance of flexibility in the social organisation of a South Indian fishing caste', *Ethnology* 27 (3): 213–30.

Schoepf, B. G. and C. Schoepf. 1988. 'Land, gender and food security in eastern Kivu, Zaire' in J. Davidson (ed.), *Agriculture, Women and Land: the African experience.* Boulder, CO: Westview Press, pp. 106–30.

Scott, J. 2009. *The Art of Not Being Governed: an anarchist history of upland Southeast Asia.* New Haven: Yale University Press.

Seeley, J. 2009. 'Fishing for a living but catching HIV: Aids and changing patterns of work in fisheries in Uganda', *Anthropology of Work Review* 30 (2): 66–76.

Sen, A. 1988. 'Freedom of choice: concept and content', *European Economic Review* 32: 269–94.

Senders, S. and A. Truitt. 2007. 'Introduction' in S. Senders and A. Truitt (eds), *Money: ethnographic encounters.* Oxford: Berg, pp. 1–14.

Shaw, R. 1996. 'The politician and the diviner: divination and the consumption of power in Sierra Leone', *Journal of Religion in Africa* 26 (1): 30–54.

Shaw, R. 1997a. 'Cosmologers and capitalism: knowing history and practising sorcery in Mayotte', *Cultural Dynamics* 9 (2): 183–94.

Shaw, R. 1997b. 'The production of witchcraft/witchcraft as production: memory, modernity, and the slave trade in Sierra Leone', *American Ethnologist* 24 (4): 865–76.

Shaw, R. 2002. *Memories of the Slave Trade: ritual and the historical imagination in Sierra Leone.* Chicago: University of Chicago Press.

Shaw, R. 2005. 'Rethinking truth and reconciliation commissions: lessons from Sierra Leone'. Special Report 130. Washington, DC: United States Institute of Peace.

Shaw, R. 2007 'Displacing violence: making Pentecostal memory in postwar Sierra Leone', *Cultural Anthropology* 22 (1): 66–93.

Shepler, S. 2011. 'The real and symbolic importance of food in war: hunger pains and big men's bellies in Sierra Leone', *Africa Today* 58 (2): 42–56.

Shepler, S. 2014. 'The Ebola virus and the vampire state', Mats Utas website, 21 July, https://matsutas.wordpress.com/2014/07/21/the-ebola-virus-and-the-vampire-state-by-susan-shepler/.

Shipley, J. W. 2010. 'Africa in theory: a conversation between Jean Comaroff and Achille Mbembe', *Anthropological Quarterly* 83 (3): 653–78.

Shipton, P. M. 1989. *Bitter Money: cultural economy and some African meanings of forbidden commodities*. Washington, DC: American Anthropological Association.

Sierra Leone Statistics. 2004. *Population and Housing Census*. Freetown: Sierra Leone Statistics Office.

Simmel, G. 1964 [1950]. *The Sociology of Georg Simmel*. Translated, edited and with an introduction by K. H. Wolff. New York: Free Press.

Simmel, G. 1978 [1900]. *The Philosophy of Money*. London: Routledge and Kegan Paul.

Simone, A. 2003. 'Moving towards uncertainty: migration and the turbulence of African urban life'. Paper prepared for 'Conference on African Migration in Comparative Perspective', Johannesburg, 4–7 June.

Simone, A. 2005. 'Urban circulation and the everyday politics of African urban youth: the case of Douala, Cameroon', *International Journal of Urban and Regional Research* 29 (3): 516–32.

Simone, A. 2006. 'Pirate towns: reworking social and symbolic infrastructures in Johannesburg and Douala', *Urban Studies* 43 (2): 357–70.

Skinner, D. E. 1978. 'Mande settlement and the development of Islamic institutions in Sierra Leone', *International Journal of African Historical Studies* 11 (1): 32–62.

Soares, B. F. 1996. 'The prayer economy in a Malian town', *Cahiers d'Études Africaines* 36 (144): 739–53.

Soares, B. F. 2005. *Islam and the Prayer Economy: history and authority in a Malian town*. Edinburgh: Edinburgh University Press.

Solomon, C. 2005. 'The role of women in economic transformation: market women in Sierra Leone'. Paper presented at the conference 'Transformation of War Economies', Plymouth, June.

Strother, Z. S. 2000. 'From performative utterance to performative object: Pende theories of speech, blood sacrifice, and power objects', *RES: Anthropology and Aesthetics* 37: 49–71.

Sumich, J. 2010. 'Does all that is solid melt into air? Questioning "neo-liberal" occult economies in Mozambique', *Kronos* 36 (1): 157–72.

Tambiah, S. J. 1968. 'The magical power of words', *Man: New Series* 3 (2): 175–208.

Taussig, M. 1980. *The Devil and Commodity Fetishism in South America*. Chapel Hill: University of North Carolina Press.

Thomas, L. M. and J. Cole. 2009. 'Thinking through love in Africa' in L. M. Thomas and J. Cole (eds), *Love in Africa*. Chicago: University of Chicago Press, pp. 1–30.

Thompson, E. P. 1971. 'The moral economy of the English crowd in the eighteenth century', *Past and Present* 50: 76–136.

Thompson, E. P. 1975. *Whigs and Hunters: the origin of the black act*. New York: Pantheon Books.

Thompson, E. P. 1991. 'The moral economy reviewed' in E. P. Thompson (ed.), *Customs in Common*. Pontypool: Merlin Press, pp. 259–351.

Tonkin, E. 1979. 'Masks and powers', *Man: New Series* 14 (2): 237–48.

Tonkin, E. 2000. 'Autonomous judges: African ordeals as dramas of power', *Ethnos* 65 (3): 366–86.

Truth and Reconciliation Commission. 2004. *Witness to Truth: report of the Sierra Leone Truth and Reconciliation Commission*. Freetown: Truth and Reconciliation Commission.

Tsing, A. 2000. 'The global situation', *Cultural Anthropology* 15 (3): 327–60.

Tsing, A. 2013. 'Sorting out commodities: how capitalist value is made through gifts', *HAU: Journal of Ethnographic Theory* 3: 21–43.

Tuan, Y.-F. 1977. *Space and Place: the perspective of experience.* Minneapolis: University of Minnesota Press.

Turay, A. K. 1979. 'The Portuguese in Temneland: an ethnolinguistic perspective', *Journal of the Historical Society of Sierra Leone* 3: 27–35.

Turner, V. W. 1967. *The Forest of Symbols: aspects of Ndembu ritual.* Ithaca, NY: Cornell University Press.

Ukwe, C. N., C. A. Ibe, and K. Sherman. 2006. 'A sixteen-country mobilization for sustainable fisheries in the Guinea current large marine ecosystem', *Ocean and Coastal Management,*49 (7): 385–412.

UNDP. 2012. *Human Development Report.* New York: Oxford University Press.

Utas, M. 2003. 'Sweet battlefields: youth and the Liberian civil war'. PhD thesis, Uppsala University.

Utas, M. 2005. 'Victimcy, girlfriending, soldiering: tactic agency in a young woman's social navigation of the Liberian war zone', *Anthropological Quarterly* 78 (2): 403–30.

Utas, M. 2008. 'Abject heroes: marginalized youth, modernity and violent pathways of the Liberian civil war' in J. Hart (ed.), *Years of Conflict: adolescence, political violence and displacement.* New York: Berghahn, pp. 111–38.

van der Geest, S. 1997. 'Money and respect: the changing value of old age in rural Ghana', *Africa* 67 (4): 534–59.

Verhoff, H. 2005. '"A child has many mothers": views of child fostering in northwestern Cameroon', *Childhood* 12 (3): 369–90.

Vigh, H. 2006. 'Social death and violent life chances' in C. Christiansen, M. Utas, and H. E. Vigh (eds), *Navigating Youth – Generating Adulthood: social becoming in an African context.* Uppsala: Nordiska Afrikainstitutet.

Vigh, H. 2009 'Motion squared: a second look at the concept of social navigation', *Anthropological Theory* 9 (4): 419–38.

Walsh, A. 2003. '"Hot money" and daring consumption in a northern Malagasy sapphire-mining town', *American Ethnologist* 30 (2): 290–305.

Walsh, A. 2004. 'In the wake of things: speculating in and about sapphires in northern Madagascar', *American Anthropologist* 106 (2): 225–37.

Walsh, A. 2009. 'The grift: getting burned in the northern Malagasy sapphire trade' in K. Browne and L. Milgram (eds), *Economics and Morality: anthropological approaches.* Lanham, MD: Rowan Altamira, pp. 59–76.

Walsh, A. 2012. 'After the rush: living with uncertainty in a Malagasy mining town', *Africa* 82 (2): 235–51.

Walter, E. L. 1917. 'Notes on the nomonlis of Sherbroland', *Journal of Negro History* 2: 160–3.

Wariboko, N. 1998. 'A theory of the Canoe House Corporation', *African Economic History* 26: 141–72.

Warnier, J.-P. 1995. 'Slave-trading without slave-raiding in Cameroon', *Paideuma* 41: 251–72.

Weber, M. 2001 [1930]. *The Protestant Ethic and the Spirit of Capitalism.* London: Routledge.

Werbner, P. 1998. 'Langar: pilgrimage, sacred exchange and perpetual sacrifice in a Sufi saint's lodge' in P. Werbner and H. Basu (eds), *Embodying Charisma: modernity, locality and the performances of emotion in Sufi cults.* London: Routledge, pp. 95–116.

Werthmann, K. 2003. 'Cowries, gold and "bitter money": gold-mining and notions of ill-gotten wealth in Burkina Faso', *Paideuma* 49: 105–24.

West, H. 2008. *Ethnographic Sorcery*. Chicago: University of Chicago Press.

Westaway, E., J. Seeley, and E. Allison. 2007. 'Feckless and reckless or forbearing and resourceful? Looking behind the stereotypes of HIV and Aids in fishing communities', *African Affairs* 106 (425): 663–79.

Whitehead, A. 1990. 'Food crisis and gender conflict in the African countryside' in H. Bernstein (ed.), *The Food Question*. London: Earthscan, pp. 54–68.

WHO. 2014. *Trends in Maternal Mortality: 1990 to 2013. Estimates by WHO, UNICEF, UNFPA, the World Bank and the United Nations Population Division*. Geneva: World Health Organization.

WHO. 2015. 'Ebola situation report', World Health Organization, 9 April, http://apps.who.int/gho/data/view.ebola-sitrep.ebola-summary-latest?lang=en (accessed 10 April 2015).

Wigen, K. 2006. 'Introduction: oceans of history', *American Historical Review* 111 (3): 717–21.

Wigen, K. 2007. 'Introduction' in, J. Bentley, R. Bridenthal, and K. Wigen (eds), *Seascapes: maritime history, littoral cultures and transoceanic exchanges*. Honolulu: University of Hawai'i Press, pp. 1–20.

Wilk, R. 2007. 'Loggers, miners, cowboys and crab fishermen: masculine work cultures and binge consumption'. Paper presented to the Yale Agrarian Studies Program, November.

Wilkinson, A. and M. Leach (2014) 'Briefing: Ebola – myths, realities, and structural violence', *African Affairs* 114 (454): 136–48.

Winterbottom, T. 1803. *An Account of the Native Africans in the Neighbourhood of Sierra Leone*. London: Whittingham.

Wlodarczyk, N. 2006. 'The Kamajor society as magic militia: understanding the role of culture and the local in military organisation'. Paper presented at the conference 'The Powerful Presence of the Past: Historical Conflict in the Upper Guinea Coast', Max Planck Institute for Social Anthropology, Halle.

Wyllie, R. W. 1969. 'Migrant Anlo fishing companies and socio-political change: a comparative study', *Africa* 39 (4): 396–410.

Zelizer V. A. 2005. *The Purchase of Intimacy*. Princeton: Princeton University Press.

Zigon, J. 2007. 'Moral breakdown and the ethical demand: a theoretical framework for an anthropology of moralities', *Anthropological Theory* 7: 131–50.

Index

Titles in the series

For EU product safety concerns, contact us at Calle de José Abascal, 56–1°, 28003 Madrid, Spain or eugpsr@cambridge.org.

www.ingramcontent.com/pod-product-compliance
Ingram Content Group UK Ltd.
Pitfield, Milton Keynes, MK11 3LW, UK
UKHW020330140625
459647UK00018B/2097